PRAISE FOR THIS BOOK

"There is something on every page of this book to make film lovers jump for joy. Brilliantly evoking the essence of Arthur Koestler's chance crossing of two unlikes, *Making the Transformational Moment in Film* packs film techniques and film theory into one seminal mashup. With Vincent Ward as his Virgil, Dan Fleming ventures below the surface of form, and guides us back to the highest function of art."
  – Barnet Bain, Emmy-nominated television and film producer; producer and writer (*The Celestine Prophecy*), executive producer (*Homeless to Harvard: The Liz Murray Story*), director (*The Lost and Found Family*), producer (*What Dreams May Come*)

"Truly helps you see film in a new and different light."
  – Matthew Terry, teacher, filmmaker, screenwriter, columnist
    www.hollywoodlitsales.com

"Like something a film school class might revolve around in its presentation of ideas, *Making the Transformational Moment in Film* gives another perspective on the art of filmmaking."
  – Erin Corrado, film columnist, musician, independent filmmaker
    www.onemoviefiveviews.com

"Dan Fleming does what few do successfully; he masterfully blends theory with practical instruction. This is what we need: more theory books that aren't just theory for theory's sake, but actually help filmmakers think in new ways to make BETTER FILMS."
  – Chad Gervich, writer/producer (*After Lately, Cupcake Wars, Wipeout*), author of *Small Screen, Big Picture: A Writer's Guide to the TV Business*

PRAISE FOR VINCENT WARD'S FILMS

"His images overwhelm with the power of an elusive dream we always wished was our own. As an international director he has redefined visual story telling"
(Phillip Noyce, director *Salt*, *The Bone Collector*, *Clear and Present Danger*, *Patriot Games*)

"A filmmaker who combines great visuals with memorable performances"
(Fred Roos, producer *Tetro*, *The Godfather Part III*)

"One of film's great image-makers"
(Jay Carr, film critic New England Cable News, and past-member National Film Preservation Board)

"A true visionary"
(Roger Ebert, film critic)

"His images have a power and strength that goes way beyond the context of the film they belong to"
(Sir Peter Jackson, director *Lord of the Rings* trilogy)

Making the
Transformational
Moment In Film
Dan Fleming

Unleashing the Power of the Image
(with the films of Vincent Ward)

MICHAEL WIESE PRODUCTIONS

Published by Michael Wiese Productions
12400 Ventura Blvd. #1111
Studio City, CA 91604
(818) 379-8799, (818) 986-3408 (FAX)
mw@mwp.com
www.mwp.com

Cover design by John Brenner
Cover photograph by Dan Fleming
Interior design by William Morosi and Dan Fleming
Edited by Paul Norlen
Printed by SC (Sang Choy) International Pte Ltd

Set in Formata Condensed, a font by Bernd Möllenstädt
Contributing illustrator Thaw Naing

Library of Congress Cataloging-in-Publication Data
Fleming, Dan.
 Making the transformational moment in film : unleashing the power of the image (with the films of Vincent Ward) / Dan Fleming.
      p. cm.
 Includes bibliographical references.
 ISBN 978-1-61593-060-9
1. Motion pictures. 2. Cinematography. I. Title.
 PN1995.F557 2011
 791.43--dc23
                          2011017959

In memory of

The absent children of the Landschulheim Caputh 1931-1938, a lost paradise,
and the school's founder Gertrud Feiertag.

Dedication

To Judy Ward
(née Edith Rosenbacher)

CONTENTS

ACKNOWLEDGMENTS

The first acknowledgment has to go to Michael Wiese. On an azure-skied June day, I attended a forum of fifty MWP authors at the Judith Weston Studio in Los Angeles where we heard Michael describe what he wants to publish: "A lot of the books have been how-to books … but they're starting to ask the question, why are we making what we're making?" That "why" set me on a course to what you now hold in your hands. This book is about an emerging "post-classical" attitude that asks why classical Hollywood narrative film has been so resistant to transformation as the world changes around it. The moment is right to be asking this.

The second kind of moment referred to in the book's title is a particular kind of cinematic moment, so I need to acknowledge the filmmakers whose creation of these moments has taught me about the possibilities: their names will emerge from the book itself. But in particular, filmmaker and artist Vincent Ward opened his life and his work to the most intimate of scrutiny, for which I am hugely grateful. The ideas expressed in the following pages are, however, my own and it should not be assumed that Vincent endorses any of them. In researching the book, I interviewed people on three continents; too many to list here but I thank them all, and again most of their names will emerge as the book proceeds. But Vincent Ward's family deserves a special mention, for generously letting me trample all over their privacy.

Michael's "why" was one seed for this book. The other was a moment of my own, when I happened to have on my desk W. G. Sebald's book *On the Natural History of Destruction*. I had just set it down in some distress after reading his account of what was found in the suitcases of women coming off a train from Hamburg in 1943. I happened to set the book down beside an old item of film memorabilia, a German magazine called *Film-Kurier*, open at a film still that you'll be seeing in the Preface. Whom do I thank for that sort of juxtaposition? It will have to suffice if I thank the late Max Sebald himself, whose writings have taught so many of us to see these juxtapositions in new ways. A couple of days later I went to hear Christopher Bollas lecture at the Institute of Contemporary Psychoanalysis and most of this book's deep structure just fell into place, so I am profoundly grateful to Dr. Bollas for the dream-work.

Thanking the people who taught me filmmaking in the early years would take too long, so I will limit it to the late Barry Callaghan, subsequently course leader at Britain's Northern Film School, at whose elbow thirty years ago I spent unforgettable days on a Steenbeck editing table, before going AWOL into the nascent community video movement.

This book was a project of Mediarena, a teaching and research facility at the University of Waikato (Aotearoa/New Zealand) that supports innovative approaches to studying and imagining the cultural impact of today's media. I am grateful to the University of Waikato for the period of leave during which the book was finished, and to the university's Research Ethics Committee for approving the interview arrangements through which so much material for it was gathered. I am grateful to the staff at the Australian National Library in Canberra where an important portion of the early work was done. Editor Paul Norlen and designer Bill Morosi turned manuscript into book with extraordinary imagination and flair. It has been my good fortune to work with such an accomplished team. Thank you gentlemen.

The alert reader will soon detect my debt to David Thomson who, indirectly, introduced me to Perkins Cobb. And so it is to Cobb that the final heartfelt "thank you" must go. As somebody says later in the book, "What the hell, I believe in ghosts."

PREFACE

You may leave the roads, or paths of high probability, and strike out over the hills of possible time, cutting through the roads as you come to them, following them for a little way, even following them backwards, with the past *ahead* of you, and the future *behind* you.

(Robert A. Heinlein, *Elsewhen*, 1941)

there must be transformation

Bresson (1967), in *Au hasard Bresson* (aka *Zum Beispiel Bresson*), documentary short directed by Theodor Kotulla, Iduna Film Produktiongesellschaft

Made a hundred years ago, D.W. Griffith's *The Massacre* includes this early moment. A young woman is introduced to a frontiersman who brings tales of western opportunity. But she realizes she has run into the house from the river without her stockings and shoes. So she hurries back to put them on. We watch as she does so. Then she returns to the interrupted conversation and, in effect, to the interrupted narrative (she will shortly marry and go west). Apart from suggesting something of her decorum, there is not much reason for this moment to have existed. Yet it does, and the image hangs on her gestural presence while suggesting layers of time that are not all harnessed to the forward movement of plot. As we watch we become briefly aware of ourselves watching... and the very nature of the cinematic moment is glimpsed. On the other hand, it may take another two hundred pages to explore.

TWO STYLES OF IMAGINING

There are three particular moments in films that I love seeing time and time again. Actually there are many of these, but three come to mind as I begin writing. In the days before domestic video-tape and DVD, I would sit in the cinema and hold my breath as moments like these approached, then wish I could go up and knock on the projectionist's window and ask him to play them back. The first is in *Touch of Evil* (1958), directed by Orson Welles. Welles plays a has-been detective in a seedy border town. Charlton Heston plays his Mexican opposite number. Heston is coming after Welles for corruption. We see Heston reflected in a small mirror on a wall full of faded matador pictures. The camera tilts down to find Welles seated below, then back up as he rises, a bull's head looming above. Then we see Heston at the doorway, as if waiting for his final entrance into the bull ring. Writing that this turns Welles into the old bull making his last stand is to render the moment too literal and misses the extraordinary feeling derived from its to and fro

movement of looks and reflections – layers of the past confronting each other.

The second moment is from Robert Bresson's *Mouchette* (1967). The girl (Nadine Nortier) who is the subject of the film is making coffee and heating milk for her bedridden mother and baby sister. It's a morning routine. At this point she flips the lid onto the coffee pot in one fluid, automatic movement. She just tosses it from several inches away, without pausing in the overall flow of her movements at the stove. She is barely looking at it. The

lid seems to hover for an instant before dropping neatly into place. There is a lightness in the gesture which is all that her routine young life has going for it at this point, before things close in and tumble her in the end towards the riverbank.

The third moment is from Andrei Tarkovsky's semi-autobiographical film *Mirror* (1975). This scene is set on a re-creation of the house in the country outside Moscow where the director spent his childhood summers. A young woman (Margarita Terekhova, playing in part a memory

of Tarkovsky's mother) exchanges a few words inconsequentially with a passing stranger. As he leaves through the field of white-flowering buckwheat he turns for a few seconds and the wind suddenly blows twice in strong gusts over the field between them, rippling the crop and the foliage, an effect impossible to capture of course in a still frame. At the start of a book about film it is perhaps foolhardy to note that there are things about film which a book can only hint at.

We can begin by setting ourselves a creative exercise about film, a warm-up exercise for the book if you will. An exercise about imagining. Take a look at the image opposite – the people on the steps – and ask yourself what film you would make that contained this moment. You will tend to think about the image opposite in one of two ways, or rather perhaps more in one way than the other.

To explain, we have to imagine somebody else looking at this picture. Let us imagine a man called Eric Auerbach in a café in the old university town of Marburg, Germany in the mid-1930s. He is leafing

Film-Kurier magazine #2473, 1936, Berlin.

with distracted interest through some copies of the illustrated magazine *Film-Kurier*. Having just been forced out of his university post by the Nazis, he is contemplating a move to Istanbul. He glances momentarily at this striking full-page still from the film *Savoy-Hotel 217*. A routine piece of entertainment in its day, the film is now long forgotten. But the image we are looking at is peculiarly arresting. Why?

As war soon roiled across Europe, the exiled fifty-year-old German Jewish intellectual was to be found dividing his time between the dusty libraries and smoky nightclubs of Istanbul. Eric Auerbach was writing *Mimesis* (1946), one of the most enduringly important books about the Western imagination's ways of representing reality (the word "mimesis" means imitation of life). Auerbach argued for a distinction between two styles: for convenience here we can term them the Homeric and the Pentateuchal. You will inevitably have adopted one style more than the other in how you thought about – how your imagination responded to – the image on the left (unless you come from elsewhere than the West and even then the cognitive styles are far-reaching).

Auerbach was, of course, referring on the one hand to the semi-legendary ancient Greek oral poet supposed to have authored the Odyssey and, on the other, to the anonymous writing of the first five books of the Bible in what we now know as Israel. Auerbach was subsequently criticized for implying two radically different "minds" at work, a distinction that might have been tempting from the perspective of a Jewish refugee trying to understand the deep roots of the hostility he was witnessing. But such a hard-and-fast distinction was not his intention. Auerbach saw reconciliation around the "separation of styles" as an ongoing challenge permeating the subsequent history of the Western imagination. Indeed what we mean by the otherwise rather suspect generalization "the Western imagination" may be deeply defined by the sometimes troubled, sometimes energizing consequences of this interconnection of styles.

The Homeric style is characterized by "uniform illumination," "uninterrupted connection," "all events in the foreground, displaying unmistakable meanings."

Auerbach (1968), 19, 23

The Pentateuchal style is characterized by "certain parts brought into high relief, others left obscure, abruptness, suggestive influence of the unexpressed, 'background' quality, multiplicity of meanings and the need for interpretation."

Now we can already see in those descriptions something that Auerbach himself never directly intended: a delineation of two cinematic styles. Without being too literal here, it is nonetheless possible to find in Auerbach's vocabulary some suggestion of lighting (uniform versus chiaroscuro), editing (smoothly connected versus abrupt), and staging (foreground versus background). If Auerbach was right in his larger explanation, then of course it is unsurprising that these stylistic distinctions have played out in all sorts of specific ways. But it is not just about style in that sense.

Both the Homeric and the Pentateuchal styles were interested in the *transformational*, or more specifically in locating the transformational in relation to the everyday. The Homeric hero found the transformational on an elevated plane, where the heroes became that special class who walked with the Gods, leaving the everyday far behind. But the Pentateuchal found the transformational in the very midst of the everyday, "in the house, in the fields, and among the flocks" as Auerbach puts it,

and rarely in heroic battles (unless those became inner battles of conscience, responsibility or self-doubt). Now consider a cinematic depiction of a Homeric hero on the way to war, striding purposefully through the house, into the fields, through the flocks, his gaze fixed on the horizon or on a mountaintop. Where epic poetry could ignore, or rather not trouble itself with imagining, the very particular expressions on the women's faces as they watched him go, or the peeling fresco on the wall, could ignore the swaying of the grass in the field, or the specific tint of the sky, could ignore the visual rhythm of the flock as it split in two to let him pass, cinema has no easy way to ignore such things other than being careless with them. For it is, of course, in the very nature of cinema's photographic basis that "background" in this particular sense will be present anyway, planned or unplanned, and with all its potential for suggestive influence.

To grasp this we can try applying to our warm-up exercise's image one of Auerbach's own descriptions of the Homeric style: "All cross-currents, all friction, all that is casual, secondary to the main events and themes, everything unresolved, truncated, and uncertain, which confuses the clear progress of the action and the simple orientation of the actors, has disappeared." Go back and forth between these words and our image and you can see that in fact the opposite starts to happen. The image arrests us, draws us in, holds our attention precisely because of its cross-currents, its casual detail, the feeling of things that are secondary to any main events, the sense of things unresolved or uncertain. And all of this surrounds any "simple orientation of the actors," e.g. towards a single story. The image is fraught with background.

We might notice the shadows on the wall to the right, or the way that the figures at the top of the steps are turning into the light, or the poorer clothes of the woman second from the left with her carpet-bag, or the glare of light through the railway station roof (how easily we know it is a railway station). And once we notice all of these things it is very hard to un-notice them again. But we could get this image under tighter control by telling one story (the film is a crime mystery set in a grand hotel) and in the forward movement of the film's story and action we would in fact start to un-notice these details. It is, however, very much in the nature of film as a medium that the details are there to be noticed and, in this case, it is difficult not to think that the director, designers and cinematographer intended as much.

We can go further. Whatever the actual story of *Hotel-Savoy 217*, it is difficult not to let our sense of what was happening in Europe at the time color our response to this image. The people on the move, the sense of dislocation, of lives crammed into battered suitcases, become something more interesting than whatever rather thin story may actually have been told. Eric Auerbach himself could have been one of these travelers (which one?). The lead actress's mother could have been one: Brigitte Horney, in the foreground, was the daughter of the subsequently famous psychoanalyst Karen Horney, by then living in the U.S. amidst Brooklyn's community of Jewish refugees.

Vincent Ward's mother, grandmother and aunt could have been among them, on their way from Hamburg to Palestine at exactly this time.

Or we could assemble some production notes about the film that might tune our response still further: director Gustav Ucicky is thought to have been the illegitimate son of the painter Gustav Klimt; cinematographer Fritz Arno Wagner's camera had been a key element on many classic German Expressionist films of the previous twenty years (including Murnau's *Nosferatu* and Lang's *M*). Indeed here one even gets the feeling that they too may just be passing through, serving their time on a routine piece of Nazi-era escapism as everything changes around them and the abysmal looms. And as we look at this image, we might even be tempted to recall director John Boorman's anecdote about the advice of an unnamed cameraman: "One good shot can ruin a bad film."

But perhaps, as our imaginations handle these cross-currents, the most potent thing going on is the contrast between the figures moving away in the background and the spilled suitcase in the foreground. As the English writer John Berger has observed, "The true stories of our time have to be able to reconcile a pile of clothes in a drawer with world historical upheavals." Knowing that the story in *Savoy-Hotel 217* may not have achieved anything so profound, indeed was not literally "about" any of this, does not stop us from seeing in this image all of that potential *if we adopt this style of imagining*.

So this is the point. By being based on the photographic process with its near incapacity to omit "insignificant" details, the film image hovers between the intersecting planes of the two great styles. The potential for a kind of current or spark to pass suddenly through the image as it jumps from one plane to the other is what gives the moment the characteristics of the qualitatively transformational.

Hollywood-dominated cinema is massively skewed these days towards the Homeric style. That has been part of Hollywood's victory culture as the dominant film industry and the definer of what so many people understand film to be. This book proposes that a re-balancing of the two styles might not be a bad thing, which is not about maintaining a distinction between "art" or "independent" film

HOMERIC

PENTATEUCHAL

Boorman quoted in Macnab (2009), 4. Berger (1985), 96

on the one hand and "mainstream" or "studio" film on the other, as that kind of distinction has tended instead to institutionalize a separation of styles.

Our "bisociation" diagram helps explain why it is necessary to weave the work of one filmmaker through this book's account of transformational moments in film. The "spark" connecting the two planes, the two styles of imagining, is about the creative process. In fact the "bisociation" diagram is adapted from Arthur Koestler's book *The Act of Creation*. If we leave the two intersecting planes unlabeled, it is a kind of empty template for creativity, where the bisociated elements can be almost anything, creativity being a label for the current that suddenly flows from one plane, one dimension to the other. The point is that we cannot look in enough depth for the creative process in pick-and-mix fashion by taking a lot of disconnected examples of moments, like the three or four we started with. So we have to plump mostly for one body of creative work. Why Vincent Ward for this? Indeed, who is Vincent Ward?

Reputation is a funny thing. Vincent's work came obliquely to the attention of one of its largest ever audiences in a recent episode of *Family Guy*, the satirical American animated TV series in which nothing is considered exempt from mockery. In an episode called "Brian's Got a Brand New Bag" the local video store is going out of business and selling off all its DVDs for a dollar each. Peter, patriarch of

the series' dysfunctional family, is lined up outside waiting for the store to open. When it does, he grabs *Road House* (fast cars, bar fights, big trucks, bigger explosions). The checkout guy makes him an offer. "As a bonus I'll throw in *What Dreams May Come.*" "No thank you." "No charge." "I do not want it." "But it's free, sir." "If that DVD even touches *Road House* I will kill you." As Peter leaves, the checkout guy looks down at the DVD of Vincent's film and says, "Don't worry, someday someone will come and take you home for their very own."

The huge spike on IMDb Pro's STARmeter at the time of *What Dreams May Come* back in 1998 is as good a representation as any of a high-point in the U.S. for Vincent's professional reputation (as tracked by searches for his name on IMDb Pro). Over a decade later, though, the very funny *Family Guy* vignette suggests it still has currency, but especially as shorthand for everything that *Road House* is not. In fact, the cleverness of *Family Guy* is often

in turning its mockery on its head. *What Dreams May Come*, and a filmmaker like Vincent, are less the objects of mockery here than is the kind of film suggested by a reviewer of *Road House* on IMDb who said "Anything for guys who like movies is in abundance."

One of the highest recent STARmeter spikes for Vincent is also revealing. When fellow New Zealander Peter Jackson made *The Lovely Bones* (2009) about a murdered girl's afterlife, a good deal of commentary recalled that Vincent Ward ten years earlier had directed a much more visually ambitious depiction of an afterlife in *What Dreams May Come*. As a result a re-review of the film by *Huffington Post*'s Alex Remington in 2010 caught the spark of rekindled interest (literally visible as a big spike on the chart): "An idiosyncratic auteur, he deserves wider recognition. Few other directors would muster the ambition to depict heaven and hell, let alone issue a compelling, original vision. For that reason alone, American audiences deserve to see more of his work." With more of the work available on DVD or Blu-ray and pay-per-view sites such as MUBI, this book reflects that interest.

Vincent's work is easy to caricature. In her directing debut, the award-winning British film *The Unloved* (2009), Samantha Morton depicts the joyless life of Lucy, a young girl in a drab English town who is taken into state care to protect her from an abusive father. Lucy's day to day existence is depicted in a flatly emotionless way, observed by a dispassionate camera. But the hints we do get of her inner life (below right) are all references to images from Vincent Ward's body of work. The "bunny ears" were a promotional image (from a deleted scene) for *Map of the Human Heart*. The white horse features in most of Vincent's films. Lucy is framed looking at a radiant sky in a shot that "quotes" a moment we will examine later from *What Dreams May Come*. These might only be a pastiche that slyly parodies Vincent's pictorial preoccupations. But on her own in the evening, in the room she shares with a girl who is being abused by one of the care workers, Lucy looks at an old book with Biblical pictures, in this instance by Hieronymus Bosch, echoing a scene in Vincent Ward's own first feature film *Vigil* where a girl of the same age does very much the same thing (there it is Gustave Doré rather than Bosch). The Bosch painting also evokes the "tunnel of light" moment in *What Dreams May Come* when the protagonist enters the afterlife. So it becomes clear that the director here is finding in Vincent's work a visual language to ask a question: is there any

kind of transcendence possible in circumstances of seeming joylessness?

Whether it is being quoted with irony in *Family Guy* or subjected to pastiche in *The Unloved*, the point these references both make is that Vincent

The Unloved (2009), dir. Samantha Morton

Ward has been one of the few film directors of the past thirty years who have used film to probe – we might even say to research – the question of transcendence. He has done so by pursuing cinematic intensities. Film offers at least two kinds of intensity: that achieved through color, light and music, and that achieved through staged and filmed acting. Vincent has pursued both kinds. (Samantha Morton acted for him in *River Queen* just before she directed *The Unloved*).

So this book will ask a related question: do what we are calling "transformational moments" in film involve transcendence? Or is there ultimately another way of understanding the transformational? We will track these questions all the way through the book.

In *What Dreams May Come*, there is a mysterious figure called The Tracker (played by Max von Sydow) who shadows the lost in the afterlife. This book has its own equivalent in the form of Perkins Cobb, first introduced to the world by the film writer David Thomson. Cobb's unfinished documentary about Vincent Ward provides biographical insights here when we need them. As a result, we will be able to see into the creative process in a way that is seldom possible.

In October 2004 Vincent Ward was fired as director from the film *River Queen* that he was shooting in New Zealand. Although he was re-hired for postproduction, for producers to fire a director half way through production is an extraordinary step. It can effectively end an international director's career due to subsequent difficulties getting "bonded" (being included in a motion picture completion guaranty or bond from a specialist insurer, something that banks and film financiers typically insist on). In fact the completion guarantor's risk manager was instrumental, along with experienced producers Don Reynolds and Chris Auty, in Vincent's removal. But at the heart of the problem was the director's working relationship with lead actor Samantha Morton.

In his own recent book, six years after the event, Vincent says he still does not fully understand what went wrong, but paints a not unfamiliar picture of Samantha Morton as a "difficult actress," while acknowledging the unusual talent that led him to insist on her for the role in the first place. As the dust settled on the controversy, its re-telling by various people turned it into a case-study in just about everything that can go wrong between a director and an actor, the kinds of thing cataloged by John Badham and Craig Modderno in *I'll Be In My Trailer: The Creative Wars Between Directors and Actors* (2006). An obsessive and perfectionist director meets a volatile, incandescent, "troubled" actor.

Sparks fly. Tempers fray. Etc. In fact, the extensive interviews done while researching this book have convinced me that there is a more fundamental, and more interesting, explanation for what happened on *River Queen*. Moreover, when we get to it later in this book, it has something to tell us about what can happen when classical narrative form on the dominant Hollywood model meets what we shall be calling "post-classical" sensibilities. The latter have the creative potential to renew and re-energize filmmaking today, but filmmakers are still looking for the best solutions to the tensions that are arising between the older forms and the newer ways of thinking about film.

The graph below charts Vincent Ward's professional reputation in the film industry, as gauged by IMDb Pro's data on searches for his name in its subscription database. In 1998 he was in the top four hundred industry professionals by this particular measure of professional interest. The subsequent graph charts the tension between Vincent's post-classical sensibility and the mainstream industry, with more recent spikes indicating that his visionary skills have not been forgotten. It is to *Map of the Human Heart* that this book will turn for the prime example of those skills.

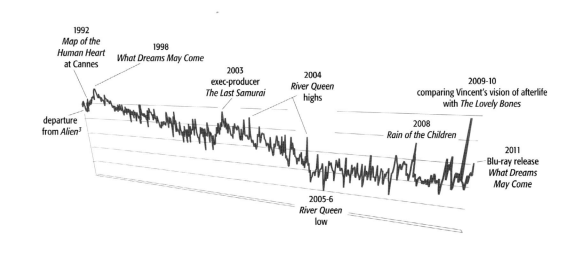

Vincent Ward's reputation graph; data courtesy IMDb Pro. The recent spike generated by *The Huffington Post* is clearly visible as a "whatever happened to Vincent Ward?" moment in the industry.

INTRODUCTION

HOW TO READ THIS BOOK

This book has to be read as an example of its own argument. In other words, it pursues its object – the transformational moment – using both "styles" outlined in the Preface. Rather like looking at our warm-up exercise's image, it is possible to jump through the book from start to finish looking for a straightforward journey (the "story") through the ideas. Hopefully those ideas can be clearly spotted in the various sections, like fast-forwarding and spotting the scenes where the obvious action is. But the book is also very much concerned with the other style. Because I am suggesting the "Pentateuchal" style is currently a suppressed one in Anglophone cinema, the book is concerned with emphasizing what it is like to function within that style. So this way of reading the book will take more time, paying attention to background, to the interweaving of material, to suggested interconnections, to layering. This includes Perkins Cobb with his parallel documentary, considered here much like a fictional "Tracker."

This approach means that there is no linear and self-contained treatment of one film at a time. We cut through and loop back across the films as necessary, depending on what aspect of the transformational moment we are focusing on.

The book covers: staging the moment; visual composition and the moment; narrative and the moment; color, light and music in relation to the moment; what it is like and the moment ("what it is like" refers to the sense of understanding what it is like to be the fictional person or persons in the film and the way things seem to them – academics call this "qualia" but we are avoiding academic jargon).

Those are the main sections of the book that can be found by fast-forwarding linearly. Aspects of film such as acting, cinematography or editing will appear, then, distributed across several of these broad sections. Along the way, the book also builds into an exploration of what it is like inside one creative process (in this case Vincent's, because one book can only scratch the surface of one person's creative process, never mind attempting to explore others), although many films and filmmakers are discussed as we proceed.

WHY READ THIS BOOK?

There is a disconnect between applied "how to" film technique books and film theory books. Stanley Cavell, in his book *The World Viewed*, talks about a seminar he ran in 1963 on film aesthetics, which set itself the aim of discussing film based on the participants' "memorable experiences of movies" rather than on "theory." However, says Stanley Cavell, the willingness to forgo theory was "too proud a vow" and the seminar kept reaching dead ends: "A frequent reaction to these dead ends

---

Cavell (1979), xxi

was to start getting technical; words flowed about everything from low-angle shots to filters to timings and numbers of set-ups to deep focus and fast cutting, etc. etc. But all this in turn lost its sense. On the one hand, the amount and kind of technical information that could be regarded as relevant is more than any of us knew; on the other hand, the only technical matters we found ourselves invoking, so far as they were relevant to the experience of particular films, which was our only business, are in front of your eyes.... Then what is the reality behind the idea that there is always a technical something you don't know that would provide the key to the experience?"

So this book is for those readers, interested in film practice, who have given up the idea "that there is always a technical something you don't know that would provide the key." The book instead moves backwards and forwards between technical "somethings" and the experience of particular films in a manner unconcerned with technical comprehensiveness. All we can really aspire to, as writer and reader, is some modest version of Stanley Cavell's own achievement: 'I had some words I could believe in to account for my experience of film."

A CRISIS IN "HOW TO" FILM BOOKS?

Filmmaking techniques get combined into film forms – particular ways of making films, ways that are not necessarily timeless. What has come to be known as "classical Hollywood narrative" is one such form. It may seem to be timeless but, in fact, clear signs have been emerging of "post-classical" ways of making films. These are not confined to the fringes of independent or even "arthouse" cinema

Inception (2010), dir. Christopher Nolan

but have been emerging right at the heart of the big-budget mainstream, for example in a film such as Christopher Nolan's *Inception* (2010), and over the past decade in the kinds of work instigated by films such as Paul Thomas Anderson's *Magnolia* (1999) or David Fincher's *Fight Club* (1999). More deliberately maverick work such as Terrence Malick's *The New World* (2005) serves to underscore the changes that have been taking place in approaches to staging, narrative, performance and character.

The crisis looming then for "how to" film books is that so many of the techniques described are still assuming a perpetuation of classical Hollywood narrative. So this book is an attempt to capture and

communicate a sense of how things have been changing. Vincent Ward, when he moved to Hollywood in the early 1990s, was widely recognized as one of the most promising post-classical Anglophone filmmakers of his generation (even if the term "post-classical" was not yet itself in vogue). So seeing the tension between classical Hollywood film form and post-classical form through the lens of Vincent Ward's films should be a good way of understanding what is at stake.

These days there is increasing debate about whether the post-classical is really a sea-change

after all, and whether classical Hollywood narrative is not simply swallowing it up without so much as a hiccup. But that debate assumes an either/or outcome: that either the post-classical will replace the classical form or it will not. Instead, it looks like what is emerging is a state of increasing tension between classical film form and post-classical pressures on that form in the interests of doing new things with it. Again, Vincent Ward's work will prove to be especially revealing here; for his nine-year sojourn in Hollywood reveals quite precisely the nature of that tension in practice.

The Hollywood of the 1990s in which Vincent worked (e.g. on early versions of *Alien³* and *The Last Samurai*) has been described by Peter Biskind as characterized by a "new brutalism," with many films conceived by and for "delayed adolescents." As Biskind points out, the influence of martial arts movies was noticeably strong. The emergence by decade's end of post-classical tendencies was in part a reaction to the marriage between classical Hollywood narrative and this "new brutalism," a marriage that may have been exciting for a while (think of Quentin Tarantino) but one which also made a particular sort of hypercharged popcorn blockbuster the de facto standard (*Speed*, *True Lies*, *Batman Returns*, *Mission Impossible*, *Independence Day*, *Armageddon*, etc.). Unsurprisingly,

more innovative approaches to film began to spring up in the independent zones (think of the Sundance Film Festival) and this helped define what we mean by post-classical, along with the growing influence of key filmmakers from outside the U.S. (Brazil's Fernando Meirelles, Germany's Tom Tykwer, Hong Kong's Wong Kar-wai, etc.). This is by no means a matter of "art" versus "commerce" but

Biskind (2005), 127

of whether the business of filmmaking can renew itself creatively.

In case all of this is sounding rather "heavy" in a book of this sort, we can clarify it quite quickly with three examples. Peter Biskind suggests that the choreography of violent spectacle in martial arts movies inspired a generation of pop culture-saturated filmmakers who got their own chance to make movies in the 1990s. In fact, the classical style of bloodlessly choreographing the screen fight in American films is usually credited to the accomplished B movie director William Witney, director of numerous routine Westerns ("B movies" were for years the bottom half of a double-feature presentation at the cinema). An almost forgotten example is *Apache Rifles* (1964), one of Bill Witney's last films, as he moved into TV.

The violence in *Apache Rifles* escalates from familiarly rambunctious fist-fights and gunplay, of the sort that Witney had staged so influentially since the late 1930s, to an unexpectedly vicious attack on an Indian village by gold miners. In the middle of the conflict is a "half-breed" woman (the film's own term), played by Linda Lawson whose subsequent career would also be in television. Falling in love with her proves to be the salvation of the previously illiberal Army captain played by Audie Murphy.

Though a minor film, *Apache Rifles* is very competently made and a good example of the classical Hollywood narrative at its most routinely effective. There are several key points to be made about it for our purpose. When the question of the woman's "half-breed" identity comes to the fore, the moment is staged as an emotional spectacle, Linda Lawson's character tearfully waiting for Audie Murphy to make up his mind, his decision about her very much bound up with the larger story of his mission to pacify the rebellious Apaches. In Vincent Ward's *Map of the Human Heart*, a similar moment hinges around an image of the "half-breed" woman (a Métisse) catching her stocking on a nail and the moment derails the male protagonist's mission to find himself by finding her. This gives us a clue about larger differences between the classical Hollywood narrative and post-classical tendencies in film. We will look at this particular post-classical moment in more detail later.

The second thing to note is that the violence in *Apache Rifles* reaches a point of B movie routine-threatening intensity in the attack on the Indian village and the film has to back off the moment somewhat awkwardly, as if the genre in this "classic" form cannot quite cope with it. The so-called "spaghetti" Westerns of the 1960s would find a stylized solution for representing this new intensity within the genre, and the violence would find other cinematic expressions (from Peckinpah to Tarantino). Attacks on indigenous communities feature in two of Vincent Ward's films (*River Queen* and *Rain of the Children*), so we will be able to track the post-classical sensibility there, against a lineage stretching all the way back to D.W. Griffith's *The Massacre*.

The replacement in the classical Hollywood narrative film of Bill Witney style bloodless fist-fights and gunplay with Peter Biskind's "new brutalism" has not in effect replaced the anodyne choreography of disinfected violence with a new realism. The stylized violence in *Salt* (2010), where Angelina Jolie's character employs just about every martial arts influenced technique to bludgeon her way through the film, is the logical outcome of the new brutalism having taken on its own unreality. If *Salt*, directed by Phillip Noyce, is a near-perfect example of the resilience of the classical Hollywood narrative, then it becomes important to ask how the post-classical sensibility handles violence differently. We will be asking this in relation to Phillip Noyce's *The Quiet American* but mostly in relation to Vincent Ward's imagining of the air war over German cities in World War Two and of colonial and post-colonial incursions into indigenous communities (variants of that village in *Apache Rifles*).

So this gives us two ways into looking at post-classical film form. The third and final one, for this book at least, is to recognize precursory examples, where the classical Hollywood narrative got tested around its margins. Our main example is the 1946 British film *A Matter of Life and Death* (aka *Stairway to Heaven*), directed by Michael Powell and

Emeric Pressburger. Peter (David Niven), a Lancaster bomber pilot, bails out of a burning aircraft after a bombing raid on a German city in World War Two. He survives, falls in love with June, the American radio operator who took his last message, but then undergoes surgery for a brain injury. In a parallel fantasy of his own mental creation, Peter has cheated death and is taken to a heavenly court in the afterlife that will adjudicate on whether he will remain there or return to his earthly life (center opposite we see him on a stairway in the afterlife with his "conductor"). Both a stunning effects-laden example of how powerful the classical "Hollywood" narrative form could be when stretched to full capacity (even if not actually a Hollywood production) and at the same time a remarkable precursor of the post-classical sensibility, *A Matter of Life and Death* sets up one of this book's main themes: the question of what it is like to imagine oneself in an afterlife. Vincent Ward's visually remarkable *What Dreams May Come* also asks this question with a stronger post-classical visual sensibility but still within a strictly classical Hollywood narrative form. So what happened there will prove to be highly instructive.

There is an intertwining of elements here: attacks on indigenous villages, the air war over Europe in the 1940s, imagining an afterlife. These contexts are revisited and crisscrossed throughout the book. The reason is that the post-classical sensibility in film seems to be attuned to time in new ways and we want to offer a practical experience of this through the pages of the book, rather than indulging in some sort of theoretical treatise.

The post-classical sensibility in its still unresolved search for appropriate forms has become much interested in "puzzle" forms. So the book you have in your hands has its own "puzzle" form, both to reflect this tendency and to explore the nature of this formal avenue.

The massacre in *Apache Rifles* (above left) is unexpectedly shocking, though kept at a discreet distance by framing through a fence, and the "half-breed" woman is positioned as the emotional object on which the story really turns. *Salt* (above right) demonstrates both the resilience of classical Hollywood narrative and the persistence of the "new brutalism" that emerged in the 1990s. *A Matter of Life and Death* (center) anticipated the "post-classical" by over half a century.

THE MODEL

The book progressively develops and explores a "model" of the transformational moment in film. You can skip forward to see the final version on page 227.

The preliminary version diagrammed here illustrates the two vital dimensions that will be fleshed out as we proceed. In *What Dreams May Come* (inset images top left and bottom right), the key character for our purpose is Marie, the young girl killed in a car wreck along with her brother. Played by Jessica Brooks Grant, Marie's imagined childhood world – in the form of an enchanting toy theater – is projected by the film into a strikingly realized afterlife through which her (also dead) father passes, intent on his own purpose. As an actor, Jessica Brooks Grant delivers one of the few largely "dry" or emotionally charged but undemonstrative performances in the film, and yet her visually imagined world takes us deep into a vivid, affecting and believable sense of what it is like to be Marie. There is a sense in which we will be arrested and briefly held in Marie's World, while her father (played by Robin Williams) passes through it. Marie's World and the father figure's (regrettably less believable and ultimately risible) mission attach themselves respectively, and to a revealing extent, to the two different styles of imagining we have introduced. Marie's World derives largely from the virtuoso visual imagining of director Ward, which projects a visionary potential into the traumatic situation. Her father's quest derives from the writerly imagining of Ron Bass, who scripted the film from a Richard Matheson novel.

In Vincent Ward's next film after *What Dreams May Come*, set in colonial New Zealand (*River Queen*), an early scene shows the destruction of an indigenous village (image below left in the model). We will shortly be analyzing this scene in detail. As the book proceeds, we will be asking about how such specifics also project themselves in time to connect with different situations (such as My Lai, Vietnam, March 16, 1968, image top right). Again, the two styles of imagining are at work – one more linked to conventional story requirements, the other to images that often have their own non-linear trajectories.

The book's overall project is to explore how these two dimensions interact to inform what we are calling transformational moments, especially those with a post-classical formal sensibility. The value of Vincent Ward's work to this project (apart from his early intuitively post-classical approach to film form and the way his later work reveals a creative tension between the two styles we have identified) is that he has consistently plumbed the nature of cinematic intensity in order to ask what happens when various kinds of intensity (of imagery, of performance, of imagining) are invested in the moment.

In this preliminary version of the book's model we have placed a question mark in the center beside the notion of generative rules. This refers to the possible existence of "rules" for generating effective filmic moments and, by extension therefore, effective films. "How to" books implicitly or explicitly promise access to such rules: the "hundred techniques" or whatever that, if mastered, will make your films great.

So we will want to ask in due course whether such generative rules are in fact at the heart of things. If you flip ahead to the later fully-developed version of the model you will find there that we have replaced the supposed "generative" rules of this kind with the rather different notion of *transformation* rules, which are peculiar to the particular creative process involved in making any specific work of art. We are still terming these "rules" because, once they have taken shape within a creative process, they become in effect its inner grammar. But they come from inside the particulars of that process, including the creator(s) of the work, not from a how-to textbook.

As we will discover later, narrative structure is an especially good place to see this distinction at work, between supposedly "generative" rules and particular transformation rules. There has been a proliferation of how-to books about the supposed rules for generating effective cinematic stories. But as Christopher Booker points out, in the best book

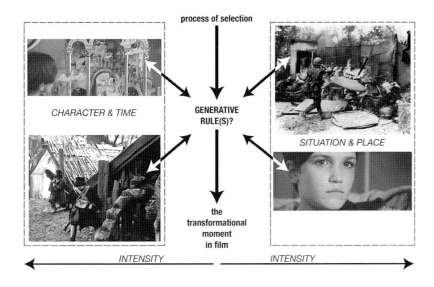

above: the intersecting dimensions of the transformational moment

written to date about the "basic stories" that lie behind most narratives, the deployment of a generative story structure as a "conscious construct" risks slavish reproduction of superficial aspects while missing from where story derives heart and soul, which is to say from the creating mind at work within the creative process. That is why this book weaves the particular story of a creative process through its model-building.

Christopher Booker points out how the ending of the original *Star Wars* film has two male protagonists bonding and walking up through a cheering crowd to be honored, "like boys walking up in front of their classmates" to receive some accolade, and how this reflects not so much a timeless, universal "mythic" narrative climax as a peculiarly American pattern of popular sentimentality twinned with a certain immaturity. Booker insightfully points out that this is characteristic of settler cultures repeatedly re-telling the story of how they escaped an "oppressively 'grown-up' old world" and of a consequent attachment to "quest"

narratives. In one sense, therefore, the aspiring filmmaker who imagines him or herself walking up onto the stage at an awards ceremony, "like boys walking up in front of their classmates," is replicating in their very imagining of a filmmaking story for themselves a broader attachment to a culturally specific "quest" for success. So perhaps we need to be quite careful about what story of creativity a book like this is implying. To be absolutely clear about this at the outset, the book will be deploying a second style of imagining this; one interested in artistry as a dense, difficult, often non-transparent process of working through its raw material in order to transform it into something moving and affecting.

So, as the inset examples in the model suggest, we shall look at both the potential world of a childlike vision and the virtual world of "elsewhens" that evoke an intransigently present and perhaps traumatic real world. The transformational moment in film, as ultimately defined by this book, is sparked by a certain level of intensity being achieved on both of these interacting dimensions.

In a remarkable essay called "The Child Director," Jacques Rancière says that the child always trumps the man (father/artist) when it comes to the directorial vision, but it will not be until page 183 and then page 228 here that we feel the full force of this insight, towards the end of this book's journey into the underworld of the film-making imagination.

Booker (2004), 382-383. The word "virtual" here is used as defined by Lévy (1998), 168-79

What is mobilized
in film's own emotional
mapping is the plan of an
unconscious topography
in which emotions can
'move' us...

(Giuliana Bruno)

PART 1

STAGING THE
MOMENT

The film
sentence is not based
on speaking but on the
juxtapositioning of shots

(Anthony Minghella)

IDENTIFYING THE TRANSFORMATIONAL MOMENT

"Go on Robin, tread on my face" (Werner Herzog to Robin Williams on the set of *What Dreams May Come*)

What exactly is a transformational moment in film? The two cinematic moments on the right are not "transformational" in the sense intended here. But the moment explained in detail on the next four pages is.

Top right is a moment from *What Dreams May Come*, the Hollywood film directed by Vincent Ward. A man searches heaven and hell for his dead family, encountering along the way, among other extraordinary things, a field of faces that he must walk precariously through. Among the faces is this one – a bespectacled stranger who thinks his son may have come looking for him. Bottom right is a moment from *Rescue Dawn*, a Hollywood film directed by Werner Herzog. A German-American U.S. Navy pilot is shot down over Laos in the early secretive months of the Vietnam War. After being tortured, he is imprisoned in the jungle but eventually escapes with a companion. The companion (squatting on the right here) is brutally killed as they try to make their way out of the unforgiving jungle, but here he has come back to his friend that night as a "ghost" – in fact an illusion conjured up by a feverish mind. Herzog told this story once before – as a documentary originally made for a German TV series called *Voyages to Hell*. And that bespectacled face from another voyage to hell is Werner Herzog himself, in a cameo role at the invitation of Vincent Ward, whom a distinguished English film critic once called "an antipodean Werner Herzog," a Herzog from the other side of the world.

Now the point about the two scenes opposite (apart from the coincidence around Herzog) is that while both are from Hollywood-favored "hero's journey" stories and both are arresting, memorable and powerfully suggestive of the two very different films' larger themes – attachment and loss – neither on its own is really sufficient to be what we mean by a transformational moment in film. For

What Dreams May Come (1998)

Rescue Dawn (2006)

one of these we need to wind back *Rescue Dawn* to an earlier moment (we will come back to *What Dreams May Come* shortly).

Dieter – the lost and imprisoned pilot in 1966 – is explaining to his friend Duane how he came to be a flier. It is a story that goes back to his childhood in Hitler's Germany, scourged by war. As written by Herzog, the story recounted by Dieter (Christian Bale) draws heavily on the real Dieter Dengler's own account from Herzog's earlier documentary. Duane and Dieter sit side by side, perched on a giant stone jar in their prison compound in a rare moment of comparative ease amidst the habitual struggles for food, for sanity, for self-preservation, for some vestige of dignity. Beyond the compound is the dense jungle of Laos, itself in reality a larger prison and ultimately just as great a threat to sanity as the actual prison conditions they endure.

Several elements come together here: an expertly crafted (casually profound) dialog by Herzog, Christian Bale's utterly persuasive performance as Dieter (he had just done a supporting role in Terence Malick's *The New World*), Steve Zahn's edgy, intense and highly complementary performance as Duane (bringing a mercurial quality to his growing friendship with the more single-minded Dieter). Duane (seated on the left) has been a prisoner much longer by this point and one quickly feels that he is already on an emotional precipice. Later it will be Duane's death – beheaded by machete – that will bring Dieter to that edge too. Unobtrusively convincing art direction by Arin "Aoi" Pinijvararak keeps the background ambiance, the look and feel of prison compound and jungle, always there in our peripheral consciousness even as our focal consciousness gets concentrated in scenes like this one. Cinematographer Peter Zeitlinger's naturalistic use of light lets the changing moods of the "Laotian" jungle and skies (actually Thailand) express themselves vividly. But it is Zeitlinger's camera that we want to pay particular attention to.

What Zeitlinger and Herzog do with the camera here is the element that really triggers the moment's transformational potential: the scene becomes more than the sum of the parts alluded to. It transforms those parts. The moment begins with the camera at position 1 (frame 1). As Dieter and Duane talk, the camera

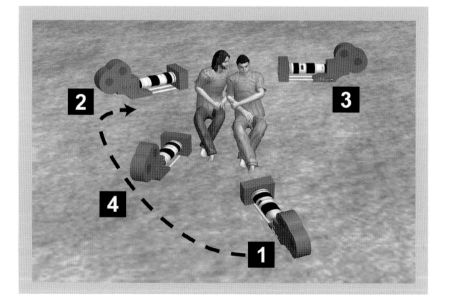

2

drifts slowly on the path marked. Frames 1 and 2 are not separate shots, but the beginning and end of this camera movement and of a single shot.

There is then a shot-reverse-shot conversational exchange between camera positions 2 and 3 (frame 3 being the reverse). But next the camera re-traces its initial movement by backing slowly away from position 2 along its original line as far as position 4 (frame 4), again in a continuous shot. All of this is unobtrusive as camera movement but at the same time it creates a very particular kind of space around the two characters, a space quite different than if it had been produced by a classical stand-offish master shot followed only by cutting between over-the-shoulder shots.

Instead, by the time we reach camera position 4 (frame 4) we have been drawn in around a semi-circle, the fulcrum of which is Dieter's story about his childhood, and then we have slowly withdrawn again. As we pull back, the two characters go immobile, caught in their own thoughts. Immobility is not an especially easy thing for actors to do, accustomed as they are to delivering something more active,

3

4

more busy in response to the camera's attention. Here, however, the immobility (frame 4) is profoundly suggestive. The lines that actor Christian Bale has just delivered are closely based on what the real Dieter Dengler says in Herzog's documentary. They have gone back to his childhood home in Germany and Dieter is remembering his village being attacked by low-flying American aircraft when he was nine years old, during World War Two. He was watching from the window with a brother.

Dieter (in documentary): *One of the airplanes came diving at our house, and it was so unusual because the cockpit was open. The pilot had black goggles that were sitting on his forehead. He was looking — he'd actually turned around — he was looking in at the window ... it was like a vision for me ... from that moment on little Dieter needed to fly.*

In the fictionalized re-telling of this, Herzog sticks closely to the original but introduces an instant of eye-contact between the American pilot and the German child.

Dieter: *It was feet away from the house ... and the canopy was open. And this pilot, he had his goggles up on his helmet and I could see his eyes. And he was looking at me, right at me. He's looking right at me and as he turns to go ... he's looking right at me still. And the thing is, from that moment on, little Dieter he needed to fly.* (They both laugh)

Duane: *You're a strange bird Dieter. Guy tries to kill you and you want his job.*

In the earlier documentary version, Herzog illustrates this moment of reversed gaze by inserting an old photograph of two children at a window. But in the

Wildberg, The Black Forest, Germany

feature film we do not "see" this memory in the same way. Instead the camera moves slowly back on its path from 2 to 4 and while it does so the two men's extended instant of immobility suggests an "elsewhen" that they seem momentarily conscious of (opposite). This "elsewhen" may be something like the scene in the old photograph (we can imagine something very like it as Dieter talks), but it is more generally to do with not being here and now, in this imprisonment, where needing to fly has an awful poignancy.

Combining the dialog and performances with that camera movement defines a space which is both literal — the space marked out by the camera — and imagined. The camera's movement affords space and time for this moment to happen. The camera's movement transforms the other contributing elements, assisting the whole to become more than the sum of the parts. When it does so, the camera movement is no longer something separate — it becomes integral to the moment. And of course a viewer does not actively notice much of this underlying construction as it goes on. Instead it is the filmic moment that is experienced. This is what a transformational moment in film depends on.

It will not always be a camera movement that is so indispensable to achieving this kind of transformation of course. There will be many other possibilities, which is what this book is about. Indeed in this example there is one further element that adds an additional transformational layer. As the camera settles back towards position 4 (below), where the re-framing reminds us again that we are in a bleak prison compound, a fragment of music is briefly introduced. It is an end punctuation for the moment. Herzog had available to him a striking cue by composer Klaus Badelt called "Hope." You can see even from the title why it might have been appropriate here. The cue is richly emotional – it builds towards a fullness of sound (the orchestral version on the *Rescue Dawn* soundtrack album is the best way to hear this) but retains a plaintiveness that is quite striking. However, rather like the old photograph, if used here it would have been trying to "illustrate" something about the moment from the outside rather than staying inside the moment.

Instead Herzog uses a brief fragment played on a *khene*, a Laotian wooden mouth organ. It gives the moment its end punctuation but it has a strangeness and sorrowfulness and fragility that belong inside the moment in a way that an intruding orchestral score could not have done. The orchestral "Hope" cue is used later, during the prisoners' escape and behind the action. So the fragile, strange sound of the *khene* here is much more powerfully evocative of a still unrealized hope. The transformational moment is complete: what have been transformed are the constituent elements that together become more than their separate parts. Or almost complete – because it is always possible with moments like these to find other "perfect" details that contribute to the whole.

Just before the camera settles back at position 4 to complete the moment, we glimpse in the background the gaunt figure of one of the other prisoners, whom we have seen here in frame 1 as well, a man teetering into madness whose paradoxical fear of leaving obstructs the escape attempt. As the camera completes its slow semi-circling movement and return, the background image of this emaciated figure passes in effect between Duane and Dieter in mute visual testimony to what they might become. In fact the fragment of music played on the *khene* begins just as this rather spectral figure appears in the background, rendered out of focus by the shallow depth of field. The *khene* playing is an example of non-diegetic music (not being played in the scene) and yet is very much of the moment.

(Original score by Klaus Badelt. Extract transcribed by David Archer, transcription copyright Soundstone Music 2010.)

WHAT THE SPECTATOR BRINGS TO THE MOMENT

Something vital does seem to enter this kind of moment from "outside." The spectator has to contribute something to it as well. We can approach the general question of what this is by "triggering" it artificially here.

If we think about the scene on the left (from *What Dreams May Come*), we may readily find ourselves thinking about it as a representation of hell. We may have other images in mind, from religious books, from art (we will come back to some of these later). *What Dreams May Come* won a visual effects Oscar for its sometimes astonishing imagery, and its depiction of "hell" is nothing if not visually arresting. Chris (Robin Williams) has lost his family — his two children to a road accident, later his wife (Annabella Sciorra) to suicide. In between these tragedies, he is involved in a vehicle pile-up in a road tunnel and finds himself … well, we will come back to where he finds himself. But at this point in the film he appears to be on a voyage to hell in search of his wife, guided by the mysterious figure of The Tracker (just visible here in the background, at the edge of the field of heads). Horribly, Chris spots his wife's face amidst all the others, he runs towards her, but before reaching her he crashes suddenly through the crusty surface into a sea of bodies. Before recognizing his wife's face, he has paused to exchange a few words with the bespectacled man, played by Werner Herzog.

But what could the spectator be contributing here? We can experiment with this by telling you about the women's voices the man hears as he picks his way clumsily through the faces, trying not to tread on too many. All around him the fragments of voices evoke past lives, traces of guilt, shards of identity. "I never took more than thirty percent from any client" pleads one woman's voice. In fact all the women's voices we hear in this scene were done by the talented voice-over actress Mary Kay Bergman, the "official" voice of Snow White for Disney since 1989. Mary Kay Bergman committed suicide in 1999, not much more than a year after she did this scene for *What Dreams May Come*.

Now that you know this "external" fact, it is probably impossible to watch and listen to this scene without *feeling something*. You may even be a little uncomfortable with our mentioning it in his context. What you are now bringing to the scene is *affect* (á,fekt with the stress on the first syllable): an initial disposition of feeling that may not yet have been representationally captured and turned into a self-consciously expressible emotion or thought (like empathy, sorrow, or an idea about whether "guilt" should attach to suicide). We have artificially injected affect into this moment, in relation to the images on the left, by pulling something in from outside. But affect can be brought to the transformational moment from "inside," not as something extraneous. We will come back in more detail later in the book (in a section called "What It Is Like") to how this is managed.

We are likely to *care* every time we hear Mary Kay Bergman's voice, now that we have imported something extraneous into the scene in order to trigger the presence of affect. This affective response is unquestionably there in the *Rescue Dawn* scene we have just analyzed. Affect materializes in the space described by that camera movement we looked at, is drawn into that space by the combination of elements and because a place is being made available where it can attach itself.

But Robin Williams' conversation with the bespectacled man (they briefly mistake each other for father and son) belongs to that part of *What*

Dreams May Come which is dominated by soupy, mawkish dialogue by Ron Bass that tries to tell the viewer what to feel, in the context of the screenplay's determinedly classical Hollywood narrative form. The third image opposite, on the other hand, an image of bodies glimpsed as the man plummets through them, belongs to the same scene but to the post-classical dimension of the film, where affect just materializes spontaneously and breathtakingly in the image and where the moment offers itself irresistibly for affective attachment. In a later

section on color, we will emphasize this other side of *What Dreams May Come*, because that is where its transformational moments are concentrated.

Affect's abundant availability to be materialized in film is clear from how important some films can be to people. It is March 1999 in Utah, five months after the release of *What Dreams May Come*. A gay Mormon boy writes this in his diary: *After sacrament, wait – during sacrament meeting yesterday, I began to feel guilty for the night before. I left in the middle of someone's talk. I drove to the top of Flat Iron Mesa, and I thought. I thought of what happened between* [boy's name removed] *and me. I drove home and stared at my four bottles of medicine. Would it be enough? Do I have the guts? I thought of the movie* What Dreams May Come*. It saved my life ... It's hard to be Mormon. It's hard to be gay. It's Hell being both.*

We don't know by what individualized connections the boy on the edge of the mesa came to care about – to invest affect so significantly in – this film (perhaps its "heaven" seemed like a Mormon one to him, perhaps its "hell" frightened him, or perhaps something about the images helped him to imagine a better escape from imprisoning and reproachful ways of thinking). We do not really need to know. The point is simply that people are willing and want to connect affectively with films. The transformational moment in film respects this fact.

http://gaymoboy.blogspot.com/ (journal entry 3/15/99 posted 8/18/05)

WHAT THE TRANSFORMATIONAL MOMENT CONNECTS WITH

Of course the kinds of moment we are interested in here do not sit in isolation within the films that carry them. Quite the contrary. All successful cinematic scenes relate closely to the scene before and the scene after, sometimes in terms of continuity, sometimes through juxtapositions that are less reliant on continuity and more on surprise. But these particular moments tend to be especially embedded in deeper structures of interconnection within a film.

The "maps" on the right are not meant to be detailed depictions of these interconnections, merely to suggest the sorts of connection that are at work here. In the case of *Rescue Dawn*, the moment we have looked at connects back to the prior scenes of abuse and imprisonment (the gaunt prisoner in the background providing a strong visual reminder). It also, very powerfully, turns out to connect forward to the "ghost" scene where the slain Duane re-appears to Dieter, deep into the escape attempt and with hope all but gone. And it connects with another "elsewhen" – not quite so literally as shown in the old photograph from the earlier documentary version but nonetheless a place of childhood and history that gives the moment its particular resonance, as two boys look through a window at the future, which gazes back at them.

What Dreams May Come is especially interesting when we start to consider the deep interconnections around that moment when the man falls through the crust of heads and glimpses those bodies. On the previous page we used an early storyboard visualization of the film's central narrative image – the figure alone, on mountain's edge, contemplating the hero's mission. That image absolutely dominates the film's narrative and forward momentum – and it is that journey which the screenplay's dialogue insists on spelling out in terms of some regrettably maudlin story ideas. So there is an arrow heading straight on here (figure right), continuing that journey with determined if misplaced conviction. But the moment's deep interconnections loop back into the film. In fact an extraordinary thing about *What Dreams May Come* is that all of its transformational moments

connect backwards rather than forwards, as if giving the forward movement over, surrendering it, to Hollywood's much worshiped Homeric hero's journey. Meanwhile it also adopts a skewed, post-classical inner structure that bends time back on itself; another (largely silent and visually stunning) film that runs in the opposite direction from the hero's mission and carries viewers' affective attachments into different times.

So the fragmentary but unforgettable moment of glimpsed bodies belongs to this other geometry and connects back through several other moments in just that way; for example to the lost woman plunging naked and rapturous into an icy lake in the "heaven" section of the film, or to a cutout paper toy-theater figure of an acrobat tucked into the edge of a picture frame containing a photo of one of the dead children. These pathways of interconnection also blur gender distinctions intriguingly, where the hero's journey remains very much caught up in gender stereotypes, often to the point of exaggerated parody except that the dialogue plays it so straight. By contrast, these other interconnections of moments are ultimately more associated with the children in the film (especially Marie), who are themselves unexpectedly androgynous figures.

Without pursuing the "puzzle" of these specific connections any further just yet, the point to be made here is that the transformational moment may connect as time-oriented images in ways that are relatively independent of the connections made by the forward narrative movement of the film, where our two diagrammed "loops" on the figures indicate these time-oriented images at work, albeit in the case of Herzog's film an "image" from another film. It must also be said quite clearly that what we are suggesting does not refer to "hidden meanings" in the film or some sort of coded secret, but rather to a map of affective attachments as a characteristic of post-classical filmic form, though here still contained by the classical Hollywood narrative form of the screenplay.

What Dreams May Come as a crash on the Hollywood Freeway

Actually, the car crash that "kills" Robin Williams at the start of *What Dreams May Come* happens in San Francisco's Broadway Tunnel, but the real "crash" here is the film itself, and that definitely happened in Hollywood. The intuitively post-classical filmmaker and Hollywood impacted loudly at this point. What this means for the book will become clearer as we proceed, but it comes down to this in summary. That impact sent the character played by Robin Williams off on his hero's mission into a "heaven" and a "hell" ostensibly both of his own making – they consist of things from his life, words said, memories clung to, regrets. Not perhaps entirely unpromising material but what classical "Hollywood" form, as channeled through the screenplay, does to this is a combination of three things: (1) the mythic structure of the Homeric journey with its recognizable stages mapped onto a three-act structure; (2) what we can call Capra's Error – thinking that drama happens when the actors cry (American director Frank Capra once said, "I made some mistakes in drama. I thought the drama was when the actors cried. But drama is when the audience cries"); (3) failing to heed what we can call Minghella's Warning about speaking not being the basis of the "film sentence." These three characteristics reinforce the classical Hollywood narrative form of the film. But where the film's extraordinary post-classical material – channeled by Vincent Ward – in fact came from and why it is so revealing about these transformational moments in film are questions that will have been answered by the end of the book.

LOOKING FOR VINCENT WARD

The page on the right is from a documentary script called *Holy Boy*, for a still unfinished film by Perkins Cobb. Perkins conjured himself up unexpectedly where I was sitting at a sidewalk café opposite the Palais Croisette in Cannes during the 2009 film festival, a moment that I would later recall as not unlike another Cobb's conversation at another such café in *Inception*. Extracts from our conversation appear in the following pages and we will use material from *Holy Boy* throughout the book as it represents one of the best sources about the creative process of Vincent Ward. Cobb was first attracted to this project when he heard that Vincent had left Hollywood, after developing an unused concept for *Alien³* (on which Vincent retained a story credit) and a project that would become *The Last Samurai* under another director. In 2005 Vincent was fired off a film he had written and was shooting in New Zealand, then was promptly re-hired to put it back together again in postproduction in London. But when Cobb went looking for Vincent Ward all of that was still unfolding.

When Perkins Cobb arrived unannounced at the *River Queen* location in the heart of New Zealand's remote Whanganui National Park, he could not shake off the recollections of Bahr and Hickenlooper's *Hearts of Darkness: A Filmmaker's Apocalypse* or Les Blank's *Burden of Dreams*. Behind-the-scenes documentaries chronicling troubled productions have become something of a genre in themselves. In addition to those about the making of Coppola's *Apocalypse Now* in the Philippines and Herzog's *Fitzcarraldo* in Brazil and Peru, the genre's highlights now include Fulton and Pepe's *Lost in La Mancha* (about Terry Gilliam's ill-fated attempt at *Don Quixote*) and Jon Gustafsson's *Wrath of Gods*, a considerably more interesting film than the one Gustafsson was documenting (a version of the Beowulf and Grendel story filmed in Iceland). The market for DVD "extras" encourages continuing interest in the genre but few can match that quartet for sheer nerve-jangling exposure of the stresses that can lie behind the screen. "This is the movie business – there is no truth – it's all lies" proclaims the DVD

```
Below Hammersmith Bridge,
River Thames, London
--duration: 1:30


HAMMERSMITH BRIDGE            VO: I am alone, filming the final
FAST-FLOWING RIVER            shots I need to open the film River
OLD DIARY PAGES FLOATING      Queen. The river is tugging at my
OVERCAST SKY                  waist, threatening to tip me off
TV SCREEN                     balance. I juggle the camera on one
TV NEWS ITEM -- VINCENT WARD  shoulder and use a stick in my
VINCENT AS A BOY              other hand to steady the old diary
WATER -- CHURNING, DARK, FAST pages I'm filming in the current.
'LAWRENCE' IMAGE OF WOMAN     The Thames is wide and swift here,
DRIFTING                      the sky a gray desolate expanse,
                              nothing like the mist-clad intimacy
                              of the Whanganui with its deep
                              green walls. By the time I
                              manhandle the camera ashore the
                              rising tide has taken hold of my
                              belongings, left carelessly on the
                              embankment, and they are being
                              swept away. I have always been a
                              strong swimmer so I don't think
                              twice before plunging in after
                              them. But the force of the river
                              drags me under. Do I imagine I
                              glimpse another figure, floating
                              there, hair streaming? For a moment
                              I imagine letting go, surrendering
                              to the river. What's the point of
                              it all anyway?

DISSOLVE OUT OF RIVER         VO (cont.) As a boy, growing up in
TRIGAN EMPIRE FRAME --        rural New Zealand, I was captivated
  'The man who was believed to by the Trigan Empire comic strip in
  be Vincent Ward...'         the children's magazine from
                              England called Look & Learn. The
                              English artist Don Lawrence's work
                              was so cinematic, so precise in its
                              capturing of moments, its capacity
                              to evoke a particular feeling.


                    - 2 -
```

Holy Boy script page courtesy of Clue Productions (dir. Perkins Cobb)

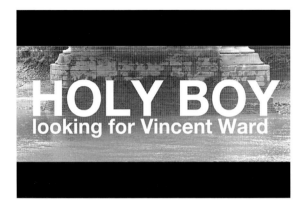

HOLY BOY
looking for Vincent Ward

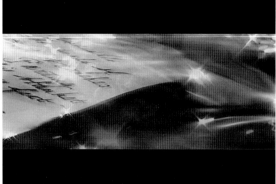

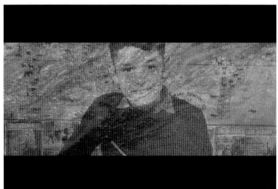

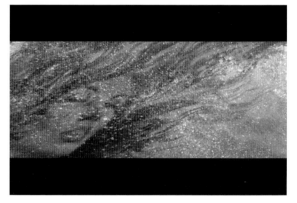

Don Lawrence's "Trigan Empire" images from *Look & Learn* (bottom row of frames) courtesy of IPC Media

The man who was believed to be Vincent Ward was given a hero's welcome on his return to Trigan City.

The man who was believed to be Vincent Ward was given a hero's welcome on his return to Trigan City.

There he is! White-haired after his nightmare journey of three years through the jungle!

cover for Gustafsson's film. Cobb was not looking for the truth that wintery day in the bush (as New Zealand's jungle-like native forest is known). In the first instance he was simply looking for Vincent Ward, whom he says he had met only once, twenty years before, at the Cannes Film Festival.

Cobb (right) was going to ask Vincent to let him make a behind-the-scenes documentary. The project, unfinished at the time of writing, would quickly expand under the title *Holy Boy*, and the weight of Cobb's own directorial ambition, into an intended exploration of what it means to be an "auteur" film director today. Perkins Cobb himself was well placed to do this. A boy wonder at film school in L.A. in the early 1970s, Cobb had done uncredited screenplay polishes for several well-known directors. Invisible "fixers" with real talent soon develop semi-legendary status in the film industry, especially Hollywood, so there was an early buzz around Cobb. His 1977 directing debut was a film loved by the handful of critics who saw it but it had no distribution outside a few film festivals and European art-house cinemas (Polish festival organizer and distributor Roman Gutek was a particular champion) and the original negative would finally be destroyed in a 2008 fire at Universal Studios. Ironically, Cobb's friend, the writer David Thomson, had remarked in 1991 that Cobb by then "was a cheerful vagrant with but one cause left" – he wanted to get into the studio vaults to destroy

the negative of his only feature film. Obsessed with the idea that the best filmmakers should make their one great film and then walk away, leaving the film itself as a physical object to decay and fade, Cobb (who never made another feature) was obsessively drawn to stories of talented filmmakers who had what Hollywood directing coach Judith Weston calls "beginner's mind" – that state of innocently intuitive confidence about filmmaking for which Cobb sees Orson Welles and *Citizen Kane* as an

archetype. He saw Vincent Ward in those terms and when he started to hear rumors that Vincent was finally losing himself up-river at the edge of the earth, Cobb's antennae started to twitch with interest.

DF: So what did you find that day in the Whanganui when you first went looking for Vincent Ward?

PC: No sign of Vincent. The director of photography in charge. A lot of burning huts. I ran into the actor Tem Morrison a couple of nights later in a place called Raetihi I think. Nearly didn't recognize him as the guy who played Jango Fett the bounty hunter in the *Star Wars* movies. Anyway, he said "none of us really knew what going to the limit meant until *River Queen*." But when the director was fired, according to Tem, the cast and crew were determined to "finish the movie for Vincent."

DF: Did you get a sense of that on location the day you watched them shoot?

PC: To some extent. I only watched them do this one setup between a nineteenth-century colonial officer and a native scout on horseback, with troops clearing a village. They were struggling with the winter conditions and especially the lack of light. What was interesting, though, was the way that the DoP (who was walking stiffly – I think he'd hurt himself) got his camera setups into the circle of action and kept things moving and fluid. But he was

Thomson (1991), 54

also pulling in on the actors from a distance with long lenses and using a very edgy mobile camera, all of which looked pretty distinctive.

DF: By the way, I thought you were dead.

PC: *(chuckling)* You mean those two April Fool articles of David's in *Movieline*? Yeah, a lot of people were taken in by those. I wanted out of Hollywood, so David said "Let's just kill you off." So he writes this piece for *Movieline* magazine where I drive off a bluff and end in a fireball. David did a follow-up a year later in the same magazine. Some people, when they spotted it was the April issues, thought the whole thing was one big lie — that I don't exist at all.

DF: So why the documentary about Vincent?

PC: Why *Holy Boy*? He's a living incarnation of that great phrase "beginner's mind." That's what I saw in Cannes in 1984. Others have come close, but Vincent really had that extraordinary early confidence and vision. If he'd then just gone on to make a string of bad films it would have been a boring little tragedy. But that's not what he did. He took two more films to Cannes, in the official selection, in 1988 and 1992 — three films in a row — how interesting is that?. He just held on to that beginner's mind longer than most people can — and then

to have him twenty years later up some far-flung river, plunging headfirst into some kind of craziness in this remote location and taking other people with him — there just has to be a story there.

DF: You haven't mentioned his big Hollywood film.

PC: *What Dreams May Come*? Well, it nearly disappeared forever in the Universal fire, until someone found a negative in Europe.

DF: Hard to read your tone of voice there. *[pause]* Let's talk about Cannes. What were you doing there in 1984?

PC: I was following up on something I'd been involved in the year before. Something very symbolic went down at Cannes in 1983. You had Orson

Welles, Robert Bresson and Andrei Tarkovsky on the stage together. Welles was presenting awards. Bresson and Tarkovsky shared the Grand Prix de Création that year. I remember one of the organizers on stage saying "A nice gathering isn't it?", which ranks as an all-time understatement. What you had there were three of the absolutely greatest examples of the three main ways of making "auteur" films — of existing as that kind of film director — the commercial system that Welles came from in Hollywood, the European system of low-profit-margin support for film as an art form that Bresson worked in — you know, Argos Films and all that — and the state-funded system that originally created Tarkovsky, even though he fought to get out of it. The bills have to be paid somehow and those three got them paid in three very different ways — three different systems.

DF: So that was 1983?

PC: That's right. In 1983 there were two Dutch filmmakers, Leo De Boer and Jurriën Rood, trying to make a documentary about Bresson — another film hoping to get at this question, what does it mean to be a film director? They took their finished documentary *The Road to Bresson* back to Cannes the next year so I went along to see it. And that was the year Vincent "arrived"....

THE PERKINS COBB THEORY

Were one to daydream the life of a film director, in that place of the imagination where we can picture ourselves living such a life, it might go something like this. You roll up to work in Hollywood in a convertible with the top down, turning in to the gates of a studio where the ghosts of past stars still seem to linger. The guard on the barrier nods you through with instant recognition. Just another day at the office but what an office – one with the biggest electric train set a boy [sic] ever had! And if you are having this daydream you probably already know who said that. Here at your beck and call is an army of producers, craftspeople, technicians and actors, all under contract to the studio. The whole setup seems to be geared towards one thing – helping you to realize your vision. In fact to keep the studio running it is necessary to keep all these people employed, to roll everything over from one production to the next. It is a factory assembly line in that respect. But you know that some great "auteurs" – filmmakers with personal vision – have entered this gate daily in the past and done great work in this factory, their artistry flourishing in the security and resources that the studio system provided.

Except that all of this is gone now. The front gates of Hollywood General Studios (right) saw directors like Alexander Korda and Howard Hughes re-enact the scene just described time and time again, Korda on his way in to direct Lawrence Olivier and Vivian Leigh, Hughes to direct twenty-eight cameramen on just one picture, with Jean Harlow in her screen debut. Legendary French director Jean Renoir, the painter's son, was driven through these gates to work. Eventually TV mostly took over here (*Beverly Hillbillies*, *The Lone Ranger*, *The Rockford Files*). Hal Ashby, Robert Towne, Warren Beatty, Julie Christie and Goldie Hawn drove through these gates to make *Shampoo*, the last feature film to be made here before an unusual new owner took over in 1980, but *Shampoo* was not using the old studio assembly-line services, merely renting the space.

The studio system had vanished by then. In fact Orson Welles' career within that system (at various studios) coincided with its slow atrophying and Welles, thanks to the fraught travails that became his modus operandi, almost single-handedly gave rise to the idea that artistic vision and the studio had become incompatible (in this myth the auteur is always trying to put one over on the studio, the studio always betraying his or her vision in the interests of commerce).

What has come to be known as Cobb's Theory (since film writer David Thomson's original article about Cobb in *Movieline* magazine) holds that, in a post-Wellesian Hollywood where every film is a one-off "package," the best that any aspiring auteur can really hope is to make the one great film they may have in them and leave it at that. David Thomson quotes Cobb saying to him, "Who has the heart to do it more than once?" but, of course, this does not stop people trying, their usually overblown attempts, according to Cobb's theory, seldom much more than attempts to repeat The One.

Thomson (1991), 54

AUTEURS AND COPPOLA'S PREDICTION

Cobb's theory is of course an exaggeration, and yet it seems to haunt his generation of auteur directors, such as Vincent Ward, as a half-truth filled with fear and confidence-crushing anxiety. Before Vincent got to Hollywood, with Cannes' accolades still ringing in his ears, there had been one attempt to recreate a studio system in Hollywood that would support the auteur filmmaker. But Coppola's attempt had failed.

The notion of the auteur film director is something of a myth in its own right. In the Hollywood context several things fed the myth, including an influential article in *Film Culture* magazine by critic Andrew Sarris, Orson Welles' personal myth-making which built up the idea of the artist struggling with the Hollywood "system," and eventually also the emergence of Francis Ford Coppola as, for a while, Hollywood's latter-day home-grown auteur par excellence. The word auteur came to imply a distinction between directors with a personal vision and those hired to do a craftsman's job on a film, but this distinction was always complicated by the retrospective re-discovery of directors such as Howard Hawks or Nicholas Ray as auteurs – directors who had very much been studio system craftsmen, and indeed were products of that system in a way that Welles and Coppola were not.

The influence of the term itself largely derives from an article in the French film magazine *Cahiers du Cinéma* by the critic/director François Truffaut and from Andrew Sarris's subsequent championing of it in the U.S. So thinking of the director as "author" of a film is a concept with a particular history and not something to be taken as self-evident at all. In fact, what is especially interesting about the notion of the auteur, whether useful or not, is the way it had become available for adoption around the time that young filmmakers like Vincent Ward came on the international scene and were being lured to Hollywood.

Coppola bought the venerable Hollywood General Studios in 1980 in order to re-create an old-style studio system but one oriented towards supporting the auteur in a way that, Coppola felt, a changing Hollywood could not. Hollywood General seemed a symbolically apt choice, as it had long functioned as a "services" studio rather than the fiefdom of the "moguls" or the power-wielding producers and executives who ran things at the major studios. However, Coppola's re-named Zoetrope Studio went out of business there less than four years later, mismatched with the new blockbuster-chasing economic realities of Hollywood film production and being too much Coppola's own personal fiefdom in the end. So in fact the signs were not auspicious for any directors arriving in Hollywood in the subsequent decade with an auteur label attached to their shirttails, especially if they were tending to take that label seriously

Interview vol. xix, no.3, March 1989.

themselves; which is exactly how Vincent Ward arrived in Hollywood (see Andy Warhol's *Interview* magazine left).

Producer-director George Lucas of *Star Wars* fame was especially prescient about these circumstances at the time of Coppola's Hollywood "auteurist" studio experiment when he said "Being down there in Hollywood, you're just asking for trouble, because you're trying to change a system that will never change." He was talking about the latest "new" Hollywood that had replaced the old studio system with its contracted armies of production personnel and assembly-line methods. Now everything was run by multinational media conglomerates, the Hollywood studio back-lots were being turned into tourist attractions as production moved away, higher interest rates were driving budgets up, and middlemen who put together deals and one-off packages around films were becoming the real power brokers. Coppola briefly tried to carve out the kind of space that a Vincent Ward might have benefited from (directors Wim Wenders, Nic Roeg and Paul Schrader were among those drawn to Zoetrope) but by the time Vincent got to Los Angeles it was gone.

Coppola himself has described what was left for the aspiring Hollywood based auteur. This is what we can call Coppola's Prediction.

So despite the huge talent he brought to making films, a young director like Vincent Ward was

> "What happens is the director embarks on an adventure, and he's basically frightened of the so-called studio because he knows the people he's dealing with are not the kind of people with whom he wants to sit and discuss what he's really going for.... Realizing his life is going to be affected with one throw of the dice, the director starts protecting himself by trying to make it beautiful, spectacular, and one of a kind...."
>
> **(Francis Ford Coppola)**

heading for a trap when he moved to Los Angeles in the 1990s after a string of successes outside the "system" as Lucas calls it.

Cobb's Theory suggests that one "auteurist" shot was all he might get in those circumstances and Coppola's Prediction suggests what the nature of that one shot was likely to be. Rather than merely seeing Vincent's subsequent filmmaking career as evidence for this, the question we want to ask is what happened to the intuitive post-classical filmmaking sensibility that he undoubtedly brought to Hollywood. The answer to this question will clarify for us the nature of the tension between classical Hollywood film form and the post-classical

tendencies that still have the capacity to renew mainstream cinema.

We will be coming back to *What Dreams May Come* but first we will take a detailed look at filmmaking in practice in Vincent Ward's *River Queen*, his next film after leaving Hollywood.

Lucas quoted in Lewis (1995), 40. Coppola quoted in Gay Talese (1981) "The Conversation," *Esquire* (July), 80

WHAT FILMMAKING IS – FROM MOVEMENT TO KNOWABILITY

Asking what filmmaking is may seem like asking the obvious. But filmmaker and writer Noël Burch, who moved from the U.S. to France in the 1950s, sounded a valuable cautionary note when he pointed out: "An American filmmaker (or film critic, in so far as American film critics are interested in technique at all) conceives of a film as involving two successive and separate operations, the selection of a camera setup and then the cutting of the filmed images. It may never occur to English-speaking filmmakers or English-speaking critics that these two operations stem from a single underlying concept, simply because they have at their disposal no single word for this concept." The French filmmaking term *découpage* (the cutting up and reassembly of space and time) identifies a synthesis of "setup" and "cutting" and superimposes this conceptual synthesis on the more concrete working tool of the shooting script.

Intuitively, the best directors probably do this whether they have a word for it or not – almost like having an imaginary screen in front of them while they are working, shooting script in hand, a screen on which in their mind's eye they can see the synthesis taking place even as the setups are being laboriously arranged (perhaps monitored on actual video screens), while the cutting may still be hours, days, or weeks away, and the hubbub of production surrounds them. Having storyboards to hand can obviously help, in a practical sense, in this process of synthesizing setup and cutting in the directorial mind's eye but an intuitive ability to see synthetically is something that undoubtedly goes beyond such practicalities. This is especially so since there will be significant differences between storyboarded visualizations in preproduction, the pragmatic choices made in setting up and shooting with actors and the assembly decisions made in postproduction. The synthetic vision is more about seeing the multiple possibilities inherent in the material as it develops while not losing sight of its potential for coherence.

Burch (1973), 4

SC.33 EXT. BURNING MAORI VILLAGE. DUSK.

The village is in flames. Huts and crops are blazing. Maori women and children are screaming; some spit furiously at the soldiers - who try to stay clear of them.

WIREMU races his horse into the village. WIREMU pulls up in front of his superior, MAJOR BAINE, and gazes around in dismay at the escalating violence -

> WIREMU
>
> Permission to call the troops off, Major!

BAINE knows this escalation could be a risky mistake - but he remains grimly determined -

> BAINE
>
> Permission denied.

WIREMU and BAINE lock gazes.

A MAORI WOMAN staggers by, cursing, one ear bleeding heavily.

> BAINE (to WIREMU)
>
> They're not your people Wiremu. This is not your tribe. Our job is to keep them off the land.

> WIREMU
>
> We're not at war with these people Major.

> BAINE
>
> Let it burn Wiremu.

> WIREMU
>
> There'll be hell to pay for this one. It'll come back on us.

> BAINE
>
> Do what you have to. Get this place cleaned up.

A problem then in writing about film technique is the tendency to concentrate only on successive and separate operations. How to think about these things simultaneously is the conundrum. And yet it is an essential thing to be able to do, especially since the "successive and separate" approach may ultimately imply that good filmmaking is achieved merely by mastering the separate operations. A central argument of this book is that the most powerful cinematic moments are always more than the sum of their separate parts, indeed that these moments transform the constituent techniques, are synergistic rather than merely additive.

To further illustrate this way of thinking about film, it may be helpful to consider a specific scene, starting with the screenplay. This scene takes place in the 1860s in the north island of New Zealand but has a more generally recognizable aspect to it as well. The spectacle of a colonial or settler army clearing an indigenous village is a not unfamiliar one and has a now disturbing historical resonance that connects the U.S. Cavalry in so many westerns with cinematic depictions of the British Empire in the nineteenth century and with cultural memories of the My Lai massacre in Vietnam or similar events today.

Major Baine is a potentially familiar figure – the military martinet (from Henry Fonda in *Fort Apache* to George C. Scott in *Patton* or Robert Duvall in *Apocalypse Now*), unbendingly ruthless in executing his duty. Wiremu is a native scout for the army, with conflicting allegiances. In the Hollywood western genre, when not merely extras these tended to be half-native characters, like John Wayne in *Hondo* or Robert Forster in *The Stalking Moon*, but Wiremu is played as Māori by the accomplished Māori actor Cliff Curtis (from NBC's television series *Trauma*). Baine is played by the experienced English stage and screen actor Anton Lessor. So the scene centers on Wiremu challenging Baine unsuccessfully, while the village burns around them and the indigenous inhabitants are dragged away or killed for resisting. The screenplay page sets things up quickly and then hinges around one key instruction to the actors ("WIREMU and BAINE lock gazes") for their exchange of words as the two characters face each other on horseback.

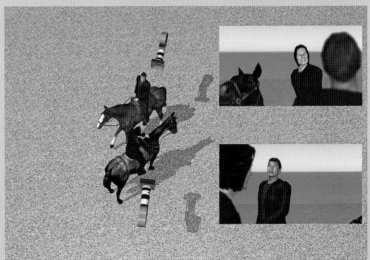

The shot-reverse-shot découpage (setup + cutting), with the "line" it establishes, is a basic building block for creating a stable sense of space and time.

(becomes pov for 9)

1 (14)

2

3

4

6/8/10

5/7/11/13

9

12

The "textbook" way of setting this up would be an establishing shot of the burning village (extras scurrying around, dramatic vignettes in the middle ground as people are dragged from their huts), then a shot-reverse-shot sequence for the conversation, with perhaps a two-shot framing both Wiremu and Baine together at some point for variation (the sequence could be fully covered in a master shot, a two-shot and from the twinned shot-reverse-shot angles). Shooting over the right shoulder of one character and the left shoulder of the other would keep their visual left/right screen relationship stable (shoulder of one character just visible when framed on the other), something that the textbooks say is manda-tory. The rest could be left to the actors. Locked gazes. A tense exchange of opinions. That approach seems entirely consistent with the screenplay. It would result in a technically competent piece of filmmaking, a "textbook" exercise with no challenges for the editor at the cutting stage. But it is not what we have in *River Queen*, with cinematography by Alun Bollinger and editing by Ewa Lind.

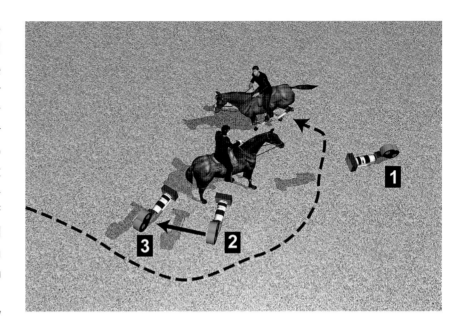

Instead of a conventional establishing shot for the first line of the screenplay page — "The village is in flames" — we are plunged straight into the flames. The first image is a sideways tracking shot, left to right, with a long lens, across a burning hut, so the visual field is completely taken up with flickering orange-red flames and half-glimpsed silhouetted outlines of soldiers and struggling villag-ers, a heat shimmer leaving us in no doubt about the intensity. The left to right movement matches that of one white woman as she walks behind a burning hut — we just pick her up at the end of the shot, framed head and shoulders in shallow depth-of-field as she moves pensively amidst the burning wreckage of the village. Then we cut to camera position 1 as Wiremu "races his horse into the village." We are looking past Major Baine on horseback as his horse shifts ner-vously amidst the chaotic scene. The long lens leaves Baine in softer focus in the foreground as his shifting figure half obscures the approach of Wiremu's horse.

The diagram shows Wiremu's approach. As he wheels around Baine to con-front him ("Permission to call the troops off, Major!") the point of view shifts to what might have been the conventional shot-reverse-shot line. But the camera

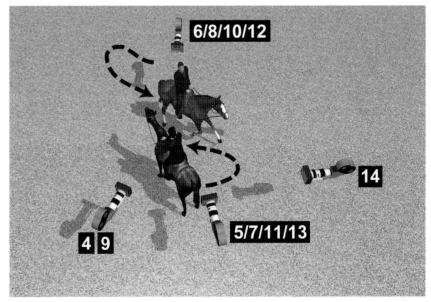

tracks from position 2 to position 3, in effect crossing the conventional line (from looking over Baine's right shoulder to looking over his left). Wiremu reins his horse round in a tighter turn and Baine simultaneously pulls his horse to the left (camera position 1). As the two characters' relative positions are established for their exchange of words, the camera positions for the duration of the shot-reverse-shot cutting (shots 5/7/11/13 of Wiremu and shots 6/8/10/12 of Baine) are held very tight to the line between them. As their horses continue to shuffle and shift uneasily, the camera in effect crosses the line several times and the overall visual effect is one of instability and tension. There is a visual "hyperactiveness" to the way that Wiremu and Baine's relative positions in the frame shift (the kind of thing that "classical" shot-reverse-shot setups are meant to avoid).

This visual impression is accompanied by an interesting variation from the screenplay's key instruction for their exchange — "WIREMU and BAINE lock gazes." In fact Wiremu stares at Baine but Baine does not meet his gaze through most of the shot-reverse-shot exchange. Actor Anton Lesser chooses instead to glance about at the out-of-frame activity in the burning village around them, which keeps his character very much anchored in what is going on off frame even though we are not seeing any of that at this point. We have two acting styles here. Cliff Curtis, playing Wiremu, has an intensity "dial" as an actor that he can modulate in very fine degrees: he can turn up and focus the intensity, which gives him a strong on-screen presence at dramatic moments like this. Anton Lesser's approach here is perhaps more technically nuanced, as he takes the scripted instruction to "lock gazes" and works with it in two ways: he holds off looking directly at Wiremu (while giving us a strong subliminal impression of the sort of scene he is glancing at off camera at this moment) and then he suddenly spears Wiremu with his look as he delivers the portentous line "Do what you have to. Get this place cleaned up." The actors bring a contrast to their interpretation of the page of script that underscores their character differences. Cliff Curtis takes the script's instructions literally and plays all three of his lines here with an intense directness. In a sense Anton Lesser is not playing his own

4B

9B

first three lines so directly — he is playing his presence in the larger scene while offering these lines in response to Wiremu's challenge. But the actor almost imperceptibly shifts the focus of his performance towards his fourth line and holds off the instruction to "lock gazes" until the very same moment.

When we overlay these performances on the camera setup as described, it becomes clear how the result is not just additive but synergistic. The "hyperactive" staging of the shot-reverse-shot exchange, with its unstable points of view (first signaled by the camera crossing the line at 2/3), gets added to by the contrasting performances in which the two actors handle differently the instruction to "lock gazes." Anton Lesser's reading of the scene turns that instruction into an instant to be controlled, having seized that instant out of the shifting relationships (both spatially and in terms of character) and out of the surrounding maelstrom of the scene. And in that seized instant a larger relationship gets suddenly focused — that between colonial power and indigenous people.

But the découpage is not finished yet. It is important to note the two points of view (camera positions 4 and 9) that are not part of the shot-reverse-shot pattern. The first immediately precedes the shot-reverse-shot sequence while the second (position 9) is inserted into it. In both cases they catch Wiremu glancing aside. In the first instance he looks at a Māori woman being dragged away, cursing and bleeding, by one of the soldiers (shot 4B). She screams at Wiremu the originally unscripted line "Shame on you, you traitor!"

In the second instance something farther away catches his attention. We see what he has seen in what is, in effect, a continuation of the scene's very first shot — the white woman, Sarah, half-glimpsed through the flames (shot 9B). These are both point-of-view shots of Wiremu's (what he is looking at when we see him in shots 4 and 9). The first was only in the screenplay as a general description ("A MAORI WOMAN staggers by, cursing, one ear bleeding heavily"). The second was not scripted at all. The cursing woman's specific exchange with Wiremu would have been a straightforward inclusion during production as the scene got developed but the second is a postproduction development. Wiremu's momentary glance out of frame in shot 9 was "found" during cutting and anchored to the cutaway of the woman behind the flames, once the decision had been made to use that image. And again the overall effect is synergistic, not just additive.

Wiremu's dead brother years before had fathered Sarah's child, a boy then kidnapped by his Māori grandfather and taken up river to be raised as Māori. Sarah has been travelling among Māori, searching for the boy for some ten years at this point. Wiremu and Sarah will eventually become lovers. Wiremu catching a glimpse of Sarah through the flames, a moment constructed almost entirely in postproduction, puts their respective identities, separated by the burning village, into the crucible of ethnic and cultural differences from which a different future will emerge for both of them. Spelling it out in this way, however, takes longer than the moment itself takes on screen. 9B is just a five-second shot but its careful and deliberate addition to the layering transforms the moment. The terrible undercurrent in Baine's "Get this place cleaned up," with all its connotations of racial separateness, is counterpointed by the momentary visual connection between Wiremu and Sarah.

The fact that she does not see Wiremu, does not return the look, leaves plenty of scope for the story to develop. But it also poses the key question of Sarah's knowability (or otherwise) and whether that knowability is crucial to the realization of a story.

Central to the classical Hollywood-influenced form is the knowability of the protagonists. Story events make sense because we come to know the characters whose personal motivations and actions either cause events themselves or cause larger reactions to events. Baine and Wiremu have this quality of knowability here, but Sarah much less so. Momentarily pulling close in on Sarah with a long lens dramatizes the question of her knowability, as she seems to evade this gaze.

We will detail the pursuit of Sarah's knowability when we return to *River Queen* throughout the book. The point to be made about it here, however, is that this will prove to be *River Queen*'s rupture point as a film that is fractured (like *What Dreams May Come*) by unresolved tension between post-classical filmmaking sensibilities and classical narrative film form.

The object of that cutaway shot (9B) – actor Samantha Morton playing Sarah – attempts an extraordinary post-classical refusal of knowability throughout the film (as we shall see in the final part of the book). But this is at odds with the film's increasingly strained efforts to "know" her through various devices (notably a diary-type voice over dubbed by another actor). The director Vincent Ward did not in fact direct the scene we have just explored. It was directed by the film's cinematographer Alun Bollinger because Vincent had just been precipitately dismissed by the producers as a result of a dispute with Samantha Morton, seen opposite at Grauman's Chinese Theater in Hollywood in 2009, four years after *River Queen*. It does not always come to such a dramatic impasse but filmmaking is this too: a complex set of professional routines and working relationships bound up with collective commitment or otherwise to specific ways of conceiving what film is. Re-employed for postproduction, Vincent did bring his synthetic directorial eye to the final construction of the scene.

So achieving the minute of screen time we have just analyzed suddenly looks anything but "textbook" in its multiple challenges, including the management of complex working relationships. But the challenge that we can generalize around here is that of negotiating a tension between classical and post-classical forms, with *River Queen* the second of Vincent Ward's two films that startlingly reveal these tensions at work.

The knowability of a central female character in the classical mode has time and again been a matter of what cultural critic Tara Brabazon calls a "womb with a view" – the construction through script and performance of wives, mothers and objects of male attention. Stereotypical emotionality is often a principal character-istic. In *What Dreams May Come*, we see Annie (Annabella Sciorra) once in her workplace – an art gallery – but only when phoning her doctor-husband Chris for his advice in the middle of an emotional crisis about paintings that have not turned up for an exhibition (he cures a girl with one hand and solves Annie's problem with the phone in the other, his patience with the relative trivia of the latter sign-posting what a good doctor-husband he really is). Placing an "emotional" woman as a sympathy-eliciting fulcrum of a film in this way is an old gender-stereotyping

Hollywood trick. Samantha Morton – one of the most interesting international actors of her generation – is certainly known as a "difficult actress," as Bette Davis once was (above, in *Now Voyager*). Asked by Steven Spielberg to wait on the set of *Minority Report* while a stand-in was used to set up lights for one of her scenes, Samantha Morton told him, "I might as well go home now." But a question to be revisited later in the book is what the balance might have been between this "dif-ficult" persona and a refusal, even if only at an intuitive level, to offer her character up as knowable in the classical way, a refusal that will turn out to be instructive for us regarding the potential of post-classical film form.

As we think about these things, it is important to bear in mind that they have their own history.

Samantha Morton and (right) Bette Davis

THE MASSACRE

COPYRIGHT 1912 BY
BIOGRAPH COMPANY
NEW YORK

"THE MASSACRE"

IN THE FAR WEST

THE SCOUT TAKES PART
IN THE SURPRISE
ATTACK ON THE INDIAN
VILLAGE

We can watch classical Hollywood film form inventing itself in a film such as *The Massacre*, made by D.W. Griffith in 1912 for the Biograph Company (left). A scout for the army sees his sweetheart fall in love with and marry another man. Sent to the frontier with the army, he then participates in an attack on an Indian village. The "rules" of frame-to-frame visual continuity are still being developed, as we can see with the shots of the woman by the river who leaves frame left and re-enters frame left in the next location (the house), which seems logical except that of course this is a reverse on her movement: "classically" she would be shot from the other side at the river in order for her screen direction to have remained consistent. In the two setups for the house exterior and interior the left frame edge on the interior and the right frame edge on the exterior are matched, so screen direction does remain consistent there and the resulting screen spaces are very stable. The soldiers' horses prance restlessly, suggesting the pent-up energy that will be released in the attack on the native village.

There is no "coverage" of scenes. Everything is filmed in static master shots, so shot-reverse-shot cutting is not yet apparent. When we watch the scout inside the house look at the couple outside, we have to wait for him to exit in order to see them; there is no point-of-view shot to reveal what he has seen. But other techniques of "identification" are being developed. Before the attack on the village, we see an Indian woman and child in the already conventional sympathy-arousing device. During the attack (bottom row left) we see her run from the tent with her baby and fall out of frame in the foreground. Then the final shot of the massacre shows them lying dead among the other bodies, a powerful image distinctly reminiscent of Timothy O'Sullivan's photographs from Civil War battlefields. The Vietnam War era western *Soldier Blue* (1970) re-staged this scene with "shockingly" explicit detail (right). But, oddly enough, the early Griffith film has just as much impact, not least because Griffith ends the scene with a lingering shot of a camp dog wandering amongst the bodies. The dog's evident confusion and anxiety is an extraordinary moment and something that only film could have achieved.

Soldier Blue (1970), dir. Ralph Nelson

Phillip Noyce

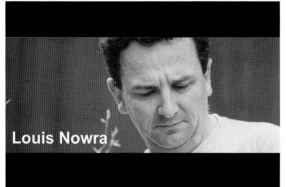

Louis Nowra

John Scott

DreamChild

```
Street
Kings Cross, Sydney, Australia
 --duration: 1:13
```

```
STEADICAM SHOT, WALKING          VO: Yes, I knew Vincent when he
ALONG STREET, CONTINUOUS         lived in Sydney before moving to LA.
FEMALE VOICE OFF                 He'd had one film at Cannes and when
SHADOWS ON WALLS                 he first came to Sydney he was
                                 waiting for funding to be sorted out
                                 so he could finish his second
                                 feature. Later he moved into the
INSERTS (MUTE):                  basement of Phillip Noyce's house in
DIRECTOR PHILLIP NOYCE           Sydney. The playwright Louis Nowra
WRITER LOUIS NOWRA               worked with him there. They stuck
EDITOR JOHN SCOTT                stuff all over the walls - pictures
                                 and notes. The editor John Scott was
                                 around at that time too.
BACK TO STREET...
                                 VO (cont.) There was a lot of
                                 waiting about for something to
                                 happen. The first place was a real
OLD SNAPSHOT OF ROOM...          dump but it was all he could afford.
                                 I remember being here one night when
DISSOLVE TO OLD TV               Australian TV ran the English film
(BLACK & WHITE)                  Dreamchild. Vincent was around but
                                 wasn't interested in it because it
SCREENSHOTS...                   was just about Alice in Wonderland.
                                 But then I remember something about
DREAMCHILD TITLE                 it really caught his attention. He'd
                                 missed most of it but I remember him
                                 saying years later that he'd made a
                                 point of renting it from Blockbuster
                                 when he got to LA. Then he was
ALICE AS OLD WOMAN               quoted somewhere saying that
                                 Dreamchild's writer, Dennis Potter,
ALICE AS CHILD                   had the genius of those who can
                                 create 'singular dreams' and share
                                 them.

(AUDIO CLIP)                     ALICE: And I shall start at the last
                                 page and finish at the first.
FADE TO BLACK
```

```
                      - 7 -
```

STAGING ROOMS

The professional working relationships that converge on any piece of cinema are not just a matter of different skills and crafts. They are also about different ways of thinking that have to be orchestrated. Writer, director, editor for instance – these three do not just work together, they bring potentially complementary but distinct ways of thinking about film to the construction of cinematic moments.

To think filmically from the inside out – as a maker and artist rather than only a spectator – is clearly an acquired ability. Vincent Ward was exposed in Sydney, at an early stage in his career, to the thinking of director Phillip Noyce who would soon be making memorable Hollywood films (*Patriot Games*, *Clear and Present Danger*, *The Bone Collector*, *Salt*, etc.) and playwright Louis Nowra, subsequently lauded as being not just at "the forefront of Australian theater" but one of the most important postcolonial dramatists working internationally. Vincent's discovery of the work of Britain's Dennis Potter would help crystallize his early belief that it was possible "to create work of the most serious intent – and yet make it accessible." Editor John Scott worked with both Phillip Noyce and Vincent Ward (as well as with other remarkable directors such as Jonathan Glazer).

Phillip Noyce is among the most accomplished practitioners of cinematic staging working in the international industry today, so we are going to take a master class from his film *The Quiet American*, edited by John Scott, before looking at a collaboration between Ward, Nowra and Scott.

Staging is the next level at which the writer's contribution is re-imagined: the first in what is a series of re-imaginings, each informed by these complementary but distinct ways of thinking about film. If everyone broadly shares a conception of what film is, there will be a progressive convergence in which differences get subsumed and complementarity starts to charge the material with the electric potential that ultimately transforms its constituent parts.

Ward on Potter in Boorman (1995), 15. Nowra in Gilbert (2001), 286. John Scott interviewed in Sydney, 05.11.10

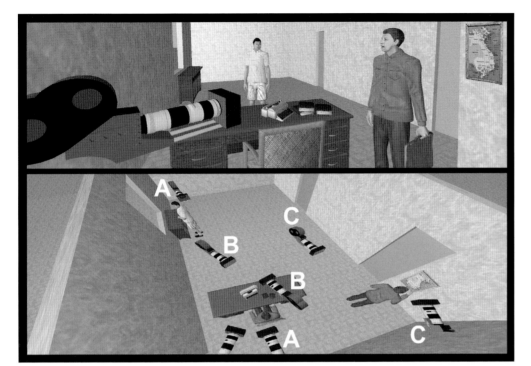

This is an early scene from *The Quiet American* (2002), directed by Phillip Noyce from a screenplay by Robert Schenkkan and Christopher Hampton, with cinematography by Christopher Doyle (*Lady in the Water*) and editing by John Scott. Based on Graham Greene's novel, *The Quiet American* follows a British newspaperman in Vietnam in the fading days of French colonial influence there (French Indochina, with its once lucrative plantations, dissolved into the partitioning of Vietnam between communist north and formerly Francophile south that in turn led to American intervention there in the 1960s). In the period when the film is set, the 1950s, the U.S. is already exercising covert influence in the region in the guise of "third force" ideas (that there is a necessary alternative to both communism and old-style colonialism), an influence that shades quickly into covert intervention. The journalist Fowler (played by Michael Caine) becomes increasingly certain that his

urbane young American friend (the "quiet American" of the title) is not just a "third force" idealist but a CIA operative. He is helping to arm a violent Vietnamese splinter group whose atrocities — including a bloody car bombing in Saigon witnessed by Fowler — will be blamed on communist insurgency.

This realization prods Fowler out of his detached complacency and he eventually colludes in the American's assassination by local nationalist activists, of whom Fowler's assistant Hinh is a ring-leader. In a 2007 speech, U.S. President George W. Bush referred to Pyle, Greene's fictional American, as "a symbol of American purpose and patriotism." So Schenkkan, Hampton and Noyce's deceptively quiet film is also quietly incendiary in its politics. In this scene, Hinh and Fowler are discussing whether Fowler might travel north to where the violent splinter group is most active, in search of a story that may save Fowler's job since he has not been producing much of late.

Fowler arrives at his Saigon office, exchanges pleasantries with Hinh (Tzi Ma) who makes tea, reads an ominous letter from his editor in London, then gets drawn to the map on the wall. The staging is on three axes: A, B and C (with an initial camera position in the corner of the room for the establishing shot). A shot-reverse-shot setup and cutting on the A axis organizes the initial conversational exchange, with the closer shots on the B axis intercut to draw us in and add emphasis. Then the C-axis camera position in the middle of the room picks up Fowler's glance at the map and follows him as he gets up to look at it more closely. As he does so, we have an utterly unexpected reverse — the camera on the other end of the C axis (in effect in the wall), completely subverting the old 180 degree rule, reversing our sense of right and left directionality in the space (see the bottom row opposite), and in effect transforming the scene.

President Bush speech, Veterans of Foreign Wars convention, Kansas City, 8/22/07

What this reverse in the staging achieves is a felt – an affective – anticipation of something not yet worked out in the narrative or characterization. Thomas Fowler by picking a point on the map where he might find a "story," is on the verge of committing himself to a course of action that will transform his understanding of both himself and the world in which he lives. What he finds at that point (opposite top) is a ravaged village in the perpetration of which it will turn out his American friend has been complicit (conspiring to arm those who did it in order to blame the insurgents and thereby justify subsequent action against them). Thomas's lesson in history vibrates with associations (opposite) – not with other films but with the histories, the places on other maps, that they in turn evoke. The fact that cinematic staging – the blocking, camera positioning and cutting of a scene – can carry this (not as a secret code or "meaning" but as *a momentarily felt shift in the fabric of the film's material reality*) is evidence of film's transformational potential.

above: *Rain of the Children*, dir. Vincent Ward, 2008

A matrix of "elsewhens": top: *The Quiet American* (2002); middle: *Soldier Blue* (1970); bottom: *River Queen* (2005) and *Rain of the Children* (2008).

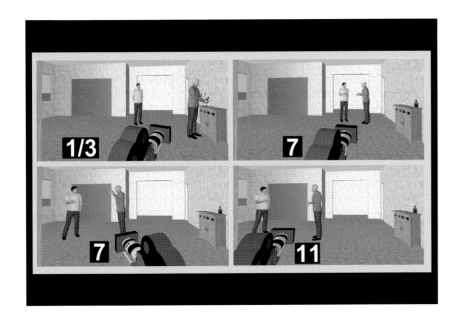

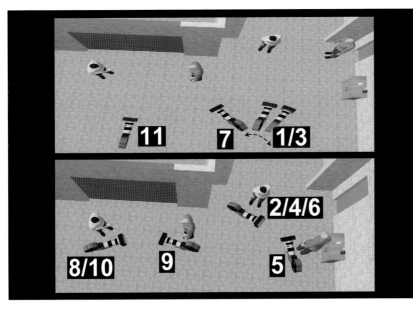

By this slightly later point in *The Quiet American*, we know that Fowler (the journalist, on right of frame 1 opposite) and Pyle (the American, frame 1 background, played by Brendan Fraser) are both involved with the same Vietnamese woman, Phuong. Their competition over her comes in some ways to symbolize their relationships with Vietnam, while Phuong's negotiation of their interest in her comes to express her own search for identity as much as it carries the burden of that symbolism. In this scene Pyle visits Fowler, with whom Phuong is then living (but she enters late in the scene).

The scene is staged on two axes again, with a third setup then disturbing that staging. A first axis is along the front edge of the scene (diagrams above left and middle left), from where the camera observes the two men arrive and pans left to follow them as they move across the space (from positions 1 and 3 through a pan at 7). A key camera position in the scene is then farther along this axis (position 11 and frame 11 opposite) as the two men face each other. The second axis is deeper inside the space (diagram bottom left), where two clustered shot-reverse-shot sequences are played out for the two portions of the men's conversation (shots 2 through 6, and 8 through 10, diagram below left). Then Phuong (played by Do Thi Hai Yen) enters.

Three things are especially noteworthy about this staging: (1) the way that Pyle (followed in the pan at 7) keeps backing away from Fowler into the room, opening up a space between them (number 7 on the second row opposite) – it is not that Pyle is apprehensive at all, rather he is being evasive and the staging communicates this even before their dialog and the actors' body language; (2) frame/position 11, which really emphasizes that space between the two men, is held for an unexpectedly long time, rather than returning to the shot-reverse-shot pattern of 8, 9 and 10 (compare these camera positions on the overview diagrams left) – in effect the staging moves out of the shot-reverse-shot arrangement and does not return to it; (3) Phuong then enters into that space between them (not literally, as she comes in the same door as they did, but in terms of the spatial arrangements in the successive frames 11 and 12). Director Noyce and editor John Scott would have worked together on cutting the scene but holding a shot like 11 is not uncharacteristic of John Scott's work. He had access to the full shot-reverse-shot coverage and could have continued cutting in that way from frames 9 and 10 onwards but holding instead on the two-shot of the men, with the void between them, makes a huge contribution to the feel of the scene. Not cutting is part of the very good editor's art. Phuong's arrival (frame 12) is then a more visually striking moment than one might have expected in so understated a scene, an "empty" space for her having been set up between them. The male gaze at a woman, and the mapping of this onto the spectator's gaze at the screen, has long been a feature of classical film form. So much so that academic film theory, to the casual observer, seems to have been dominated to an extraordinary degree by its interest in the gaze; often at such a level of psychoanalytically-informed abstraction as to have been off-putting for those filmmakers and others who might otherwise have been interested in film theory. But we can sense why it is important when, in *The Quiet American*, the camera and the two men instantly direct their gazes at Phuong.

However, frame 13 is particularly interesting because we see their gaze rather than seeing Phuong via their gaze. Noyce and cinematographer Christopher Doyle cleverly set up a first person point-of-view shot for Phuong as she moves into the room. As spectators, we become suddenly aware of being on the receiving end of the male gaze, rather than ourselves invisibly sharing in it.

The "gaze" we are thinking about here can be given very definite forms in Western culture. It was there when Charles Dodgson, whose pseudonym was Lewis Carroll, gazed with an unsettling intensity at the female child (a "gaze" that was transformed into *Alice in Wonderland*). It was there in Greek myth when Orpheus journeyed into the underworld searching for his dead wife Eurydice and secured her return on condition that he would not look at her, but he did. Twentieth-century feminist thinking, understandably, linked the male gaze to the objectification of women more generally. Mainstream cinema seems to have been invented around it. But it is also important to note

that the male gaze in film, as here, is worked out in terms of the specifics of a scene and of a particular film.

So the bottom row of three frames on the previous pages (frames 11, 12 and 13) represents a staging of the gaze in a way that resists any simplistic generalizations, as does this scene from Vincent Ward's *River Queen* (below) where Wiremu is taking Sarah up-river.

STAGING THE GAZE

We have now looked in detail at staging and scene coverage and related this to the synthetic notion of découpage (staging/camera positioning + cutting). Our diagramming of this has suggested the organized matrix of camera positions involved in the coverage of a scene, from which the editing constructs the final sequences, and how all of this if done with craft and artistry can work synergistically to transform the constituent parts. We have begun to see how, as a result, the film's material reality can momentarily transform itself by the apparently simplest of means but in doing so can powerfully suggest "elsewhens" (the instant of stillness and memory in Herzog's *Rescue Dawn*, the reverse on the map in *The Quiet American*). We have suggested that these "elsewhens" can connect images in ways that lie outside the classical organization of the particular découpage, allowing other kinds of connection to be made. We have found the first traces of an "elsewhen" in Vincent's *What Dreams May Come* (when the man falls through the crust of faces and we glimpse another web of images in the film, running against the grain of the multiplex-friendly Homeric journey). And finally we have identified the gaze as a key component in the matrix of the découpage.

We have begun looking for Vincent Ward along the way, so we will shortly bring all of this together in a detailed consideration of one scene from his *Map of the Human Heart* (1993), co-written with Louis Nowra and edited by John Scott (who cut *The Quiet American* as we have noted). But first it will be helpful to look at how Vincent stages the gaze in *River Queen* (2005), especially around the character played by Kiefer Sutherland (top right).

The scene on the right is the most explicitly violent staged by Vincent Ward in his filmmaking career. The British colonial army in 1860s New Zealand is continuing to hunt for the Māori insurgents, now deep up-river (following the village clearances we looked at earlier). This contingent, among which is Doyle (Kiefer Sutherland), an Irish sergeant, unexpectedly comes across an idyllic scene of half-naked Māori girls playing with a skipping rope under a tribal banner. The

girls are a lure and an explosive crossfire suddenly rakes the soldiers, the first to die taking a bullet in the head.

Doyle, who has been in love with Sarah (Samantha Morton), survives this ambush but is fatally wounded soon after. Sarah finds him stripped naked and in trauma in the forest (top left opposite) and helps him back to camp. Subsequently she nurses him in a cabin by the river. Though friends since Doyle first worked with her father, an army surgeon, Sarah has never returned Doyle's love. But she lets him watch as she puts on a wedding dress she has been saving in her meager belongings. As she returns his gaze he finally looks away in distress and pain.

Sarah leaves the cabin, picks her way across the wet moonlit rocks and makes love nearby to Wiremu, the disenchanted Māori scout for the army who had challenged Major Baine's policy of scorched earth. When she returns, Doyle has died, a small fluttering bird landing on his unresponsive chest where he had been feeding it millet seeds.

These successive scenes – the violent "punishing" of the soldiers' gaze and then the disappointment, deflection and displacement of Doyle's – suggest how the gaze as an organizing principle of découpage is available not just for unquestioned application but for re-working within the specifics of the particular film.

Here, in the moments before death, the gaze is revealed as a fantasy and its informing principle as trauma. That sounds like a "difficult" summation of the illustrated scenes, but we can take it quite literally for the moment – the soldiers' instant of fantasy is traumatically interrupted and Doyle's few minutes of fantasy are supplanted by his substitution and death. The visual organization of these fantasies around the gaze entails that the gaze itself is momentarily exposed as traumatic in nature.

However, Hollywood film's commitment to the fantasmatic gaze as "normal" has been almost total and *River Queen* has enough of the "Hollywood" form about it for the gaze to be largely recuperated throughout the film (except, as we shall see, in one or two coherence-threatening moments when Samantha Morton, the "difficult actress," refused to do what may have been expected, whether through petulant instincts or conscious intent).

The screenplay (in what would have been a much more conventional moment) has Sarah lie beside the still sleeping Doyle and hold his hand. She sleeps briefly, then wakes: "He is dead. Her eyes are brimming as she sits, still holding his hand." But Sarah is not holding his hand when he dies alone and her point of view (below) emphasizes instead the absent touch by putting him so clearly out of reach now, the gap between them a kind of wound.

Imagine standing looking out a window just before it gets dark. Everything seems laid out for you to look at, arrayed and framed for your visual satisfaction, a whole world. The brightness out there, through the window, contrasts with the protective shadows in your room. That is the fantasmatic nature of the gaze. But imagine it getting dark. Gradually the light fades outside, becomes darker than the light in your room. You begin to feel uneasy. You begin to feel that it is you being looked at. Now you feel certain that a look is being directed at you out of the darkness. If there were curtains you would close them. Suddenly you glimpse your own reflection in the glass and it only serves to reinforce the feeling that you are now the object being viewed. That is the traumatic nature of the gaze.

Vigil (1984), dir. Vincent Ward.

TRANSFORMING THE GAZE

In many ways this scene is very similar to the one we looked at from Phillip Noyce's *The Quiet American* – two men parry verbally in a room, sidestepping what they really need to say, not least about their competition over the same woman. The staging plays out very differently though and the differences are instructive.

From Vincent Ward's *Map of the Human Heart* (1993), this scene is from the middle of the film and shows Avik, an Inuk who has become a World War Two bomb-aimer on night raids over Germany, seeking help from Walter, a senior air force planner for the bombing of German cities. Years before, Walter had been an aviator, surveyor and map-maker in northern Canada where he had met the boy Avik, whom he rescued from tuberculosis – a white man's disease. In the sanatorium where Walter deposited him for a cure, young Avik had fallen childishly in love with a Métis girl, Albertine. In the early years of the war, Avik and Walter met again when Walter was back in Inuit land searching for a German

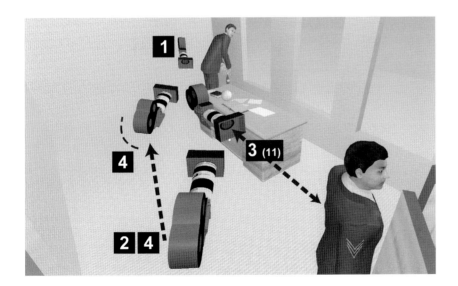

submarine stuck in the ice. Avik asked him to look up Albertine (in fact to return a crumpled X-ray of her that Avik had kept from the sanatorium). Inspired by Walter, Avik joins the air force and ends up on a British bomber. He also finds that Walter did go looking for Albertine and that they are now living together, but Avik and Albertine renew their friendship in England and it develops into something more.

In this scene Avik (Jason Scott Lee) is asking for Walter's help because his bomber crew has been assigned to one more mission despite having completed their tour of duty. But suspicion begins to dawn on Avik that Walter (Patrick Bergin) may have colluded in the assignment to get him out of the way. Walter's room at Bomber Command's planning headquarters is full of maps – maps of all kinds, everywhere, and not just for the attacks on Germany. Avik is impressed as they enter the room (covered from camera position 1). Walter closes a closet door on the map-adorned far wall but, as Walter moves up the room, Avik goes to take a look in the closet.

Cutting to position 2 sees Walter pouring drinks and glancing back at Avik. Technically there is a double action at the end of shot 1 and the beginning of shot 3 – Avik starts to open the closet twice. But it is deliberately cut this way to prolong the moment. The spectator does not notice the overlapping action as a discontinuity but feels the moment hanging suspended in time. What is revealed is an automaton – a mechanical figure, a life size female "doll" covered in fragments of maps. As Avik turns slowly to stare at Walter and then back at the automaton, evidently struggling to understand what he is seeing, the camera at position 3 dollies slowly in past Avik to "look" at the automaton, which has been triggered by the door opening. The figure clanks and whirrs into motion and turns its back, the camera dollying out again along its line at 3 as Avik crosses its path to go for the drink Walter is now holding out.

There is nothing like that axis at 3 in the staging of the similar scene we looked at from *The Quiet American*. What the camera does here on this axis creates a third presence in the room. The spectator is unlikely to be overly conscious of this at the time but it colors how the entire scene feels. One way of "explaining" this axis would have been with a reverse to show the automaton's point of view as it were. We have all seen shots where a character reaches into a closet, a refrigerator or a safe and inexplicably the camera is in there looking out. Almost always these are pointless visual gimmicks in the setup. But here, cinematographer Eduardo Serra, editor John Scott and director Ward refuse such gimmickry. Instead the movement in and out along the axis at 3 resists attachment to any eyes within the scene, even the automaton's in the closet. In fact the camera passes Avik's own look on its way towards the automaton.

The camera at 4 moves with Avik towards the other end of the room and pans slightly there to follow Walter as he moves between the desk and the windows. We hear the sounds of soldiers drilling outside.

What follows is entirely conventional shot-reverse-shot coverage of the conversation between Walter and Avik. The frames on the right condense this sequence of shots but the cutting and camera positioning will be self-evident from the selected frames. The eight shots of Walter during the conversation are all literally over the shoulder as shown in the diagram, as is a shot looking down at photographs of Dresden on the desk. The seven reverse shots on Avik are offset somewhat from Walter's position and the close shots, because the lens has been zoomed in from there, have a shallow depth of field that throws the background into softer focus (frame far right middle).

Avik eventually refers to the automaton, glancing over at it (far right middle). Walter briefly turns to look at it as well (frame bottom left). Shot 11 – of the automaton – is now from Avik's point of view and also aligns his position with the other end of that axis established by camera position 3 (previous diagram). So that earlier point of view is retrospectively picked up by Avik. The overall effect is to have made that gaze involving the automaton the central organizing axis of the staging – much more powerfully so than the position at 2 with the movement (4) from there into the scene. The establishing shot (at 1) is never returned to, unlike its more normal establishing of a baseline axis in the last

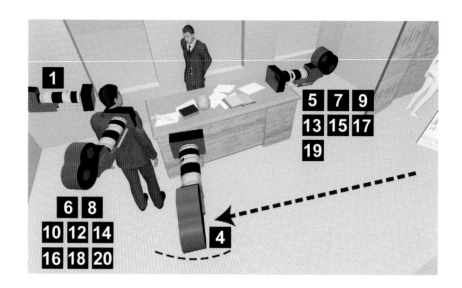

scene we looked at from *The Quiet American*.

So the staging of this scene establishes a gaze involving the automaton object around which the rest of the setup organizes itself. Although Avik eventually "adopts" that gaze (and only in a brief sideways glance), it preexists his doing so.

When Walter looks back at Avik (the final frame on the right), actor Patrick Bergin delivers one of the most intense monologues of his career. It is, in large measure, this monologue and the automaton-gaze that combine to transform this particular moment in *Map of the Human Heart*. The depth and unsettling intensity in Patrick Bergin's performance at this point needed the staging to have set up the situation in this way, both by creating a focused space around him through the convergent lines of the staging and by linking that space to the third presence in the room through the establishment of what we have called the automaton-gaze.

As this has been the book's final "lesson" focused on staging, we can finish it by moving beyond staging in order to understand more fully what has just happened in this scene.

ROSTRUM
EARLY 20th CENTURY POSTCARD
SOUNDS OF STREET, FEMALE VO

AERIAL PHOTO OF CITY
(LABELED 'HAMBURG')
AIR RAID SIREN STARTS TO WAIL

'FLY' SLOWLY NORTH OVER PHOTO
PULLING IN CLOSER,
OVER ST. NIKOLAI, TOWARDS
EPPENDORFERLAND STRASSE...

CLOSER, BRIDGES...

MANY BUILDINGS RUINED...

A PARTICULAR BRIDGE...

A CYCLIST JUST VISIBLE

END MOVEMENT ON
RUINED BUILDINGS
REFLECTED IN RIVER.

ARCHIVE SHOT
(BODY BLACKED OUT]

DISSOLVE FROM 'BODY' TO
RIVER IN MOTION, LIGHT DANCING,
JAGGED SKYLINE REFLECTION
JUST VISIBLE IN WATER.
OTHER MOVEMENT RESOLVES INTO...

FILM OF CARS SPEEDING BY
ON AUTOBAHN

VO (narrator): Vincent's maternal grandparents, Gertrud and Leo Rosenbacher, lived a comfortable life in pre-war Hamburg until - as Hitler rose to power - Leo took the family to Palestine.

VO (cont.): Sixteen year old Inge Einspener, who had been a neighbor of the Rosenbachers, heard the Hamburg sirens start up at 9pm on July 24th 1943.

VO (old woman, German accent): We were caught in a big, big fire. The houses were all coming down on us. We didn't know where to go. Bombs were everywhere... Everything was burning, even the paving stones in the street. We were blind from the fire. Burning dust. Ashes. People were burning. I saw a child stick in the tar in the street. And it didn't come out again. And the mother tried to save her child. But she couldn't. She made one step. That was all. A woman was watching the girl burning and the mother sticking. Then she herself started to burn on her back, so she jumped into the river.

VO (narrator, cont.): A German archive has a photograph of a woman's body dragged in a tin basin out of the river in Hamburg after that raid, an image too terrible to be shown here. Vincent hitchhiked across Germany in his 20s to find his grandparents' house in Hamburg. Trying to cross a busy autobahn he got stuck on the median reservation.

- 4 -

Holy Boy script page courtesy of Clue Productions (dir. Perkins Cobb)

STAGING THE "ELSEWHEN"?

As this further extract from Perkins Cobb's unfinished *Holy Boy* documentary suggests, both historical and biographical elements inform the scene we are looking at from *Map of the Human Heart*. It would be a mistake, of course, to "explain" the scene in those terms.

In fact both the historical and the biographical get transformed within the scene into something specific to the film, not least to its material organization of images and to the function of the gaze (specifically the automaton-gaze) within that material organization. But they also tell us about the double orientation of the gaze around which the scene is constructed – it is both a fantasmatic gaze (projecting the fantasy of control onto both the woman and the mapped places) and a gaze troubled by its own potentially traumatic reversal, where the unreproducible archival image far left suddenly occupies the place of the woman in Walter's closet. Or rather, like the old photograph of two boys looking out a window in Herzog's documentary moment when Dieter Dengler watches aircraft attack his childhood home in Germany, the image makes specific here something that the film evokes as an "elsewhen."

It becomes clear then that what we might think of as *sheets* of time can be staged in this kind of post-classical moment, not as epic imagery of "historical" reenactments as has so often been the case on the screen, but as "elsewhens" informing the now of the filmic moment, even inside rooms.

What Avik realizes in the scene we have just looked at is that Walter now reduces everything – the woman whom they both love in their different ways, the people in the German cities – to objects that he aims to dominate. But not only that – Avik realizes he too has become an object to Walter, not just an object to be "rescued" as a child from his Inuit community in the Canadian north and deposited in a sanatorium but an object now to be assigned one more mission over Germany. Avik does not share Walter's gaze at the automaton – Avik joins the automaton as another object. It is in this realization of his own

Documentary source for "Holy Boy" images opposite, Michael Foedrowitz archive, Berlin

WALTER is clearly enjoying himself. There is not only
something menacing about his talk, it's as if he's really
talking about something else. AVIK motions to the
mechanical doll.

>   AVIK
>   If someone entered this room and
>   destroyed her would it break your
>   spirit?
>
>   WALTER
>   If she were made of flesh and
>   blood it might.

A BEAT.

>   When you kill a seal you have to
>   personally slit its throat, don't
>   you?

AVIK nods.

>   All big decisions are personal.
>   When I was a student in Dresden I
>   fell in love with a beautiful
>   girl. I found out she was two-
>   timing me. She said I hate your
>   obsession with maps. I hate the
>   way you fuck. I hate the way you
>   smell. I hate the way you eat.
>   Well as far as I know Avik she's
>   still in Dresden.

PAUSE.

AVIK realizes something.

objectification that Avik experiences the reversal of the gaze and feels, not its fantasmatic illusion of control, but its traumatic nature.

The quality of the writing and Patrick Bergin's remarkable performance throughout the film both render Walter as a complex, multi-dimensional (and for the most part not unlikeable) character, so this moment is all the more quietly shocking.

At this transformational moment Avik also realizes that he is not on a journey of his own making — that his life is threading in and out of Walter's progress which is itself a growing perversion of the hero's journey towards fulfillment of his goals. Avik is off-centered not just in relation to that story but also in terms of the larger historical events in which that "hero's journey" is embedded.

THE VOGLER MEMO

In 1985, the year Vincent took his first feature *Vigil* to Cannes, Christopher Vogler, then a story analyst at Walt Disney Pictures, wrote a seven-page in-house memo that still has a somewhat legendary status today. Little did Vincent know that his own subsequent arrival in Hollywood, after *Map of the Human Heart*, would coincide with the dominance there of ideas that the "Vogler Memo" captured. The *Holy Boy* documentary (right) includes a storyboard reconstruction (following pages) and a description of a key moment from *West of the Rising Sun*, a project that subsequently became *The Last Samurai* starring Tom Cruise (a film on which Vincent Ward had an executive producer credit). There are many differences between *The Last Samurai* and *West of the Rising Sun*, which was co-written by Robert Schenkkan, the Pulitzer Prize-winning playwright who co-wrote the screenplay for *The Quiet American* (as well as four episodes of *The Pacific*, HBO, 2010). But the most interesting for our purpose is this scene.

The hero (much like the character played by Tom Cruise in *The Last Samurai*) is a Westerner hired in Japan for his skills, though in this instance he is driving a herd of imported cattle needed to relieve a famine. As a character, Merritt could have walked off the set of any old Delmer Daves or Anthony Mann western onto these pages. Along for the trip is Rebecca, an independent-minded woman based on adventurous Victorians like Isabella Bird who visited Japan in the 1870s. The presence of a Japanese orphan boy, from the village they are headed towards, seems to promise a ready-made family if Merritt's interest in Rebecca follows the conventional storyline.

But the Schenkkan-Ward screenplay arrives at this moment — at the remote village where the samurai for whom Merritt is working will make their last stand against the pursuing imperial forces — and Merritt is suddenly killed. This is the mandatory story stage of last-minute dangers on the hero's journey that have to be overcome before he triumphs. So where is the hero?

STORYBOARD

--duration: 1:09

ROSTRUM
FEMALE VO

STORYBOARD IMAGES FROM
'WEST OF THE RISING SUN'.

LARGE HERD OF LONGHORNS
COLORED RIBBONS ON THE HORNS...
  (FX SOUNDS OF HERD)

SAMURAI AND THEIR SERVANTS
DRIVING THE HERD...

MERRIT, A WHITE MAN,
WITH TARO, AN ORPHAN BOY

REBECCA, A WHITE WOMAN,
SPIRITED, FOCUS OF MERRITT'S
ATTENTION...

VILLAGE, IDLE SILK FACTORY,
STARVING VILLAGERS...

SHARPSHOOTER IN THE HILLS...
  (FX CRACK OF SHARPS RIFLE)

...FIRES AND HITS MERRITT.

VILLAGE, NIGHT, BARRICADED.

REBECCA AND TARO LOOK OUT
AT MERRITT's BODY, WATCHED
BY KENICHI...

VO (narrator): One of the projects Vincent had in development in Hollywood was a kind of Western set in Japan. He co-wrote his final version with Robert Schenkkan. An American Civil War veteran called Merritt is trail boss on a herd of imported longhorn cattle being taken from the port at Yokohama to a famine-ravaged rural part of Japan in 1872. He's in the employ of a samurai lord called Kenichi. Each samurai is responsible for a section of the herd, identified by colored ribbons on their horns. They are accompanied by Rebecca, an adventurous white woman who has been making a life for herself in Japan since it opened up, and by Taro, a Japanese orphan boy.

VO (cont.): Kenichi and his traditionalist supporters are in rebellion against the young modernizing Meiji emperor who has sent troops in pursuit. The herd arrives at the village of Niwa in late evening. Its silk factory is lying idle and deserted, the villagers starving, 'western advancements' designed to modernize the peasant economy having happened too fast. From the overlooking hills, a sharpshooter from the pursuing imperial force kills Merritt. As Kenichi and the samurai barricade the village and prepare to defend it, Rebecca and Taro look out to where Merritt's body still lies beyond the perimeter. Kenichi watches her with interest...

- 15 -

Holy Boy script page courtesy of Clue Productions (dir. Perkins Cobb)

Storyboard by Thaw Naing for *Holy Boy: Looking for Vincent Ward* (unfinished documentary) dir. Perkins Cobb, illustrating *West of the Rising Sun* (unmade film written by Robert Schenkkan and Vincent Ward).

We have already looked at Vincent's later film *River Queen*. Clearly Rebecca from *West of the Rising Sun* becomes Sarah in *River Queen*. There is also the potential here for Kenichi, the samurai watching her in the last frame, to equate with *River Queen*'s Wiremu, Sarah's lover. (The names are interesting: in the Old Testament, Sarah was Isaac's mother and Rebecca his wife.) So unresolved potential from one film carried over into the other, while *West of the Rising Sun* was replaced as a project by *The Last Samurai*, a film that shared some of the core concepts but started over with a fresh screenplay.

Rebecca gazing out in the moonlight at Merritt's body, beyond the village's now barricaded perimeter, equates with Sarah looking at Doyle's body (Kiefer Sutherland) in *River Queen*, a scene we have already illustrated (indeed the screenplay describes Merritt as Irish-American). Kenichi's presence in the background equates with Wiremu's presence outside the cabin in *River Queen*: except that Wiremu and Sarah consummate their relationship whereas here the latent potential in unresolved. (See Exercise on page 121.)

Nor in fact would it be resolved, because it was impossible for Schenkkan and Ward to write that in 1990s Los Angeles with any real prospect of it being accepted. What the Vogler Memo did was articulate and help sharpen for many people Hollywood's growing collective faith in a standardized mythic story structure especially suited to turning out the multiplex blockbusters then needed. *Star Wars* had established the model: big Homeric stories delivering big story arcs with predictable emotional satisfactions. Myths have always tended to function in the same way, so unsurprisingly a self-reinforcing loop soon got established between a "mythic" story structure and high-concept movies packaged for the deal-makers' blockbuster mentality. Smaller films then got caught up in the myth-oriented mood that seemed to be promising a winning formula.

The Vogler Memo was written by Christopher Vogler during a week in New York with fellow story analyst (and theater director) David McKenna. It summarized the ideas of Joseph Campbell (writer on comparative mythology) whose work Vogler had looked at while in the cinema studies program at the University of Southern California. He recognized the influence of Campbell's ideas on George Lucas's construction of *Star Wars*. In seven pages Vogler distilled this down to stages in the hero's journey (such as becoming aware of a challenge, resisting the necessary change, crossing a threshold, confronting obstacles, making the big leap, challenges stacking up, re-dedicating oneself to the task, facing last-minute dangers, etc. – there are various ways to describe the phases and transitions Campbell had found in the world's mythologies).

Fax machines seemed to have been purpose-made for leaking this sort of memo and it soon escaped the confines of Disney, where it had already gone to people like producer David Hoberman (*Good Morning Vietnam*, *Stakeout*) of Disney division Touchstone; by all accounts then spreading through Hollywood's agencies and executive offices as a uniquely succinct expression of something that was very much in the air. For example, it was picked up at Paramount at the offices of production executive Dawn Steel (*Top Gun*, *Fatal Attraction*); Disney head Jeffrey Katzenberg (later the 'K' in DreamWorks SKG) apparently embraced it with enthusiasm (Vogler went straight to work for him on *The Lion King*); and soon the memo was being widely quoted elsewhere to endorse the view that a good movie story has a definable myth-like shape that a writer ignores at his professional peril. It is not so much that the Vogler Memo caused any of this; rather it has come to symbolize what became part of the "common sense" understanding of story in Hollywood at that time, and to a great extent still today.

So in *West of the Rising Sun*, Merritt lies in the darkness and is approached by the sharpshooter who downed him. The screenplay continues: "He unsheathes his sword... Merritt raises his right hand holding the derringer and...." The hero, obeying a "mythic" rule, rises from the (pretended) dead, kills his assailant, takes part in the heroic last stand of the samurai, wins the woman, adopts the boy.... The Hero's Journey reinstates its authority. In fact the project then evolved towards a yet more "perfect" version, one less troubled by other possibilities, and this became *The Last Samurai*, a textbook application of the approach to story that had been so effectively crystallized by the Vogler Memo.

STORIES AND LOGLINES

A "logline" is a short, pitchable statement of what a film is about. Usually it is only one or two sentences long. The type of logline today's industry expects to see will name a protagonist, suggest their main character trait, set up what their goal is and what forces oppose attainment of this goal. The main character trait will often just be a single adjective (courageous, bored, unhappy, etc.). The goal is often linked to an "inciting incident" ("Stripped of his power and sent into slavery by his tyrannical arch rival, brave Roman general Commodus must do [x] to achieve [x]," *Gladiator* (2000)). What the protagonist must do might be a series of linked things ("avenge the death of his family, rise through the ranks of gladiator school, re-instate the authority of the deposed Senate," etc.) but the logline typically subsumes these into one more abstract statement ("must fight to survive and to avenge the wrongs done to him and to the Roman people").

The logline will imply the sorts of event that will occur in the film but does not need to list them. Instead, it sets up the framework within which certain events and actions are likely and suggests what links them. A good logline of this type will be clear about where a film is really headed: in *Gladiator* is it really in the end about revenge or about restoring justice or both? ("Must fight to survive, to avenge the wrongs done to him and bring justice to the Roman people.") So even a small tweak to the wording can make a big difference.

In recent years, loglines – which is to say the stories that people are wanting to make into films – have tended to conform more and more closely to variants of the "Hero's Journey" template – a modern distillation of the structure of myth. The Vogler Memo which captured this tendency has been developed into a book that elaborates the stages. If you do not have access to the book, there are numerous summaries online, including "The Writer's Journey" Wikipedia entry and at the official website *http://www.thewritersjourney.com*.

This structure is based on the passage from a protagonist's ordinary world into and through a "special" world of some kind and an eventual return to the ordinary world. The "journey" is triggered by a "call to adventure" (which the protagonist may initially resist), then (in the "special" world), encounters with tests, allies and enemies on the way to an ordeal and a reward, which puts the protagonist on the road back (rededicating him or herself to the goal). There tends to be one final hurdle to get over (and sometimes an associated crisis of self-doubt) before the goal is achieved. So we can see in *Gladiator* that Commodus's ordinary world (honored Roman general and family man) is overturned, the life of a slave and then gladiator becomes his "special" world, but the goal requires his striving to return to the world from which he came in order to achieve what he wants. (*Gladiator* was written by David Franzoni, John Logan and William Nicholson. John Logan was screenwriter on *The Last Samurai*, developed from the earlier idea we have looked at as *West of the Rising Sun*). The "special" world is conceived as including a place or crucible (or "inmost cave") of transformation, so we will want to think in due course about whether or not we are using the word "transformation" in the same sense here.

This structure of myth tends to be taken in two directions. There are simplifications of it (life is normal, something happens to disrupt normality, things get really bad, hero overcomes the bad stuff and returns to a new normality). And there are immensely detailed elaborations of it, adding sub-stages and specifying relationships between protagonist and various allies and enemies (mentor, trickster, father-figure, etc.) The elaborate versions are often driven by the notion that the "transformation" is some kind of transcendent rite of passage that returns the protagonist to the ordinary world a better person in some way. Many aspiring and established screenwriters now use this as a system of generative rules for generating new screenplays.

Now consider a possible logline for Francis Ford Coppola's off-Hollywood film *Tetro* (2009), a film written by Coppola himself.

Eighteen-year old Bennie arrives in Buenos Aires and finds his long-missing older brother Tetro, a once-promising writer who is now a remnant of his former self. Bennie's discovery of his brother's near-finished play might hold the answer to understanding their shared past and renewing their bond. Against his brother's wishes, Bennie finishes the play.

There are several problems with this in terms of the now conventional "Hero's Journey" type logline we have been considering. First, who is the "hero" here? Is it Bennie or Tetro? Second, Bennie's literal journey (to Buenos Aires) is over right away – he has already found Tetro (and as he works on a cruise ship that has docked there he didn't really choose to make this journey in any straightforward sense). There is clearly the potential for another kind of journey – "finding" Tetro in a different sense, discovering what it is like to be Tetro – but this is not mapped onto an actual journey (in fact there is a journey, but late in the film instead). And where is the inciting incident, the call to action?

Now there are two key questions we should ask ourselves about these two loglines (for *Gladiator* and *Tetro*). First, do they make us want to watch the films? I would suggest that the answer is yes in both cases.

Stripped of his power and sent into slavery by his tyrannical arch rival, brave Roman general Commodus must fight to survive, etc. This sounds like an exciting film, promising much by way of interesting action (and if you have seen the film you will know that is what it delivers).

Eighteen year-old Bennie arrives in Buenos Aires and finds his long-missing older brother Tetro, a once-promising writer who is now a remnant of his former self, etc. This sounds deeply intriguing and poses more questions than it answers. Why has Tetro not finished the play? What is it about their

Tetro (2009)

past that needs to be understood? Why has Tetro gone AWOL from the family in the first place? Why has the brothers' bond broken down? What will happen to their relationship when Tetro discovers that Bennie has finished the play? And what is in the play?

So if a logline is intended to make us want to see the film (thus a producer to want to make it), then both of these are successful. But the one we have written for *Tetro* breaks the current rules in terms of the structure of myth. So the second important question is, from the loglines can you guess what the film is going to be like? In the case of *Gladiator*, the answer is very clearly yes. We fully expect the hero to survive, to avenge the wrongs done to him and bring justice to the Roman people. Even if we have not seen the film, we can imagine the sort of character that he is and the sorts of scene that will occur along the way. In a sense we have seen this film before precisely because it is another Hero's Journey.

In a letter to subscribers in Landmark Theaters' e-newsletter, Francis Ford Coppola says that his own main criterion for enjoying a film is "that I never saw it before or anything quite like it." And it is in fact utterly impossible to anticipate what will happen in *Tetro* – you have to see the film to find out.

The loglines for *Gladiator* and *Tetro* do have things in common. Both tell us *who the story is about, what they strive for,* and *what stands in the way*. So in a fundamental sense, this is all that a logline has to include if, at the same time, it succeeds in making us want to see the film. Of course, if a generation of production executives comes to expect one form rather than another – and a generation of audiences is trained to be reassured by the familiarity of that form – then alternatives to that form may have to bide their time.

EXERCISE

Taking the image from the Preface (page 15), write the loglines for two different films based on it, but having the following in common. Imagine that all the people in the picture (reproduced again below) have just died in a bombing raid on a German city during World War Two (perhaps Hamburg or Dresden). They are now in some kind of "way station" on their way to an afterlife. This is the beginning of the imagined film. The three people in the foreground are the central characters.

Your first logline should reflect the principles of the Hero's Journey structure (structure of myth). Your second logline should do something else. (You may wish to review the preceding section of this book.)

Things to Think About

Is one of the three foreground characters going to be your main protagonist? What are their relationships with each other? Did they know each other in life or have they just met?

Now take your second logline and story concept. Script one page each for two scenes that follow on directly from the scene on the steps. One scene should be an exterior. The other should be an interior. Think of what you are producing as, broadly speaking, one minute of each scene. (There is an example of screenplay formatting on page 78.) The only "rule" for this part of the exercise is that both scenes should include the woman

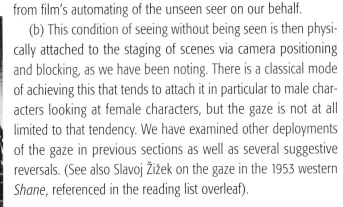

from the center foreground of our picture, even if she is not one of your main protagonists.

Finally, in visual form block out the actors' and camera's positions and movement for your two pages of screenplay. If you have access to it, you can use the software FrameForge Previs Studio to produce the kinds of visualization used in this book. Otherwise, drawn sketches will do perfectly well. Here the only rule is that you should think about the gaze and try to include a moment of "gaze reversal" as we have described it. This should not be anything quite so literal as the use of mirrors (as in that moment from *Touch of Evil* at the start of this book). Instead you can try keeping these two ideas in mind.

(a) Stanley Cavell suggests that in general "our natural mode of perception is to view, feeling unseen" (if we feel "seen," except in certain situations of deliberate self-display, we begin to feel uncomfortable). Viewing a film then "makes this condition automatic" (so we can relax and accept that this is a "natural" way for us to perceive things). Cavell explains the distinctive feeling of relaxation and surrender that comes with settling down to watch a film as in large measure derived from film's automating of the unseen seer on our behalf.

(b) This condition of seeing without being seen is then physically attached to the staging of scenes via camera positioning and blocking, as we have been noting. There is a classical mode of achieving this that tends to attach it in particular to male characters looking at female characters, but the gaze is not at all limited to that tendency. We have examined other deployments of the gaze in previous sections as well as several suggestive reversals. (See also Slavoj Žižek on the gaze in the 1953 western *Shane*, referenced in the reading list overleaf).

Can you stage a moment that taps the transformational power inherent in a reversal of the "normal" situation just described?

Cavell (1979), 102

Reading

Gulino, Paul Joseph (2004) *Screenwriting: the Sequence Approach* (New York: Continuum), "How a Screenplay Works," pp. 4-12. Introduces four basic "tools" of screenwriting: telegraphing, dangling cause, dramatic irony, dramatic tension.

Seger, Linda (2003) *Advanced Screenwriting* (Los Angeles: Silman-James Press), chapter 4, "Making a Scene," pp. 51-79. Sensible, undogmatic, practical advice on writing different types of scenes.

Geuens, Jean-Pierre (2000) *Film Production Theory* (Albany: State University of New York Press), chapter 5, "Staging," pp. 111-147. Includes an excellent discussion of découpage and very good practical advice.

Thinking about the "tools" described by Paul Joseph Gulino and applying them to a scene type identified by Linda Seger is basically all you need to draft two great scene extracts for this exercise. Then Jean-Pierre Geuens' advice on staging will help you think about how to put your scenes in front of the camera.

Ruffles, Tom (2004) *Ghost Images: Cinema of the Afterlife* (Jefferson, NC: McFarland & Co.). Mostly focused on "ghosts" on Earth, there is a short section on "Depictions of Heaven and Purgatory," pp. 133-136, and a very useful discussion of the film *A Matter of Life and Death* (1946), pp. 151-159, plus an excellent filmography.

Dixon, Wheeler Winston (2006) *Visions of Paradise: Images of Eden in the Cinema* (New Brunswick NJ: Rutgers University Press), chapter 4, "The Uses of Heaven," pp. 128-157. An excellent short history and discussion of cinematic depictions of a "heaven," in a book concerned with various kinds of cinematic paradise.

Walters, James (2008) *Alternative Worlds in Hollywood Cinema: Resonance Between Realms* (Bristol UK: Intellect). It is useful to think of "afterlife" films as variants of the "alternative world" that has long preoccupied filmmakers, as James Walters demonstrates.

Stam, Robert and Toby Miller (2000) *Film and Theory: An Anthology* (Malden, MA: Blackwell Publishing), Part IX, "The Nature of the Gaze," pp. 475-538. This section of a hefty film theory textbook is the state-of-the-art introduction to the gaze (and includes Laura Mulvey's classic essay on the topic), but the gem for the present purpose is a two-page discussion by Slavoj Žižek of the gaze in the 1953 western *Shane*, pp. 528-530.

For the historical background, an excellent source is Friedrich, Jörg (2006) *The Fire: The Bombing of Germany 1940-1945* (New York: Columbia University Press). There is also W. G. Sebald (2004) *On the Natural History of Destruction* (New York: The Modern Library); pp. 88-89 of this edition includes an unsettling discussion of suitcases.

Viewing

Afterlife stories offer some of the most ambitious of "special world" settings complete with threshold crossings and fantasies of transcendence. So they provide a good context for an exercise of this kind, concerned as it is to pose some fundamental questions about our styles of imagining. These are perhaps the four most innovative and challenging afterlife films:

A Matter of Life and Death (1946) dir. Michael Powell, Emeric Pressburger (UK), aka *Stairway to Heaven*
After Life (1998) dir. Hirokazu Koreeda (Japan)
What Dreams May Come (1998) dir. Vincent Ward (USA)
Wristcutters, a Love Story (2006) dir. Goran Dukic (USA)

Later in this book we will be looking in more detail at aspects of *After Life*, *Wristcutters* and *What Dreams May Come*.

PART 2

COMPOSING THE MOMENT

Compositionally, the primary interest in a visual field often has a dynamic quality. In the sketch, the top element on its own has a distinctive force and a sense of moving towards us and to the left. On its own, this is unquestionably the primary interest. It draws all of our attention to the right of the visual field it occupies, while its orientation towards the left promises some secondary interest there. When, on the second row, we add a further element, do we now have two areas of primary interest in the composition? The answer is quite definitely "no." What happens, even in this very simple example, is that the relationship between the two elements now becomes the primary interest, compositionally. We immediately start to feel the space between the elements taking on an energy and interest of its own. This is the dynamic nature of the primary interest in compositional terms.

In this scene from *Map of the Human Heart*, the Inuit boy Avik (Robert Joamie) is being bounced by his friends on a trampoline of walrus skins. As he takes to the air he sees an aircraft approaching. It is 1931. We are in the far north of Canada.

(In this and the following sequence of pages a key image from a scene appears first, then a compositional sketch referring to the images on the *opposite* page.)

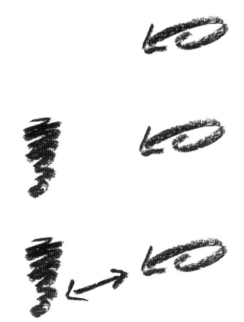

The biplane aircraft, with its slow, steady motion towards us and slightly to our left, dominates the frame entirely.

But Avik's bouncing into the frame sets up a second area of interest. As he appears, disappears, reappears, and the aircraft comes closer, it is the space between them that takes on the primary interest in this moment.

This intrusion into Avik's world is set up compositionally before it takes on any narrative or thematic significance. This dynamic space between two compositional elements within the frame constitutes one basis on which the entire film then builds its story of two worlds.

The planar structure of a composition can, for convenience, be summarized as foreground, midground and background, but of course there are many possible planes between these convenient segmentations of the represented space. In sectional perspective the planes sit parallel to each other, like a series of surfaces through which the eye moves as it travels into the space. Compositionally, a powerful device is the altering of the distances between planes (e.g. with different lenses). If we imagine reducing all of these planes to only one then we have imagined the core of the volume being spatially projected by a composition's spatial structure. This imagined core – a central plane through the represented volume – is itself seldom represented directly. Instead, depth is created in front of and behind it by the compositional arrangement of other planes.

Walter has arrived by aircraft in (from his point of view) the remote lands of the Inuit. A surveyor, he sets out with his assistant to map the area with his instruments for measuring space. Avik is intrigued.

Sometimes the most powerful deployment of planar structure in a composition is its deliberate collapsing onto the core of the represented volume. Here the use of an extraordinarily long lens completely collapses foreground, midground and background onto a single plane. When Walter is distracted, Avik clambers over his surveyor's theodolite, to see what it does. Walter explains how it captures the dimensions of a space. Looking through the theodolite Avik, to Walter's amusement, exclaims "Holy Boy!" which will become Walter's nickname for him.

Meanwhile, the ice, instead of being "background," takes on a material presence in the composition — bulbous, cold, overpowering, dwarfing the human figures. The suggestion of lives played out against the presence of greater, impersonal forces is compositionally expressed when nothing in the story, dialogue or characterizations yet suggests this.

The degree of lightness or darkness across areas of a composition — its range of values — gives a compositional organization to the surface of the image even where that surface is representing considerable depth in planar terms. For example, the physical contrast of dark figures against a light background provides strong compositional areas of interest. The values of the three "figures" in the sketch will not change even if they are reduced in size to suggest they are receding away from us in space.

Walter is now obtaining information and assistance for his surveying from Avik's extended family group and hunting band.

In a busy foreground scene, Avik, his grandmother (left of frame) and other members of the Inuit band play music, dance and carve up a seal. But the figure of Walter in the background is an insistent presence, overshadowing even from a distance the feeling of community and of an unchanging way of life being expressed in the foreground.

The feeling of an intrusion is muted but palpable. The question of what Walter's presence will mean for Avik is already in the air even though nothing has yet been said or done to suggest what this might be or that Avik's simple life might not continue unaltered.

The convergent lines of the Inuks, their tupiks (hide tents), boat, etc. tend to draw our eyes back towards the figures on the skyline, despite all the activity going on in front.

A visual composition can be thought of in terms of areas. In the sketch there are three areas — the two dark areas and the V-shaped area between them. Once representational detail is added — once the two dark shapes become something recognizable — we tend to be less conscious of the third area. But compositionally it retains just as much potential as the other two areas and that potential can be re-activated.

Avik is playing ball with his friends when he coughs up blood into his glove. He takes off determinedly with the ball — almost an act of physical defiance against the momentary sign of illness — but Walter realizes something is wrong and runs after him.

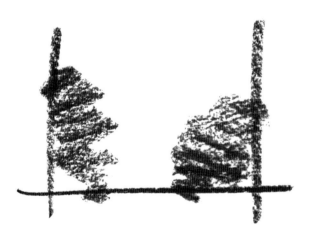

As Avik collapses on the snow, coughing up more blood, Walter grabs him. Blood splatters Walter's face. He wipes it off and stares at Avik, realization dawning that the boy has tuberculosis.

Re-framing the moment in close-up and against a blank background charges the space between white man and indigenous boy with a sense of now unsettling proximity and connectedness, its implications physically manifested in Avik's spume of blood.

The air-borne bacterial lung disease tuberculosis, or "consumption," was introduced to the Inuit by contact with whites, eventually leading to thousands of Inuit children being shipped south for treatment, many never seeing their families again.

A framed composition becomes a field of forces once elements are introduced into it. Cultural and psychological predispositions lead to these forces being perceived in particular ways. In the first sketch the object feels as if it is tending to slip out of the frame to the bottom left. To a Western eye this quadrant of a frame always tends to harbor this sort of feeling. But the second sketch shows an object that seems suspended energetically in the space. The top right quadrant of any such field always tends to feel more like a place where the forces are energized, where the object is floating within the compositional field rather than moving out of it. In other words, the bottom and left edges of the frame seem to have more power of attraction, pulling at objects. The right and top edges of the frame do not "pull" in the same way so the object seems freer.

Walter is flying away again. Avik's grandmother (Jayko Pitseolak) does not want Avik to leave but, at the last moment, he clambers aboard the aircraft, leaving her disconsolately below, watching it climb into the sky.

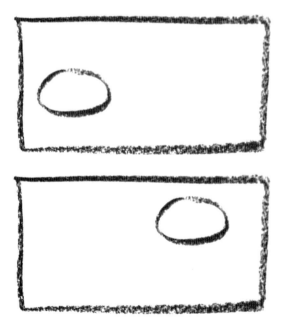

The scene leaves Avik's grandmother looking compositionally "abandoned" as Avik's excitement at flying takes over from any apprehension he might have had. Drawing the figure of Avik into the top right quadrant of the frame expresses his compositional suspension in the field of the frame, just as he is representationally suspended in the sky and also in a liminal moment between two worlds, his grandmother's and the white man's. Leaving that top right quadrant so visually empty in the shot of the grandmother serves to underscore the compositional effect. Even a composition can have poignancy.

Composition in relation to interior spaces can be thought of as working within a box-ended prism. Spaces can then be thought of as a series of "rooms" within this shape. Placing a plane within this prism, as shown in the sketch, creates the "picture box" used by painters since the early Renaissance, as well as by theater designers working for a traditional proscenium-arch stage. Openings on the sides or back of this box then link notionally or actually to other interior or exterior spaces. The representational elaboration of this compositional framework into rooms, doors, windows, etc. soon takes over from the underlying compositional framework, and the adoption of varied points of view tends to reduce the effects of parallel lines, notional vanishing points and box-like compositional framings. But those elements can still be used compositionally to striking effect.

Walter deposits Avik at the sanatorium in Ottawa for treatment of the boy's tuberculosis and leaves for Europe where he will be doing research in Dresden, Germany, on map-making and city planning.

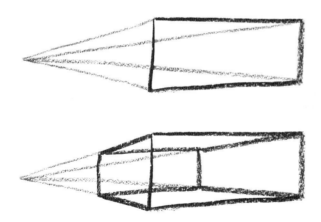

Avik experiences the hospital as a series of boxed spaces, from the corridors with their framed arches to the closet where he plays with his new friend Albertine (Annie Galipeau), the Métis girl (and where a disapproving Sister Banville finds them). The compositions emphasize Avik's introduction to the white man's world of enclosed spaces and parallel lines — a new geometry of space for an Inuit boy accustomed to the Arctic. This culminates in the perfect "picture box" composition of a storage room where one wall is a giant map of Canada.

The map as back wall of a "picture box" composition ironically evokes the very spatial expanses blocked off for the children by these walls. They find that Avik's home is not named on the map, suggesting another kind of tension between the two worlds.

Compositionally, exterior spaces can be thought of not as a continuous depth but as areas organized around the planar divisions of the space (e.g. the planes of foreground, midground and background). In plan view (i.e. from above) the planes are no longer visible as such but their compositional relationships come more clearly into view, as in this sketch. Starting from the bottom of the sketch (where the actual point of view will be located, not this bird's eye view), the foreground can be thought of as the area marked by the first arrow. A midground is then roughly a doubling of this first area. A background area is then, in terms of a useful compositional method, a doubling of those first two areas taken together. And a deep background space is in turn a doubling of the first three spaces together. Actual dimensions will vary of course depending on the context.

This creates in effect a series of "stages" that are compositionally related to each other in a balanced way. In the sketch the foreground "stage" is empty. Three figures (left) are placed at the rear of the midground "stage" and two figures (center) are positioned at the notional transition between background and deep background "stages." Hills define the deep background (the backdrop) in this example.

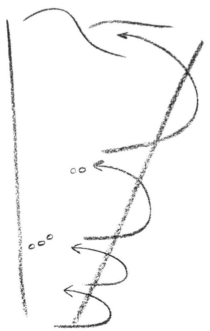

The time comes for Avik's new friend Albertine, now recovered, to leave the hospital and go off to school. To stay the moment, the two children take off across the fields at dusk and in the rain, pursued by three adults, including Sister Banville (Jeanne Moreau), who eventually drag them back.

The composition of the master shot (above right) leaves the foreground empty and places Avik and Albertine almost exactly where a doubling of the foreground and midground areas creates a compositional "stage" that dramatizes the feeling of attempted escape, without putting the figures into the deep background and severing our feeling of connection with them. Sister Banville and the two men enter the composition at the rear of the midground "stage."

Even the use of long lenses to get into the circle of action when the children are caught does not reduce the compositional feeling of space already created. Paradoxically perhaps, the intensity of emotion seems more vivid in this larger space than if the camera had stayed with the children throughout, like a moment of intensity on a theatrical stage viewed from the back of a theater — all the more striking because expressible across that distance.

Shapes are the basis of many powerful compositional effects. The most potent shapes create and channel active forces on the compositional field.

It is almost impossible to see the pair of lines on the top row of the sketch as anything other than leading upwards and away.

The triangle also has a powerful channeling effect, creating a sense of force towards the apex.

The oval contains and constrains the space it encloses and separates it from the surrounding compositional field.

So even these simplest of shapes, if embedded in a composition, create effects at the purely compositional level that can then be harnessed representationally.

As Albertine is bundled into a car to be driven away — the children will not see each other again until they are adults in war-wearied Europe — Avik watches from a hospital balcony. The striking use of a triangular composition (top right) formed by walls and paths in the hospital forecourt, combined with the strong compositional element of the road, creates an inexorable sense of potential motion off into the gloom, even before Albertine is pushed into the car and driven away.

Avik is framed in an oval that emphasizes his entrapment, along with the more obvious representational elements of wrought iron balustrade and heavy architecture.

So before any actual movement apart of Albertine and Avik the compositions are absolutely saturated with the feeling of their impending separation.

In a moving image the composition becomes dynamic. The field of forces can shift and change as action takes place within the frame.

Strong static graphic elements can anchor these compositional dynamics, becoming points on the visual field around which shifting patterns and forces change. Here (sketch) a strong element of this sort becomes a kind of hinge around which two compositional diagonals are articulated. In the top version an initial line is established but the two moving elements that form it shift across the frame into a second alignment with both the "anchor" and a new element in the right foreground.

Such movements feel neither random, on the one hand, nor artificially choreographed, on the other, but the overall effect is of compositional dynamics that have a purpose, once the representational details of a scene harness their purely compositional effects.

Avik is now a healthy young man and has returned to his northern community. However he is having difficulty re-integrating. It is 1941. Unexpectedly Walter shows up again. Unknown to Avik, he is now in the wartime military and, because of his cartographer's knowledge of the area, has been sent to find a German submarine that has been trapped in the ice, its crew dead by now but its code books hopefully intact.

As the newly returned Walter climbs the hill towards the inunnguaq (cairn), an excited Avik by his side, they form a strong diagonal across the frame, emphasizing behind them the vastness of the Arctic tundra over which the inunnguaq, sentinel-like, stands guard. But the camera cranes slowly down to find Avik's grandmother waiting for them. When Walter and Avik reach the top the new diagonal, from inunnguaq to right foreground, aligns the four figures strikingly. What also gets brought into view here, as it were, is the complex set of relationships between traditional life and the new world that Walter will be telling Avik about. The human or cross-like figure of the inunnguaq is a newer development of the traditional Inuit inuksuk cairns, already the beginnings of a negotiation with the white world's representational conventions.

Yet again Avik is going to be drawn away into that other world, although his grandmother's increased dependence on him gives him pause at first.

There is a kind of *understanding between dynamic forces* in the compositional field that can produce a complex feeling. This is often connected with how the eye is encouraged to move across the visual field. Composition takes the eye's natural tendency to roam and captures it. Producing the complex feeling is then a matter of what connections are possible between capturing the eye and everything else that is going on: narratively, performatively, affectively.

Out on the tundra with Walter's search party, Avik hears Albertine singing. Realizing where the sound is coming from (the radio operator in the previous shot has tuned to a channel from Ottawa), Avik runs and leaps crazily over the ice formations trying to get there before the signal vanishes again. A hand-held camera tries to keep him in frame but he bounces all over the place. However, through all the movement the framing orientates itself around the same place in the frame as the radio operator occupied. So, as we rush with Avik towards that compositional point, we feel both the frenzy and the focus in his astonished reaction, with all that it means for his future.

The compositional capacity to distract the eye can be as important as focusing it. The visual field can be put in motion compositionally so that the complex feeling is one of uncertainty, fluidity, shifting points of attention, narrative hiatus.

For this feeling to be effectively used, it has to be captured as it were. The immediate visual pleasure of a busy, complex, shifting field of view, gets followed by a shot or shots assigning the point of view to its "owner" in the narrative field. Compositionally, the sketched "eye" below is not permitted to float freely, as perhaps it does in the viewing of a painting in a gallery.

When Avik, now in the air force in wartime England, goes to an elegant dance to find Albertine, not knowing that she will be there with Walter, he feels out of place. As people very different from Avik dance around him, the camera shares his confusion visually. Spatial relationships become compositionally uncertain. The eye gets distracted by this blur of movement, that passing shape. Albertine, when he sees her, is not a stable object held by his and the camera's gaze but a glimpsed figure with whom his compositional relationship has become suddenly uncertain.

That relationship will not clarify itself until what we shall call a *meta-compositional* moment, which we are now going to look at in more detail.

The Meta-Compositional Effect

In *Fail-Safe* (1964), the director Sidney Lumet, cinematographer Gerald Hirschfeld and editor Ralph Rosenblum gave us perhaps the best two intercut counter-dollies in cinema history. After more than an hour of seeing the two central characters in a rigid composition (top left), the final minutes of the film deploy two agonizingly slow dollies from profile to frontal shots of their faces. The dollies produce a formal effect that we can call "meta-compositional" because it depends for effect on the previously established composition.

THE META-COMPOSITIONAL MOMENT

Compositional elements, as we have seen in the preceding examples, slip rapidly behind their representational elaboration (from left hand page to right hand in each of our examples). So each of the simple circular compositional elements below becomes instantly an object in the sequence opposite and on the next two pages. Following his disorientation at the dance where he discovered that Albertine has been with Walter, Avik arranges to meet her after his next flight. When they do meet he thinks he has only one more bombing mission over Germany in his tour of duty. Compositionally, the scene begins to organize itself around a series of circular shapes.

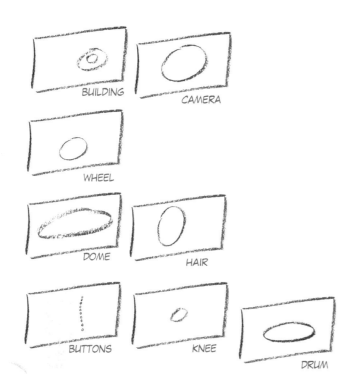

In themselves, these very simple but insistently present compositional elements do not express anything other than a growing circularity occurring within the visual field.

The viewer will not "see" this circularity but, as the previous examples have demonstrated, composition quickly sets up forces and dynamics within the plane of the image. What happens quite strikingly to these forces here is that they take on their most dynamic physical presence when Albertine and Avik start spinning slowly round an iron column in the middle of this unusual space.

What is constituted here (and roughly represented in the sketch above) is a meta-compositional moment in which the circularity has built up a kind of insistent pressure within the visual field's pattern of forces. The camera movement picks this up by semi-circling the figures outside the "cage" of iron lattice-work in which they spin and then dance. So a sort of compositional vortex is created by "seeding" the images with this circularity and then releasing it in one central action, on which other aspects of the film also converge.

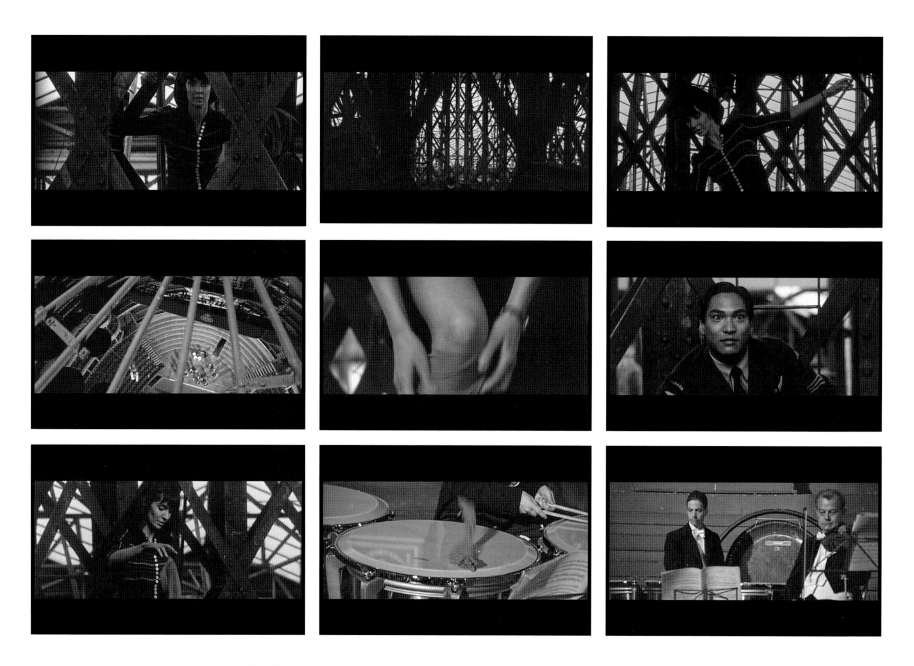

109. INT. ROYAL ALBERT HALL. DAY.   **109**

There is an explosion and a couple of glass squares
shatter, covering them with glass, but not harming them.

They laugh at their escape, it is almost hysterical
laughter.

They wipe glass from one another and then, almost *not
realizing what they're doing, they kiss, gently, briefly.*
She pulls away from him.

> AVIK
> After this mission we'll be
> together...

She knows what he is going to say and puts her finger on
his lips to shush him.

> ALBERTINE
> No. I dreamt I would be married
> with a white man.

> AVIK
> There's nothing special about a
> white man.

> ALBERTINE
> Do you know what being a half-
> breed is? Being poor and dirty.
> Thinking you're stupid and ugly.
> Living on a dirt floor in some
> filthy shack. And all the time,
> all the time, white people
> sneering at you, calling you a
> half-breed. I want to live like a
> real, white, person. Never be
> hated again.

> AVIK
> You think you're the only half-
> breed?

> ALBERTINE
> I can get away with looking
> white.

Though one's objects are prized and "precious," they are no less objects and no less defined by being possessed. Avik, the Inuk rescued by Walter the map-maker turned military planner, and Albertine, the Métisse whom Walter has taken to London as his lover, have both become objects in Walter's world. The worlds they have come from are respectively that of the Inuit, the indigenous people of the Arctic, and that of the Métis, a Canadian "first people" of mixed European and aboriginal descent. Children together in the Catholic sanatorium and orphanage in Ottawa, Albertine and Avik were separated when the girl was taken away to be fostered by a white family. They meet a decade later in London during World War Two and, thanks in different ways to Walter's influence, are both now working in Bomber Command. England is "carpet bombing" German cities with massed night-time bomber raids. Germany, the aggressor now on the defensive, is launching rocket-propelled drones known as "flying bombs" or "buzz bombs" against London.

A bomb-aimer on a Lancaster aircraft that the crew has nicknamed "Holy Boy" after him, Avik knows that Albertine is a photo analyst interpreting daily images taken by on-board cameras over German cities. On the way back from what should be his penultimate bombing mission, he sends her an invitation to a secret tryst by photographing the Royal Albert Hall in London. He waits for her there the next evening.

Opened by Queen Victoria when her Empire was at its height (and named for her late husband), the red-brick confidence of the Royal Albert Hall was reportedly described by the Queen at the time as looking "like the British Constitution." In 1936 it hosted a celebration of the "Youth of Empire," attended by thousands of young people from Britain's then still precious "possessions" and "dependencies" across the world. The Hall's wrought iron and glazed dome was designed by an English architect also known for designing a famous iron-framed hotel in Bombay and a bridge in Singapore: those were the days when British Empire builders were followed by builders and planners of all kinds, a legacy that Walter inherited. Albertine climbs up to the dome where Avik waits (the frames on the preceding pages). The "floor" of its iron cage is an open grille. Far below a section of an orchestra rehearses.

Albertine catches her stocking on a piece of wire. She takes it off, so as to balance better with her bare feet as she precariously crosses the dome's grille. She lets the stocking drop through, drifting down towards the musicians. It lands on a timpani drum, to the evident bewilderment of the musician. Albertine shakes her long, unruly hair out of the net it has been done up in. Then Albertine and Avik use the dome's central iron shaft like a carousel, wheeling around it as they talk. They dance. A buzz bomb interrupts the moment, its explosion nearby shattering panes in the dome and showering Albertine and Avik with chalky dust and shards of debris. They laugh, as much with relief as anything, but then, in the gloom, the question of who and what they really are unexpectedly surfaces like a repressed thought that has been released by the explosion.

Albertine's very name carries the same imperial echoes as the Hall's (while also the name of Proust's orphaned object of attachment, trapped by his narrator but also by her own longing for status, in the multi-volume novel *In Search of Lost Time*).

How quickly compositional elements that are purely visual take on increasingly dense layers of meaning. We could identify other features of the composition here – especially the ways in which diagonals and frames derived from the dome's iron "cage" are used to direct the eye. And we could block out the staging and camera positioning as we have done for other scenes, especially the use of a hand-held camera as Albertine balances on the grille. But the point here is to emphasize how composition becomes another layer to the moment, and in particular how a meta-compositional layer (or second order form of composition) draws simpler compositional elements into being more than the sum of their simple parts and into an intimate relationship with what the moment is expressing.

It is, of course, very tempting to interpret the "cage" in which Albertine and Avik are represented here as the "cage" of Empire, Albertine's bare-foot

letting go of decorum and their dance in the darkness as a reassertion of identities. There is some considerable justification for such an interpretation. But jumping too quickly to it tends to miss how the moment feels. Indeed the fact that Albertine and Avik do feel is what comes across most strongly here. The momentary vortex of feeling they find for themselves, before the bomb wrenches them back to a sense of reality, is as much physical as it is a "meaning" to be interpreted in terms of displaced and assimilated identities re-expressing themselves. Appropriately then the viewer *feels* the question of identity more than intellectualizes it, which is entirely characteristic of how Vincent (above) works.

What comes clearly into focus in this scene from *Map of the Human Heart* is the subaltern status of two of the three main characters. Albertine and Avik both wear the uniform, both are being used by the white world in ways that have little to do with who they were before. Except that both have willingly sought out these roles. And Walter is not some one-dimensional oppressor. He has been, in many ways, their friend. In Albertine's "I can get away with looking white," as the dust lies shroud-like on her hair, resides an entire, complex exposure of how the dominant white world constructed a "universal human being" in its own image and then made it seemingly natural for others to aspire to that image.

Shortly afterwards, Avik discovers that his crew is being sent on an extra mission, to fire bomb the German city of Dresden. He goes to see Walter and, for the first time, sees the object that he himself has become. (We looked at that scene in detail earlier in the book.)

General Hospital, Beirut, Syria, 1942

```
OLD PHOTOGRAPHS
Poland & Middle East, 1939/1942
 --duration: 1:27

ROSTRUM
1942 MAP OF MIDDLE EAST.
FEMALE VO

ARCHIVE PHOTOS
 (PAN/ZOOM SLOWLY ACROSS,
  KEN BURNS' STYLE...)



RUSSIAN TROOPS ROUNDING
UP POLISH 'UNDESIRABLES'...

POLISH REFUGEES...




SOME OF THE 'TEHERAN CHILDREN'
- JEWISH ORPHANS AMONG THE
  POLISH REFUGEES.


DISSOLVE TO...

THE DESERT ROAD TO DEIR EZ ZOR
IN SYRIA...

PHOTO FROM NZEF/ASC ARCHIVE
OF CPL. WARD'S TRUCK ON FIRE.






HOSPITAL

PULL IN ON LONDON GAZETTE
PAGE SHOWING PAT WARD'S NAME,
MENTIONED FOR GALLANTRY.
```

VO (narrator): In 1942 the New Zealand Expeditionary Force's Army Service Corps sent its reserve transport companies on an extraordinary mission. 110 trucks were to take drugs and other medical supplies, including perishable serum, from Egypt through Palestine and Syria to Teheran which had been flooded with 115,000 Polish refugees from Russian labor camps. Three years earlier, Soviet Russia and Nazi Germany had partitioned Poland. While the Germans embarked on ethnic cleansing, the Russians deported 'undesirables' to labor camps. When Russia entered the war against Germany it agreed to release the Poles, among them many Jews. While some of the men were recruited into a reconstituted Polish army to guard the oil fields and others headed West hoping to enlist in the Allied army in Palestine, the women, children and elderly stayed in Teheran, many weak and ill with dysentery, typhus and scarlet fever after the deprivations of the labor camps. People were dying daily.

VO (cont.): The New Zealand convoy, which would have to travel nearly 2,000 miles to reach them, promised a lifeline. Corporal Patrick Ward was driving one of the convoy's fuel trucks when it overheated and caught fire on the desert road to Deir ez Zor. Knowing that a burnt-out truck could block the road for hours he stayed at the wheel as his truck turned into an inferno, steering it off the narrow road into the soft sand. Vincent's father sustained severe burns to over a third of his body. He would spend two months in a hospital in Beirut before he was well enough to be moved.

- 5 -

Holy Boy script page courtesy of Clue Productions (dir. Perkins Cobb)

THE "UNIVERSAL HUMAN BEING"?

The writer Gayatri Spivak, thinking about her own upbringing in the education system in India, remarks that the "hero" of the Western traditions she was exposed to "was the universal human being." Moreover, she says, "we were taught that if we could begin to approach an internalization of that universal human being, then we would be human." With an Irish Catholic father whose grandfather had left a tenant farm in Ireland owned by an absentee English landlord after famine made life untenable, and a German Jewish mother whose father had got the family out of Germany in the 1930s, Vincent Ward's own "internalization of that universal human being" was never going to be an absolutely straightforward one. The half-glimpsed circumstances behind his father Patrick's trauma on the road to Deir ez Zor on his way to Teheran, in this iconic family story (left), and Vincent's trip to Hamburg looking for his maternal grandparents' house, both have the potential to chip away at any easy adoption of the "universal human being" as the model of how to "be human"; not least because an iron-clad commitment to versions of that universal figure had produced the victims, the "undesirables," who populate the background of those historical circumstances.

This telling of a fragment of "family history" in the first ten minutes of *Holy Boy*, the documentary, raises questions about memory, time and story. Though the Russian soldier aiming his rifle at the Polish woman and child – a fragment of a larger moment that would put Pat Ward on the road to Teheran three years later – has a hair-raising sense of tension and terror about it, it remains difficult not to see that image and the others as mostly here to represent something abstract – "refugees," even "history." But what if we pick out one detail – those muslin drapes over the beds in the Syrian hospital (far left), and see the story from there?

Spivak (1990), 7. Documentary source, War History Branch, Dept. of Internal Affairs, Wellington NZ

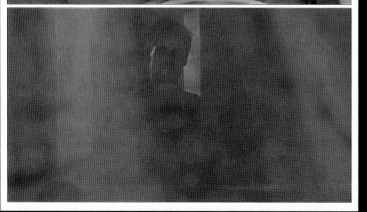

The English Patient (1996) dir. Anthony Minghella

The infiltration of story includes the "English Patient" quality in our imagining of Pat Ward's burned body being taken first to an Arab hospital in Deir ez Zor before transfer to Beirut (coincidentally, Anthony Minghella was an admirer of *Map of the Human Heart* and used the same composer, Gabriel Yared, when he directed *The English Patient*). But what if, perhaps with the help of that last association, we pick out one detail here – the look and feeling of those muslin drapes over the beds in the Syrian hospital in the documentary frame overleaf, the faintest evening breeze from the windows fluttering them almost imperceptibly?

When archival images document a history more loyally, what does cinema do instead? There is something about cinema's rendering of things – not just of detail but of the larger fold of cloth, the way things hang in space and shift in time – that might seem a loyalty to realism and a fidelity to documenting but is in fact rather different. Where one aspect of the archival images on the previous pages moves outwards towards a generalization about lives and times, the "Pentateuchal" style of imagined moment (as we want to think of it) compels us to feel differently, and to shift our attention inwards instead. There is an automatism about the succession of archival images. They manufacture a sense of time according to familiar conventions and organize their historical objects in recognizable ways to do so. Add on top of that a story with a familiar shape and the moment is no longer arresting in the same way, especially if we are watching moving images rather than still frames. Even the faces of the "Teheran Children" on the previous pages hover somewhat uncertainly between these two possibilities: that they are individuals who might speak to us across the intervening years about ordinary things, or that they are refugees whose faces only speak to us in the collective about horrors in response to which we must wring our hands one more time.

The photograph of the beds in the Syrian hospital is less archivally insistent about making a general point. So we can linger for a moment over those muslin drapes. In doing so, don't we momentarily come closer to Patrick Ward who lay in one of those beds in 1942 while his burns began to heal, listening at night to the unfamiliar sounds of a Beirut street outside while the muslin rippled? The word "gallant" put into the mouth of the King in the *London Gazette*, in that ritually ventriloquistic gesture, seals a process of "Homeric" generalization instead. A deserved acknowledgment of course but also an archaic word attached to Spivak's "hero."

Whether in Anthony Minghella's *The English Patient* (left) or in *Map of the Human Heart* (above), when Albertine catches her stocking on a barb of wire, the cinematically arresting moment does two things. First it tells us that we could be present in that moment were it not for time. The moment feels physically, spatially present to us in all its subtle materiality. It is not so much that we are not there. It is that we are not *then*. And second? Well, the book hasn't quite got to that point yet; but it is going to be about what Kathleen Stewart means when she refers to "the sure knowledge that every scene I can spy has tendrils stretching into things I can barely, or not quite, imagine." As we will discover, there is a risk in such moments of turning inwards instead (especially through actors looking for a truth within themselves) when the transformational orientation is properly outwards.

Stewart (2007), 128

SUMMARY #1

What have we found out so far about the transformational moment in film?

(a) It happens when a cinematic moment becomes more than the sum of its parts.

(b) It includes what the viewer brings to the moment, which is a readiness to feel something about the moment – an affective potential.

(c) This affective potential does not necessarily need to go into large on-screen emotions – in fact the directing of affective potential into prominent "emoting" by characters, though common, may misdirect it away from the kinds of moment we are interested in.

(d) Among these kinds of moment, there may be connections that are organized along different lines than the plot ("plot" as a particular interlinking of story events) – our transformational moments may further a plot but they may at the same time be organized along different lines within the film, and sometimes they may not actually further the plot at all.

(e) The synergistic combination of different techniques informs the construction of these moments – they are not reducible to the effects of one technique.

(f) Staging is an important first place to look for how the transformational moment in film is actually constructed, although the French filmmaking term *découpage* is even more useful as it emphasizes the indivisibility of staging and cutting (which tend to be thought of separately in the English-speaking world).

(g) The "gaze" is a key effect of staging and cutting and a fantasmatic gaze (based on being the seer rather than the seen) is a now familiar, omnipresent feature of how "classical" cinematic form attaches its staging and cutting to a particular point of view and offers that point of view to the spectator.

(h) There is potential for a reversal within the gaze that is inherent in every staging of it and being able to tap into this potential is a key resource to have

available, where appropriate, in constructing the post-classical transformational moment – the potential for reversal is always there but relatively seldom accessed.

(i) The screen that carries the transformational moment is a field of forces, among which compositional factors play a significant role in setting up the affective potential even before objects on the screen take on represented identities, and even though that happens instantaneously – meta-compositional forces intensify this potential.

(j) The transformational moment in film is subject to various kinds of containment capable of blunting its potential or erasing it entirely – and among these is a tendency to harness story to mythic structure and to the idea of the "universal human being," both of which suit Hollywood's understandable interest in finding a global narrative transparency (product that travels well) but both tend to limit the possibilities.

(k) Time is an important dimension to the kinds of moment we are interested in, and these moments are often capable of evoking "history" in a way that differs from mere historical re-enactment – by suggesting connections across sheets of time.

(l) f + i gives us a good example of e.

(m) When g combines with the kinds of containment identified in j we are likely to have an example of mainstream movie-making at its most formulaic. But there are other formulas…

(n) b + h promises a powerful combination.

(o) d + k promises another powerful combination.

(p) Starting to wonder about b + d + h + k ?

We have also been tracing one filmmaker's navigation of these possibilities in his own life, along with the work of some of his friends, because it is not as a textbook exercise that these things become actual, only as practical and creative solutions.

This, the book's second exercise focused on creative solutions, is concerned with using visual composition to express some of the meaning that a scene has. At its best, this can produce what we have termed a meta-compositional effect, where the other elements in a scene do not have to spell out absolutely everything for us because the visual composition is communicating so powerfully.

Look back at the storyboards for the un-made *West of the Rising Sun* and at our related discussion of the frame below, as well as the plot summary contained in the page from the *Holy Boy* documentary (pp. 79–82). Merritt, the western-style hero working in Japan in the 1870s, has been killed. In our version he is not just feigning in order to trap his assailant! Rebecca Bryson is an adventurous widow who has been travelling with Merritt and the samurai Kenichi.

On the next page we have written an imagined scene to follow on from this storyboard frame. (Left is a nineteenth-century postcard of a samurai or member of the Japanese military nobility like Kenichi.)

The exercise is to storyboard the scripted scene, with an emphasis on visual composition. Rough sketches are fine for compositional purposes (artists' charcoal sticks or felt-tip pens are good sketching media as they make it quick and easy to shade areas and block out shapes).

We are using this print by Japanese landscape artist Hiroshige as the basis for the setting where the scene is to be shot. Empty it of Hiroshige's people (and mentally remove the decorative prints on the interior walls). With the houses on right and left and the trees beyond, this is the space you have available for compositional purposes. How can you use this space – and the visual elements it offers – for compositional effect? Think about framing and angles. How many shots do you need for the scene? Will the camera move, thus changing the composition?

Thaw Naing

Tarui, from the series *Sixty-nine Stages of the Kisokaidō* 1835-42, by Utagawa Hiroshige.

```
SC.105 EXT. EDGE OF VILLAGE. DUSK.

KENICHI watches as REBECCA and TARO return from the
improvised barricade where they have been looking out at
MERRITT'S BODY. REBECCA gives the boy a tender hug, then
sends him off to one of the houses.

                    KENICHI
              Mrs Bryson...

She stares at him, not really seeing.

                    KENICHI
              It is a war, Mrs Bryson. You did
              not start it.

He touches her sleeve but she pulls away -

                    REBECCA
              I have to go. I have to leave
              here...

                    KENICHI
              It is too late. They are almost
              on us. You cannot go back alone.
              You must...

He doesn't finish. She stares straight ahead. KENICHI goes to
the side of one of the houses and picks a small bunch of
white chrysanthemums. He carries them, flowerheads downwards,
back to REBECCA and holds them out to her with both hands. At
first she does not react. Then she stares at the flowers.
KENICHI looks uncomfortable.

                    KENICHI
              For Mr Merritt.

Without taking the flowers, REBECCA turns and walks away. But
she stops a short distance away. Her back is still turned to
KENICHI. TARO is secretly watching the scene from a shadowy
doorway. REBECCA walks on, into one of the houses. TARO runs
out and surprises KENICHI by bowing in front of him and
accepting the flowers. TARO disappears after REBECCA, leaving
KENICHI alone.
```

Reading

Giannetti, Louis (2010) *Understanding Movies* (Boston MA: Allyn & Bacon). In its 12th edition at the time of writing, the chapter on mise-en-scène (with a section on composition) is still one of the best overviews available, with excellent illustrations. (Mise-en-scène refers to the arrangement of elements within a three-dimensional filmed space with a view to its still typically two-dimensional representation on screen. Composition is a key element of mise-en-scène.)

Block, Bruce (2008) *The Visual Story: Creating the Visual Structure of Film, TV and Digital Media* (Burlington MA: Focal Press), second edition. This is the "bible" for visual composition on screen, especially the first four chapters. Bruce Block always relates composition to other aspects of the visual construction of the image.

Things to Think About

Where is the moment with most compositional potential here? Rebecca pulling away? Kenichi picking the flowers? The awkward few seconds between them? Rebecca walking off? The boy running out to accept the flowers? Kenichi standing alone at the end of the scene? These are all important aspects. But is there one part of the scene where you can specifically use composition to say something that the characters are not saying or that even their actions are not fully expressing? (Hint: one possibility is the moment when Rebecca walks off but stops briefly, her back still turned to Kenichi....)

Viewing

Tokyo Story (1953), dir. Yasujirô Ozu (Japan). For some very four-square compositions with the camera always three-feet off the ground and a use of empty space that has extraordinary power. Profundity without showing off.

narrative and the moment

The Navigator: a Medieval Odyssey is available for viewing at http://mubi.com/

THE TRANSFORMATION RULE IN NARRATIVE

The Navigator: A Medieval Odyssey (also released on video in the U.S. as The Navigator, an Odyssey Across Time) was Vincent's second feature and second official selection in competition at the Cannes Festival (1988). It had taken four years for the young director to make, in the context of tax incentives and loopholes that had made the first half of the 1980s a relatively risk-less boom period for Australasian film production but a period brought rapidly to an end by changes to the tax regimes in both New Zealand and Australia that saw many investors pull out. While Vincent waited in Sydney, producer John Maynard pieced together the needed funding in fits and starts and the film finally emerged as the first official co-production between the two countries, sweeping the boards at the Australian Film Institute Awards that year. Vincent and John Maynard's previous Cannes selection, Vigil (1984) had begun a remarkable reputation-building process internationally – it shared the billing at Cannes with films such as Wim Wender's Paris Texas and Lars Von Trier's The Element of Crime – and encouraged important pre-sales to international film distributors for the next film. The New Zealand Film Commission, a government agency set up in the late 1970s to channel public money into developing and sustaining a national film industry (as happened in many countries due to concerns about viability in the face of Hollywood's international dominance) made its then largest yet commitment to supporting a single film. Nonetheless, production faltered for financial reasons partway through, reportedly when private investors who were crucial to the overall package pulled their money out and put it into a Broadway musical. With Australian Film Development Commission support the film did get completed and when Navigator was released it consolidated its then thirty-three-year-old director's growing reputation. Major London publisher Faber and Faber published the screenplay (by Ward, Kely Lyons and Geoff Chapple) with an introduction by film journalist and critic Nick Roddick (then editor of trade paper Screen International) who said, quite simply, that Vincent Ward had now become "a major-league film director."

Griffin (Hamish McFarlane)
Searle (Marshall Napier)
Arno (Chris Haywood)
Villagers (14th century)

Connor (Bruce Lyons)
Ulf (Noel Appleby)
Martin (Paul Livingston)
Foundry workers (20th century)

Griffin's first vision. 3:38

Cumbria, 1348. The village. The boy Griffin is teased for being a dreamer. Discussing omens and threat of approaching plague. Waiting for Connor's return. Connor's back! Community meets. Plan for journey to make offering at the 'great church in the west'. Watch boatload of 'refugees from the east' being driven off by men from a neighboring village, their boat burned out on the lake. Length 13:53 (running time 19:31)

Griffin's second vision. 00:36 (20:07)

Decision to go down the great pit (Connor, Griffin, Searle, Ulf, Arno, Martin). Preparations. Leaving the village. Ulf brings rough little carved figurine of Virgin Mary. Discovery of the wooden tunneling engine at the great pit. Tunneling to the far side of the world. Breaking through to the sewers of the (modern!) city. 9:42 (29:49)

Arrival at the surface, overlooking city. Crossing the road. Ulf gets stranded. Connor goes ahead on his own. The others look for a foundry. Convincing foundry workers to make the cross for the church spire. Want to raise the cross before daybreak. Cross has to be cooled so Martin stays with the three workers. Searle, Arno and Griffin decide to go ahead: must cross the harbor by boat to reach the church. 16:36 (46:25)

Stealing a white horse (for roping to a pulley when they get to the church and hoist the cross). Rowing across the harbor, with horse on board. Encounter with a nuclear submarine (USS Queenfish). Includes Griffin's third vision (00:46), immediately after 'Queenfish' encounter. Griffin tells the others that somebody will die falling from the church spire. 8:05 (54:30)

In the city. Connor encounters monstrous machines and gets carried on front of a train. Includes Griffin's fourth vision (00:56). Connor finds himself at the church and starts to climb the spire. Martin arrives at the church with the foundry workers. Griffin jumps into the water and wades ashore. Searle scrambles the horse off the boat and rides it ashore. Running through the deserted nighttime city streets. Griffin encounters a wall of TV screens. Griffin says he can 'see too much' and asks Searle to blindfold him so he can lead them to the church. 12:45 (1:07:15)

At the church. Connor struggles with ropes and old wooden ladder on the spire. Griffin and Searle rush through the church. The winch rope on the foundry workers' truck frays and breaks, leaving Connor clinging. Griffin and Searle climb the staircase in the spire. Searle climbs out onto the ladder with Connor but the rungs snap and they both cling on precariously. Griffin climbs out to help. On the ground, the others rope the horse to the pulley. Griffin climbs up to drag the cross, held by the ropes, into place on top of the spire as the sun comes up. He succeeds. Back at the village they hear bells. Griffin falls from the spire. 7:48 (1:15:3)

Morning, back at the mine. It was all a story, told by Griffin as the men waited for dawn. Griffin tells Ulf that in the end he tunneled under the road and 'showed the little Virgin celestial city'. Daybreak finds the village without the expected signs of plague. Celebration. Griffin dances joyously with the others but suddenly feels unwell - he has the marks of plague. 4:56 (1:19:59)

The revelation that Connor had come back to the village at the beginning with the plague ('There was nowhere else for me to go'), unintentionally infecting Griffin. Connor has recovered, believing that Griffin's story has saved them, but Griffin is now dying. We see (Griffin's final vision) Connor push his small coffin off into the lake, bearing the symbol of their cross from the spire. 5:30 (1:25:29 + credits = 1:27:00 running time)

The Navigator is itself in some ways a parable about storytelling, so it affords an ideal opportunity to consider the nature of cinematic story and narrative (the way a story is told).

The main sequences in The Navigator are summarized on the left, with timings for each section. The film is set in late medieval Cumbria, a then isolated, mountainous region in the northwest of England. "Medieval" here means less the actualities of that long historical period between Roman Empire and early modern world and more a modern imagining of simpler, inward-looking communities eking out meager but honest existences with little concern for anything beyond their own horizons. The people in this kind of imagined community are versions of the peasant figure that historian Kathleen Biddick has called a "melancholic object" invented by later medievalists, impoverished yet innately noble in spirit, craftspeople rather than alienated functionaries of industrialization, superstitious but in a way that can elicit modern empathy. Kathleen Biddick recounts how the first issue of The Ecclesiologist (monthly journal of a Victorian society dedicated to returning church architecture to the luster it had had in the Middle Ages) carried an appeal from the Bishop of New Zealand for working drawings of medieval church design, including moldings, doors, arches, etc. so that these could be imitated in the colonies, a task for which pattern books were eventually produced in England and distributed everywhere from New Zealand to the West Indies. So the pairing of the idealized medieval peasant figure and a religious medievalism opposed to the perceived corruptions (especially visual corruptions) of modernity has had a potent history in the English-speaking world. The Navigator's central fantasy is that a group of these medieval peasants, threatened by plague, tunnel through the Earth (and time) on a pilgrimage to find what turns out to be one of those modern churches that evoke the "medieval" for its anti-modern connotations (in actuality St. Patrick's Cathedral in the city of Auckland, New Zealand). Ironically, the exported medievalism that offered the colonial world an imagined picture of pre-modern spiritual clarity is re-worked by a post-colonial filmmaker in The Navigator.

Ward (1989), x. Biddick (1998), 34

At the center of the film are two brothers – nine-year-old Griffin and his older brother Connor who has been lured away by the temptations of the outside world but returns disenchanted and with news of the chaos being caused by the plague. Griffin is having visions – disjointed images that begin to take on the form of "flash-forwards" to a journey that the brothers and four men from the village (Searle, Ulf, Arno, Martin) will embark on. Threatened by the steadily approaching Black Death, a pandemic sweeping across the known world, the community wants an offering to be made at the rumored "great church in the west." They work copper mines in the mountains where they live and, in desperation, Connor leads the small band down a great pit where they toil overnight with a massive wooden tunneling machine, breaking through unexpectedly into the sewers of what turns out to be a modern city. There they hope, before dawn, to find the church they are looking for and hoist on its spire a great copper cross, the template for which they have brought with them, along with chunks of smelted copper ore to cast the cross if they can find a foundry.

Thinking they have found some sort of "celestial" city, the group discovers that it presents some unique terrors – from crossing a multi-lane highway to encountering a nuclear submarine while rowing across the harbor, from getting stuck on the front of a speeding train to getting overwhelmed by a wall of TV screens. But they do find three metalworkers (who come to Griffin's aid when he is struck by a hit and run driver). Their industry crippled by recession (this was the mid-1980s we need to bear in mind), the three foundry workers are on a work-less night shift, their last before becoming unemployed. Caught up in the visitors' otherworldly passion, they cast the beautiful cross for them in one last act of craftsmanship.

The film's set pieces are stunningly visual experiences. Ulf gets caught in the middle of the road, his reverie over the prettiness of all the lights suddenly exploding in a frenzy of traffic noise and near-misses. Out in the moonlit harbor, Searle, Arno and Griffin, with a white horse they have stolen to work the pulley when they hoist the cross, balance precariously in a small rowboat when the monstrous shape of the *USS Queenfish* surfaces beside them and then disappears again into the darkness. The casting of their offering in the foundry fills the screen with the golden glow of molten copper as the form of the cross appears. Connor, who has gone ahead alone, gets stuck on the front of a speeding suburban train that carries him on a brief but terrifying journey into the city. Running through the city streets to find the church, Griffin is confronted by a bank of TV screens whose images offer their own visionary juxtapositions (including the Grim Reaper in an Australian television public information film about AIDS).

The narrative that binds the film's visual set pieces together, and structures the story, is organized in a way that becomes superficially recognizable according to the various theories of effective screenplay structure. On the right, the narrative structure of *The Navigator* is explained using core concepts from Paul Joseph Gulino's sequence-based approach, Robert McKee's explanation of the story-driving "gap" between protagonists' expectations and the results of their initial actions, and Dara Marks' description of a transformational arc at work in powerful stories. These are some of the best ideas in the burgeoning (and not always so helpful) field of advice for screenwriters about how to structure a film, and these three sources overlap in significant respects so it becomes possible to map one level of the narrative structure of a successful film like *The Navigator* by drawing on all three. The film of course pre-dates any of these theories so, in a sense, its partial compliance with their models actually validates them. The breakdown on the right is very much a composite model, borrowing elements where appropriate and putting them together.

A number of things become very clear. Inciting incident and "call to action" are embedded in just enough exposition of background for the setting and the characters to be quickly believable and engaging. Breaking through into the modern city is a key moment, defining the film's central fantasy and setting up the relationship of past and present. But the encounter with the highway, which presents a terrifying barrier and sensory overload for the visitors from the past, is a moment of awakening – getting to the city is only the beginning of their challenge.

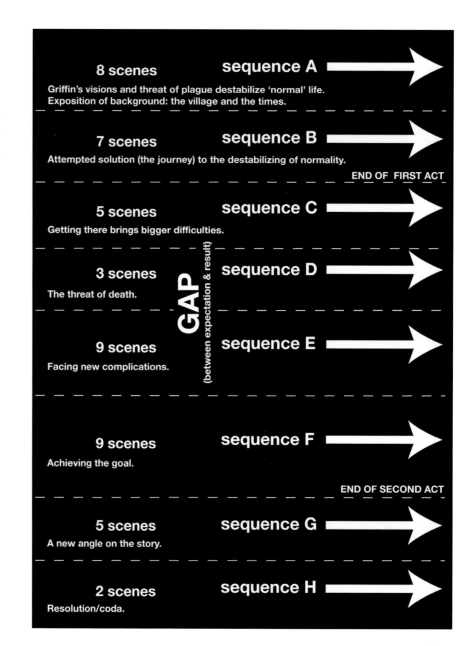

Griffin's first vision. 3:38

Cumbria, 1348. The village. The boy Griffin is teased for being a dreamer. Discussing omens and threat of approaching plague. Waiting for Connor's return. Connor's back! Community meets. Plan for journey to make offering at the 'great church in the west'. Watch boatload of 'refugees from the east' being driven off by men from a neighboring village, their boat burned out on the lake. Length 13:53 (running time 19:31)

Griffin's second vision. 00:36 (20:07)

Decision to go down the great pit (Connor, Griffin, Searle, Ulf, Arno, Martin). Preparations. Leaving the village. Ulf brings rough little carved figurine of Virgin Mary. Discovery of the wooden tunneling engine at the great pit. Tunneling to the far side of the world. Breaking through to the sewers of the (modern!) city. 9:42 (29:49)

Arrival at the surface, overlooking city. Crossing the road. Ulf gets stranded. Connor goes ahead on his own. The others look for a foundry. Convincing foundry workers to make the cross for the church spire. Want to raise the cross before daybreak. Cross has to be cooled so Martin stays with the three workers. Searle, Arno and Griffin decide to go ahead: must cross the harbor by boat to reach the church. 16:36 (46:25)

Stealing a white horse (for roping to a pulley when they get to the church and hoist the cross). Rowing across the harbor, with horse on board. Encounter with a nuclear submarine (USS Queenfish). Includes Griffin's third vision (00:46), immediately after 'Queenfish' encounter. Griffin tells the others that somebody will die falling from the church spire. 8:05 (54:30)

In the city. Connor encounters monstrous machines and gets carried on front of a train. Includes Griffin's fourth vision (00:56). Connor finds himself at the church and starts to climb the spire. Martin arrives at the church with the foundry workers. Griffin jumps into the water and wades ashore. Searle scrambles the horse off the boat and rides it ashore. Running through the deserted nighttime city streets. Griffin encounters a wall of TV screens. Griffin says he can 'see too much' and asks Searle to blindfold him so he can lead them to the church. 12:45 (1:07:15)

At the church. Connor struggles with ropes and old wooden ladder on the spire. Griffin and Searle rush through the church. The winch rope on the foundry workers' truck frays and breaks, leaving Connor clinging. Griffin and Searle climb the staircase in the spire. Searle climbs out onto the ladder with Connor but the rungs snap and they both cling on precariously. Griffin climbs out to help. On the ground, the others rope the horse to the pulley. Griffin climbs up to drag the cross, held by the ropes, into place on top of the spire as the sun comes up. He succeeds. Back at the village they hear bells. Griffin falls from the spire. 7:48 (1:15:3)

Morning, back at the mine. It was all a story, told by Griffin as the men waited for dawn. Griffin tells Ulf that in the end he tunneled under the road and 'showed the little Virgin celestial city'. Daybreak finds the village without the expected signs of plague. Celebration. Griffin dances joyously with the others but suddenly feels unwell - he has the marks of plague. 4:56 (1:19:59)

The revelation that Connor had come back to the village at the beginning with the plague ('There was nowhere else for me to go'), unintentionally infecting Griffin. Connor has recovered, believing that Griffin's story has saved them, but Griffin is now dying. We see (Griffin's final vision) Connor push his small coffin off into the lake, bearing the symbol of their cross from the spire. 5:30 (1:25:29 + credits = 1:27:00 running time)

Inciting incident

Call to action

Defining moment

1st turning point/Awakening

Moment of enlightenment

MIDPOINT

Death experience

2nd turning point

'Transformational' moment

Climax

Resolution

RESISTANCE

RELEASE

The long sequence based around the encounter with the foundry workers (which takes the film to its midpoint in terms of length) produces a moment of enlightenment for the three metalworkers, who get drawn into the visitors' vision and for a while discover that they can be something other than the passive victims of circumstance (economic decline and unemployment). At this point, the people of the medieval village and the disenfranchised modern people represented by these workers become, in a way, a single collective protagonist in the film. The encounter with the impersonal forces of the modern world then takes on overtones of impending death, especially in the surreal encounter with the nuclear submarine. Finally, Griffin, whose visions have been impelling his companions forward and at the same time warning them, realizes that he is seeing too much and losing his way as a consequence. Blindfolded, in the film's second turning point, he gets them back on track and they reach the church. There they find that Griffin's brother Connor, who has gone on ahead while the great copper cross was being made, is now imperiled on the church spire, leading to the climax of Griffin raising the cross just as the sun comes up, and his fall from the spire seconds later. In the narrative resolution Griffin and his companions are revealed to be still in the mine, listening to the boy tell the story we have just witnessed. A coda sees Griffin's death from the plague that his brother had brought back from the outside world at the very beginning of the film.

While this exercise is extremely informative about how a good screen story begins to work in terms of narrative structure, there is a problem with this whole approach if we leave it there. These classical ways of understanding narrative structure (typifying a now dominant approach to story in Hollywood) are all based on an Aristotelian focus on plot at the expense of what can be termed experientiality. The Aristotelian conception of plot (or what Aristotle called Mythos) as the first principle of drama was based on the idea of carefully articulated parts connecting beginning, middle and end. This Aristotelian view has been progressively elaborated into contemporary "systems" for describing the parts and how they articulate, especially in a film industry looking for successful formulas, to the point where these approaches to narrative structure seem to be identifying generative rules for storytelling. In other words, instead of describing some features of stories that already exist (as here) they seem to describe underlying rules for generating new stories.

But generative rules are not themselves the basis of effective storytelling. As literary scholars such as John Holloway have demonstrated, *transformation rules* have a much stronger claim to explaining how narrative works at its best. Generative rules will tend to produce sameness, which may not matter much in the context of myths and legends that actively seek to produce a reassuring sense of the same symbolic "truths" being repeated time and time again, but works of novelistic or cinematic imagination and originality need considerably more than this, especially in relation to experientiality or the question of what it is like to be in the particular story. This is something that many films which, in their screenplays, slavishly follow the supposed generative rules of narrative structure then fail to communicate. So all the right moves are there but there is very little depth to the experientiality (though spectacular effects-driven action can often be used to cover this absence, at least superficially).

In order to grasp what a transformation rule is we can look more closely at the narrative of *The Navigator*, as its compliance with the supposed generative rules of classical cinematic narrative structure (as mapped on the previous pages) is in fact quite a superficial aspect of this film's narrative effectiveness.

Paul Joseph Gulino, who is much less guilty than most of implying that his narrative analyses identify generative rules, makes the very informative point that even a typical eight-sequence feature film structure, or any variation upon it, derives from the old days of film "reels" on single projector theater setups. When projectionists had to change reels of approximately fifteen-minute lengths, structuring filmic narratives into these segments made a lot of sense. Though we have now largely forgotten why, and the sequences have drifted away from the

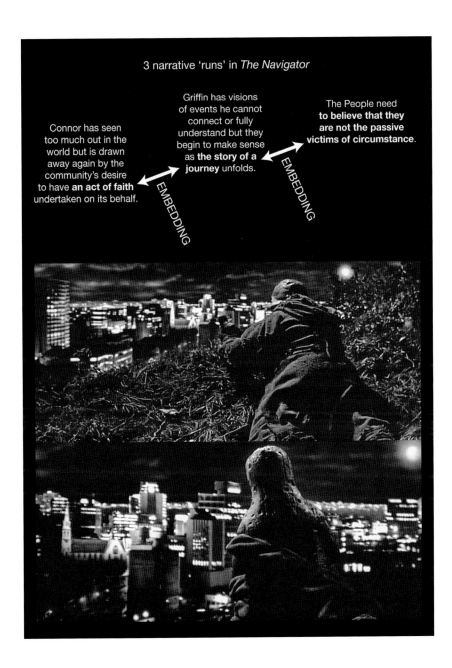

3 narrative 'runs' in *The Navigator*

Connor has seen too much out in the world but is drawn away again by the community's desire to have **an act of faith** undertaken on its behalf.

Griffin has visions of events he cannot connect or fully understand but they begin to make sense as **the story of a journey** unfolds.

The People need **to believe that they are not the passive victims of circumstance**.

EMBEDDING

EMBEDDING

strict fifteen-minute durations, this structure has tended to persist to a remarkable degree. This is a salutary reminder, if one were needed, that many of the seemingly generative rules of "classical" narrative may be describing how things have tended to be rather than how they have to be.

For example, instead of only the linear end-to-end approach (from inciting incident through to resolution), we can think of a narrative structure in terms of parallel "runs" (top left) and then the embedding of these runs inside each other. Three such runs make up the narrative of *The Navigator*: Griffin's, Connor's and one that brings the medieval villagers and modern workers together as one collective protagonist (called "The People" here for convenience).

"Embedding" operations can be thought of as being rather like relative clauses in sentences. We could re-write each of the "run" statements opposite with the other two statements as relative clauses, except that the resulting sentence would be an impossibly clumsy one. So the act of faith in Connor's "run" contains and is contained by the story of the journey, so too The People's belief, and so on.

What the particulars of this specific film establish as the film works through its material is that the act of faith is ultimately an act of faith in seeing (the city, the great church). At the very end, this is underscored when Griffin adds a coda to his own narration by telling Ulf that he (Ulf as a character in the story) finally tunneled under the terrifying road and, on a hill overlooking the city, showed the church to the little wooden Virgin (left). One of the most powerful and affecting moments in the film, this is not explained by any of the generative rules of narrative structure, other than the rather mundane one of tying up loose ends at the resolution. But there is a transformation rule running through this particular film that does explain the moment's deep impact, and that informs the embedding operations interlinking the three main narrative runs.

This transformation rule can be expressed in the following way. When seeing reaches a point of sublime intensity it risks "seeing too much" and becomes traumatic.

<u>Griffin's first vision</u>. 3:38

Cumbria, 1348. The village. The boy Griffin is teased for being a dreamer. Discussing omens and threat of approaching plague. Waiting for Connor's return. Connor's back! Community meets. Plan for journey to make offering at the 'great church in the west'. Watch boatload of 'refugees from the east' being driven off by men from a neighboring village, their boat burned out on the water. Length 13:53 (running time 19:31)

<u>Griffin's second vision</u>. 00:36 (20:07)

Decision to go down the great pit (Connor, Griffin, Searle, Ulf, Arno, Martin). Preparations. Leaving the village. Ulf brings rough little carved figurine of Virgin Mary. Discovery of the wooden tunneling engine at the great pit. Tunneling to the far side of the world. Breaking through to the sewers of the (modern!) city. 9:42 (29:49)

Arrival at the surface, overlooking city. Crossing the road. Ulf gets stranded. Connor goes ahead on his own. The others look for a foundry. Convincing foundry workers to make the cross for the church spire. Want to raise the cross before daybreak. Cross has to be cooled so Martin stays with the three workers. Searle, Arno and Griffin decide to go ahead: must cross the harbor by boat to reach the church. 16:36 (46:25)

Stealing a white horse (for roping to a pulley when they get to the church and hoist the cross). Rowing across the harbor, with horse on board. Encounter with a nuclear submarine (USS Queenfish). Includes <u>Griffin's third vision</u> (00:46), immediately after 'Queenfish' encounter. Griffin tells the others that somebody will die falling from the church spire. 8:05 (54:30)

In the city. Connor encounters monstrous machines and gets carried on front of a train. Includes <u>Griffin's fourth vision</u> (00:56). Connor finds himself at the church and starts to climb the spire. Martin arrives at the church with the foundry workers. Griffin jumps into the water and wades ashore. Searle scrambles the horse off the boat and rides it ashore. Running through the deserted nighttime city streets. Griffin encounters a wall of TV screens. Griffin says he can 'see too much' and asks Searle to blindfold him so he can lead them to the church. 12:45 (1:07:15)

At the church. Connor struggles with ropes and old wooden ladder on the spire. Griffin and Searle rush through the church. The winch rope on the foundry workers' truck frays and breaks, leaving Connor clinging. Griffin and Searle climb the staircase in the spire. Searle climbs out onto the ladder with Connor but the ropes snap and they both cling on precariously. Griffin climbs out to help. On the ground, the others rope the horse to the pulley. Griffin climbs up to drag the cross, held by the ropes, into place on top of the spire as the sun comes up. He succeeds. Back at the village they hear bells. Griffin falls from the spire. 7:48 (1:15:3)

Morning, back at the mine. It was all a story, told by Griffin as the men waited for dawn. Griffin tells Ulf that in the end he tunneled under the road and 'showed the little Virgin celestial city'. Daybreak finds the village without the expected signs of plague. Celebration. Griffin dances joyously with the others but suddenly feels unwell - he has the marks of plague. 4:56 (1:19:59)

The revelation that Connor had come back to the village at the beginning with the plague ('There was nowhere else for me to go'), unintentionally infecting Griffin. Connor has recovered, believing that Griffin's story has saved them, but Griffin is now dying. We see (<u>Griffin's final vision</u>) Connor push his small coffin off into the lake, bearing the symbol of their cross from the spire. 5:30 (1:25:29 + credits = 1:27:00 running time)

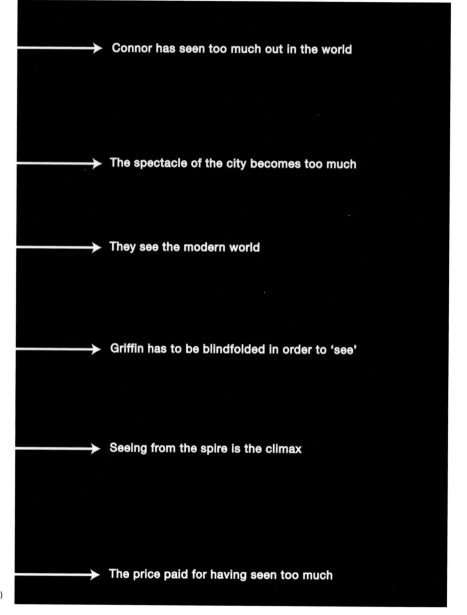

Connor has seen too much out in the world

The spectacle of the city becomes too much

They see the modern world

Griffin has to be blindfolded in order to 'see'

Seeing from the spire is the climax

The price paid for having seen too much

All statements of transformation rules tend to be specific to the film (or novel) that has been elaborated around them (and there may be several transformation rules operating in concert). They do not become "rules" for generating other stories (i.e. generative rules), except perhaps in the filmmaker's own body of work. Some advocates of the various generative rule systems of narrative structure tend to view such aspects of a film as "subtext" – the place where the writer and director can put all their clever stuff if they want to, so long as the main "text" is obeying the "classical" generative rules. The implication is a take it or leave it attitude to "subtext," as if it does not really matter too much whether these aspects are there at all. But we are not talking about disposable "subtext" here. This transformation rule is what turns *The Navigator* into such an unforgettable piece of instinctively post-classical cinema. And it does so by indissolubly wedding the narrative to the image-making, which is of course something that cannot happen at the level of a screenplay alone.

Where does a unique transformation rule come from? From a writer or director putting it on a post-it note to themselves when they sit down to make a film? Undoubtedly not. All the evidence available from close scrutiny of the creative process suggests that the vital transformation rules, which transform narratives from the inside, develop deep inside the creative process in ways that are frequently not expressible by the creators.

We can identify its principal transformation rule in operation at several key points in *The Navigator* (left). Connor, having returned to the village from the outside world, describes in vivid detail what he has seen there – growing chaos and scenes of human despair caused by the plague. When the group arrives at the city it looks first like an entrancing spectacle, glowing with lights, but crossing the highway turns into a visual assault on their unaccustomed senses. When the great menacing shape of the nuclear submarine rises out of the harbor in the darkness, something of the immensity of forces at work in the modern world comes literally into sight for a moment. Then the city's further assault on the senses culminates in the vast wall of TV screens encountered by Griffin, their

disjointed imagery both compelling attention and warning of dangers loose in the modern world (nuclear proliferation, AIDS). Ascending to the top of the spire at dawn gives Griffin a climactic view as the strange world he has entered begins to fill with color.

Integral to, and immediately preceding, each of these moments, the film offers images of sublime beauty or strangeness: the figures from the village dwarfed by the snow-covered "Cumbrian" landscape; the night-time cityscape blazing with light like a vision of something self-evidently "celestial"; a white horse on a rowing boat in the moonlight; a hawk in flight and lunging onto a bolting rabbit on the TV screens; the morning sky reddening over the city. Griffin's visions themselves, interspersed through the film, belong to this catalogue of especially intense imagery. And each time, as the visual intensity approaches its sublime apotheosis, the film effects an immediate transformation into the traumatically overwhelming, Griffin's eventual blindfolding in order to help him "see" the way more clearly becoming an explicit recognition of these transformations within the narrative itself. And Griffin's eventual death from plague is the final traumatic resolution of the series of visions that have informed the film as a whole.

Now, there is a sense in which asking what this means is to ask the wrong question. Structurally, within the narrative of *The Navigator*, its own unique transformation rule is what melds the narrative so powerfully and affectingly to the image. So identifying a further extractable "meaning" is unnecessary for this effect to have been achieved. It is always possible, of course, to think about a further level of meaning anyway. So it becomes possible, for instance, to wonder if a critique is being offered here of that "society of the spectacle" that the modern world has become. Or if a parable of the storytelling act and of creativity in general is being offered – one in which the especially creative vision becomes unbearable for the society and has to be excised, driven out in the end. But here we are in the realm of our own responses, our own speculations, our own "readings," rather than the realm of the film's own narrative organization as such.

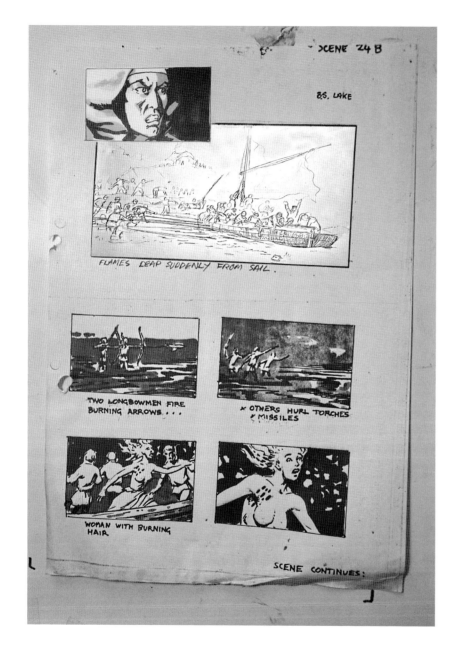

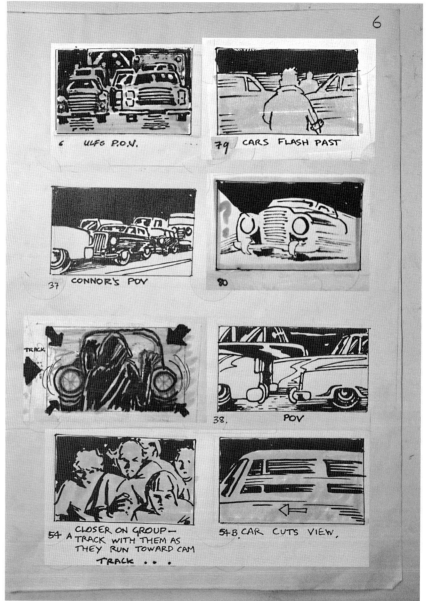

Preproduction material courtesy of Arenafilm, Sydney

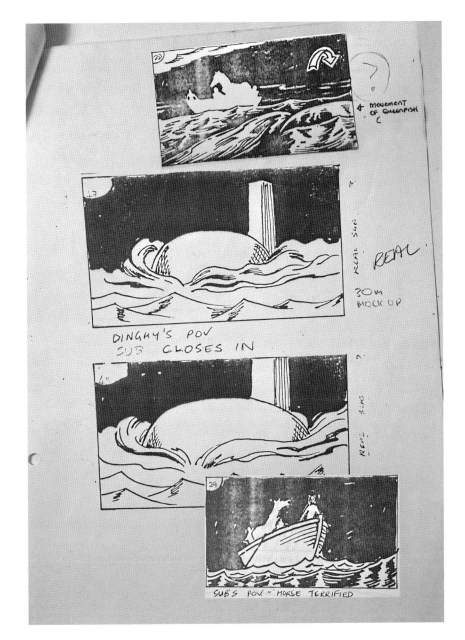

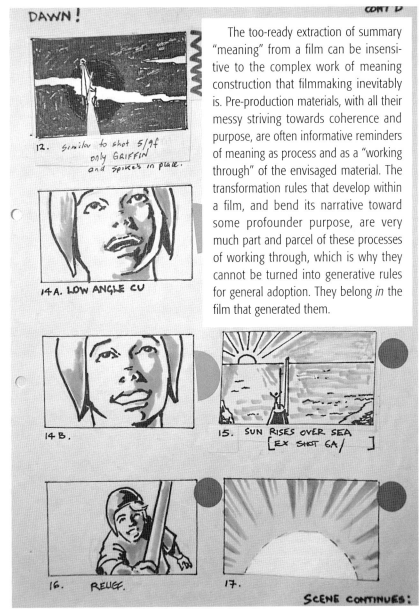

The too-ready extraction of summary "meaning" from a film can be insensitive to the complex work of meaning construction that filmmaking inevitably is. Pre-production materials, with all their messy striving towards coherence and purpose, are often informative reminders of meaning as process and as a "working through" of the envisaged material. The transformation rules that develop within a film, and bend its narrative toward some profounder purpose, are very much part and parcel of these processes of working through, which is why they cannot be turned into generative rules for general adoption. They belong *in* the film that generated them.

The principal transformation rule we have identified at work in *The Navigator* (when seeing reaches a point of sublime intensity it risks "seeing too much" and becomes traumatic) becomes especially clear in the following examples.

Connor returns to the awe-inspiring landscape of his mining community having been shocked by what he has seen in the outside world. He has clearly been a young man eager to get away but the plague has brought social chaos to the wider world and, at first, the village he returns to looks reassuringly safe and familiar. But when he talks of what he has seen out there – the people dying by the roadside, children becoming beggars, monks on "pilgrimages" that are their means of getting away – it becomes clear that these things are coming nearer. The sublime images of the natural environment are immediately followed by these intrusive verbal evocations of what Connor has seen. And then it becomes very real in the form of a boatload of refugees from the east, out on the lake. Repelled and then set alight by men from a neighboring village, while Connor and his companions watch from the shore, this boat full of the ill and the terrified brings home the traumatic nature of what is happening. Connor says he is sick of all that he has seen out there. But community pressure and Griffin's visions convince him to lead an expedition to find the great church being built in the west and make an offering there.

Cumbria March 1348

For people who believe the earth is flat, arriving at what appears to be a "celestial" city after a night of tunneling in their deepest mine makes sense: they have broken through on the other side of the world. The city's lights make an enchanting spectacle from a distance. Even the lights of the vehicles on a busy night-time highway are, at first, full of beauty. Ulf stands enchanted in the middle of the road.

But suddenly the reality of where he is breaks through his moment of reverie. As car horns blare and vehicles streak past him at perilously close quarters, Ulf becomes trapped and terror-struck amidst what seconds earlier had seemed like a dreamscape. The force of the sudden reversal is palpable, as sounds and images blur menacingly and Ulf does not know which way to turn, until his companions drag him back to the side of the road. For the group as a whole, the road suddenly makes it all too apparent that more trauma lies ahead than they might have imagined.

While Connor goes on ahead to look for the church, the others find a foundry to cast the copper cross they intend to place on its spire, having carried chunks of ore with them from their mine. Then Martin stays with the foundry workers waiting for the new cross to cool, while Searle, Griffin and Arno steal a horse (for working the pulley that will hoist the cross) and begin rowing it across the harbor to the other part of the city where the church is.

The surreally beautiful visual spectacle of a white horse in a rowing boat in the blue moonlight is interrupted when, gazing out into the darkness, they sense a presence in the water around them. Suddenly a massive submarine partially surfaces near them, then disappears again, only to resurface on the other side of their boat, terrifying the horse, almost capsizing them, and expressing by its very presence a feeling of how immense and incomprehensible the forces are that characterize the modern world in which they have found themselves.

The incomprehensibility attains its visual apotheosis in a bank of TV screens that Griffin encounters as they hurry through the streets after clambering ashore. Both captivating and then shocking, the TV screens almost hypnotize Griffin. A hawk swoops on its prey. A nuclear submarine appears with a commentary about how, in effect, there is nowhere to hide from the realities of the modern world, not even in some remote place in the hope of remaining detached and uninvolved. The parallels between Griffin's medieval world and isolationist pockets of the modern world become clear. Then the stylized figure of the Grim Reaper swings his scythe in an infomercial about AIDS. Griffin, having touched the screens in momentary engrossment, turns and runs from the spectacle.

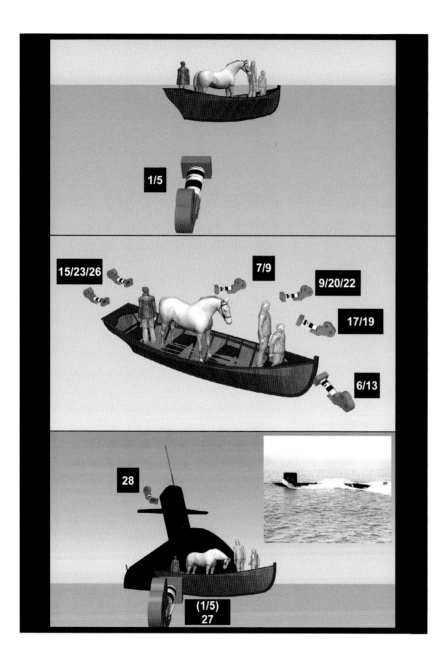

Of the four examples just discussed, each embodying in different ways the film's own transformation rule, the encounter with the nuclear submarine is especially interestingly placed within the film's narrative structure, as it represents a second act near-death experience. In terms of narrative, this kind of moment crystallizes the gap between expectations and results in the middle of a film, emphasizing how strong the resistance really is to what the protagonists want to achieve.

It is also, though, worth considering exactly how this scene is internally constructed, as it represents not only the film's main transformation rule in action but an instance of what we have earlier identified as a traumatic reversal of the gaze.

In a 27-shot set-piece, the film organizes the space of the encounter in a very specific and carefully controlled way (left), even though the visual effect on screen is deliberately chaotic. The first shot in the segment we are concentrating on is the one reproduced on the previous pages – a very low angle "bobbing" shot from the surface of the water, showing the white horse particularly clearly in side profile in the darkness. This camera position is returned to five shots in to the segment and again in shot 27, though by then the submarine itself has appeared. These shots initiate the growing feeling that Griffin and the others are being watched.

All the non-identified shots interspersed through our numbering series on the left are of Griffin and the others gazing out into the darkness, trying to see what is initially only a disturbance in the water. So the labeling on the diagram identifies the shots that are looking at them, so to speak. These shots move progressively round one side of the boat, though with some cutting back to earlier camera positions for visual continuity. So the camera in effect shifts in a series of steps until it has taken up a position off the rear of the boat, which is exactly where the submarine reappears. Almost subliminally, it becomes apparent that position 1/5 (top left) was in effect a periscope view from the submerged submarine. In fact a mirror image shot (25) is used just before the submarine surfaces and looms over them. And at that point the elevated camera position at 28, looking down at

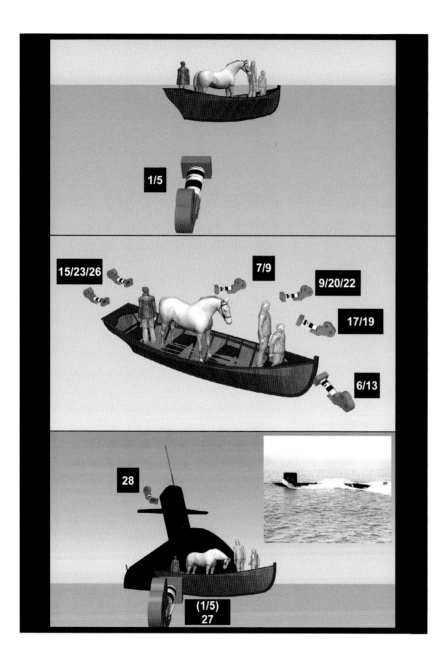

And in the context of the film's insistent emphasis on what the protagonists are seeing, this reversal of their gaze feels especially powerful.

The *USS Queenfish* (inset photograph on opposite page) was a nuclear attack submarine of some notoriety after its Cold War operations became known about. It clandestinely mapped the previously uncharted sea routes under the polar ice pack and along the Siberian coastline for military purposes should war occur between the Soviet Union and the West. During the Cold War, the Arctic ice pack on top of the world became a covert theater of operation for nuclear missile-carrying submarines from both superpowers. The Arctic cartographer who becomes a mission planner for the bombing of cities in *Map of the Human Heart* is an unsettling echo of the *Queenfish*.

the boat, makes it retrospectively clear that in effect we have been seeing them from the submarine's point of view. In one sense, none of this is unusual. We have seen water-level shots ostensibly from periscope point of view in numerous war films, and the "stalking" effect is even a little reminiscent of *Jaws* (indeed shot 4, not illustrated here, looks up at the keel of the little boat from deep below it in an homage to Spielberg's dramatic use of this angle). But here it is an unusually impersonal point of view (no crewman peering through the periscope, nobody on the conning tower), as if the machine itself is doing the watching.

In *The Navigator*, the transition from a protected pocket of medieval Cumbria to the realization of Griffin's vision out in the world is also a transition from black and white to color.

light, color, music, and the moment

Vertigo (1958)

Hitchcock's *Vertigo* (1958) offers this small but rather comprehensive master class in lighting and color (above). Scottie, the ex-detective played by James Stewart, is following Madeleine (Kim Novak) at the request of her husband, a wealthy businessman and old college friend of Scottie's. Madeleine has, it seems, been behaving strangely – going for long drives and wandering aimlessly around San Francisco. This is early in the film and Scottie follows her through a back-alley entrance into what turns out to be a flower shop.

The director and the cinematographer Robert Burks (a Hitchcock regular) light Stewart in the gloomy storeroom between alley and shop with classic key and fill lights. The key, towards which Stewart is oriented, provides overall illumination, especially on his face, while the fill brings up detail in the shadow on the other side of his face. This is not quite the classic three-point lighting setup of the

textbooks though, as the diffuse light in the "alley" area behind the set is used instead to frame Stewart where a backlight might have been used to pick out the edges of his form and separate it from the background. But as Scottie moves into the storeroom Stewart moves out of the key light into the shadows and a backlight is used to pick out his outline, with only pale illumination on the wall behind to maintain a sense of depth to the space.

Then when Scottie slowly opens the door through which Madeleine has gone, a strong key light without fill is used to represent the light flooding in from the flower shop. And as the door opens, seen now from Scottie's point of view, a blaze of intense color from the massed flowers fills the screen, amidst which we now see Madeleine. As she turns, Kim Novak is given the three-point lighting treatment, with key, fill and backlight modeling her figure and lifting if off the

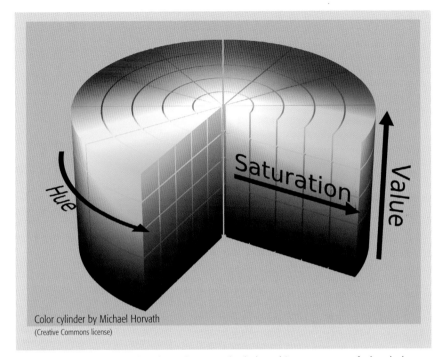

Color cylinder by Michael Horvath
(Creative Commons license)

A number of excellent textbooks (especially Benjamin Bergery's *Reflections*, Jacqueline B. Frost's *Cinematography for Directors* and Alexander Ballinger's *New Cinematographers*) provide the levels of detail that will be skimmed over here. However, this basic example has the virtue that it reminds us of some fundamental principles. What we see Burks and Hitchcock do here, over a matter of only seconds and two or three shots, is constantly fine-tune and adjust the relationships between lighting and color. So whatever the technical tools being used, the basic notion of "tuning" these relationships remains valid. In the *Vertigo* example, the relatively low intensity of the fill light in relation to the key in the first shot, the absence of backlight and of general illumination in the space create a low-key look, whereas moments later the key, fill and backlight are brought into a more equally balanced contrast ratio and, along with general illumination of the scene, create a high-key look that emphasizes the saturated colors. Art direction, costume design and make-up provide the on-screen materials on the basis of which the cinematographer's tuning of light produces the color that we respond to: Madeleine's cool gray suit contrasting with the intensity of the flowers, Scottie's dark coat and hat merging with the shadows.

Once this kind of visual "tuning" or relative adjustment of elements is in place, no matter what the contemporary tuning tools being deployed in the specific instance, it becomes possible to think about light and color in ways that are less tied to specific techniques and technologies. In particular, we want to think about the intensity of the visual experience being created through the use of light and color. Intensity is the real point of the *Vertigo* example. In front of the cinema screen we are almost knocked back in our seats by the shift from low-key in the top row of frames to the intensity of the visual field revealed in the second row of frames. Placing Madeleine within that intensity is communicating something about Scottie's growing fascination, as well as about whatever it is that simmers just below her cool exterior. (It should be noted that Bernard Herrmann's score makes its own contribution to the intensity at precisely this moment, but we will come back to music in due course.)

background. The final shot here is one of Hitchcock's moments of visual showmanship, as he places a mirror beside the door so that we see both Scottie's secretive vantage point and Madeleine as he gazes at her.

Although there is of course a very great deal more to lighting than this, it remains useful to think of this scene as a kind of primer. As lighting technology has changed, the basic notions of "key," "fill" and "back" lights have been converted into various combinations of specific lighting units for particular situations, correlated with choice of film stock or the digital medium being used. The "fill" is often various sorts of reflector or "bead board," the "key" might be natural light or banks of lighting units, with carefully placed "cross keys" illuminating different characters, depending on the color palette and the look required. On-screen source lighting within a scene will often be part of the mix. Filtering and diffusion of various kinds may be used in front of lighting units to modulate their effects.

In terms of color, what we mean by "intensity" is a product of ratcheting up the scale on any or all of the three axes indicated in the color field diagram: hue, saturation and value. When we see color anywhere, not just in film, we are seeing colored light. And what we term "color" is the interaction of these three components: hue, which is in effect the "rainbow" subdivided into all its distinguishable differences (based on the wavelengths of light); saturation, which is the degree of brightness or paleness of a hue (like pouring more or less colored paint into a white base paint); and value, which is the degree of "grayness" or otherwise (like a black and white photograph with various shades of gray on which hues then get overlaid). Different kinds of intensity – which is to say different sensations of intensity on the part of the viewer – are created by ratcheting up any one of

these scales. In interaction, they form the powerful expressive means of visual communication that we experience as color.

So the pre-visualization artwork for Vincent's (unrealized) version of *Alien³* (top left above), while very limited in its range of hues and relatively limited in terms of saturation (except for the shadows), achieves its striking intensity on the value scale. The underlying range of grays in the image runs the full gamut from nearly black to nearly white, something this "look" shares with classic German Expressionist cinema (such as *Pandora's Box* (1929), above left). Value exists independently of hue (think of adding those blues from *Alien³* on top of the *Pandora's Box* image), so affords an underlying expressive layer of considerable potency. As we increase the range of hue and boost the saturation

– like "pouring" more red into Avik's hat in the frame from *Map of the Human Heart* – we start to code the visual field. In other words, increasingly specific meanings begin to suggest themselves on the level of color. In this instance, Avik's hat marks him out as different in the Arctic world of grays, blues and whites, a difference that at this moment gets literalized when he coughs red blood onto Walter's face and we realize he has tuberculosis.

In *Navigator*, when Ulf gets stuck in the middle of the modern highway, the saturated reds of the torches reflect off the wet roadway and the speeding cars to underpin with an intense visual sensation the equally intense psychological moment that we imagine him to be having. So just these few examples are enough to demonstrate the three axes of color operating both independently and in concert.

But it is important to note that color is also in our minds. The white horse in Fritz Lang's *Siegfried* (1924, middle left) stands out in our minds as much because of the idea of a white horse, an idea that has its own kind of intensity. Similarly, the white horse cantering unexpectedly down the highway in Fellini's *Roma* (1972) is an unforgettably vivid image even though the actual screen image is all desaturated hues in rather insipid natural light. The intensity in these instances is in large measure a psychological sensation just as much as it is a literally visual one.

The white horse has cultural associations that contribute to this response (mythological versions appear around the world), but color on its own as it were also needs to be understood as having a psychology. Whatever shortcomings the much-quoted Rorschach "inkblot" tests might have as tools of psychological investigation, the tenth and last card in the set (Card X, reproduced here) is still a revealing reminder of the suggestive power of color.

It is more or less impossible not to respond to Card X. Look at it and see if you can prevent yourself from having feelings about it. Even before people start to "see" crabs, lobsters, spiders, snakes, rabbits' heads, caterpillars, seahorses, the Eiffel Tower, a spine and pelvic bones or any number of other things, they are having what we may take to be a series of emotional responses as they scan the color field (although we are going to be more careful in due course about distinguishing emotion and affect). Visual shapes are what start to give form to the "seeing" of things in the image (as with the predominantly black-and-white cards in the Rorschach set as a whole), but the colors here are what trigger the immediate feelings, before any imagined representations of things start to take over as one looks at Card X.

And some "representations" if they occur – like broken eggs with blood – then start to reclaim the color in ways that many people begin to find uncomfortable. It is not too difficult to generate in oneself a small maelstrom of feelings just by looking long enough at Card X, although equally some people can gaze contentedly at it for a long time and see only pretty pastel colors. Whatever way you are tending, there is still perhaps no better example of the affective nature of color sensations. We want to say affective here – rather than psychological or emotional – because any other vocabulary conspires too quickly with the representational appropriation of the sensation. "Psychological" moves too quickly towards representing and labeling supposed states of mind (which after all is what the original Rorschach test is for), while "emotional" moves too quickly into telling stories about what we feel. ("That's disgusting" is a story wanting to be told.) The term affect, on the other hand, identifies an important pre-representational and non-verbalized layer of response on which these other elaborations are then built.

Caspar David Friedrich, *Man and Woman Contemplating the Moon* (1830s), Alte Nationalgalerie, Berlin

Robin Williams in *What Dreams May Come* (1998), with (inset) Thomas Kinkade, detail from *Beside Still Waters* (updated) and Albert Bierstadt *Donner Lake from the Summit* (1873). Kinkade detail (top) used by permission of Pacific Metro LLC

J28E-31-pinktree.0127.sgi

J28E_23_multiscale.0101.sgi

./0278

Habitat (1997), dir. Rene Daalder

Pierre Jasmin and optical flow in *What Dreams May Come*

The interaction of color-based and affective intensity is a powerful aspect of human response to the visual. Surprisingly, the interrelation of cinema's represented and affective worlds has not been much studied and may not yet be fully understood, although directors such as Hitchcock, Michelangelo Antonioni, Andrei Tarkovsky and Alain Resnais and cinematographers such as Sven Nykvist and Rodrigo Prieto have used color in ways that suggest an especially deep intuitive grasp of the affective dimension. (Of course many more have deployed color "symbolically" in films, with this character wearing red for "passion" and that scene looking desaturated to suggest "depression" but such rather literal understandings of the affective world on film are perhaps the more cliché-prone end of the spectrum.)

When French urban scenographers Skertzo (Hélène Richard and Jean-Michel Quesne) devised a high-tech digital laser projection system to recreate the medieval paintwork on the front of Amiens Cathedral (right top), they revived a lost affective dimension in our response to such a building, normally experienced as gray stone. They refer to the "beacon" effect that the color creates before any specific religious representations take over. The cathedral's Portal of the Virgin quickly re-introduces its dense religious iconography, but Richard and Quesne are right that the color when present seems to come first (partly because visible from a distance where represented detail cannot be discerned with any clarity). The affective dimension to this is undeniable when experienced. The palette of hues and the rich saturation produce an intensity that is then only secondarily channeled into Christian representations of prophets and angels.

This representational channeling of the intensity that light and color can affectively generate is one key to understanding the great European tradition of Romantic painting, as exemplified (p. 148) by Caspar David Friedrich's *Man and Woman Contemplating the Moon* (1830s). Although reproduction does not

capture the particular intensity of the light in this painting (the original is in the Old National Gallery in Berlin), enough of the sensation is reproducible here to make the point that affect, once produced, is available to be channeled in ways which rapidly turn into narrative that borrows or inherits the feeling of intensity.

The painting is a considerable step up in terms of representational specifics from Rorschach's Card X, but again we can test our own response to it. This time, the question is whether you can resist the entry of story into the visual field. It is very difficult not to wonder who the man and woman are. Do you start to imagine the man as somewhat older? Is she his daughter? Are they traveling further into this landscape? Or do they seem poised on the edge of a different landscape, perhaps a "spiritual" one? At this point a tradition of narratives about spiritual journeys starts to infiltrate our response to the picture, a tradition invoked by German Expressionist printmaker Ernst Barlach in these details (left) showing the man alone in the landscape as a metaphor for the human spiritual condition or the spiritual traveler treading on the heads of lost souls.

All of this connects with our present purpose, of course, when we think of Robin Williams playing this man. If we "narrativize" the Friedrich painting by taking the woman away (let us say she is his daughter and she has died), and we add something of the anxiety (as well as the specific imagery) from the Barlach prints, we are in the worlds of *What Dreams May Come* (1998). I say "worlds" because I want to hold on to the idea of both represented and affective worlds. The represented world of *What Dreams May Come* is regrettably mawkish at the level of classical narrative exposition. But the affective world is an extraordinary experiment with the limits of visual – and especially color-based – intensity. As such, the remarkable visual excess leaves the pedestrian exposition of story far behind and reveals a post-classical sensibility at odds with its classical Hollywood narrative form.

Ratchet up the color on all three dimensions of hue, saturation and value and you are in the world where Chris finds himself after he dies in a car crash. This turns out to be one of his wife's paintings before depression drives her to suicide. It is also a world characterized by what essayist and novelist Joan Didion has called the "Kinkade Glow," in reference to the highly marketable "inspirational" paintings and prints of contemporary American painter/entrepreneur Thomas Kinkade (detail on p. 149 from *Beside Still Waters*). Supposedly the most collected living American painter and an instantly recognizable brand for many Americans, the Kinkade company's specialism has been the creation and selling of a luridly and lushly exaggerated image of unnaturally luminous nature. Joan Didion also points out the obvious debt, in the use of light, to the nineteenth-century German-American painter Albert Bierstadt (*Donner Lake from the Summit*, 1873, inset p. 149). Bierstadt took Friedrich-style light over "Romantic" landscapes and turned up the value to maximum in order to suggest, as Didion puts it, that the scenes are "divinely illuminated." It is this unsubtle trick that Thomas Kinkade a century later married to saturated hues, creating a popular craze for prints of his paintings in the process.

The "Kinkade Glow" was at its commercial height when *What Dreams May Come* was made, so it is impossible not to see the film's experimentation with intense color as "quoting" both Kinkade and predecessors like Bierstadt. Put more simply, the film asks what happens when intensity is pursued through color. How far can this kind of intensity be pushed and what are the affective results? These remain important questions for anyone interested in the cinematic use of color.

Joan Didion, comparing Kinkade and Bierstadt, suggests in passing part of an answer to these questions: after a certain point the intensity itself becomes somewhat sinister. Look long enough at the reproduced detail from *Beside Still Waters* and the intensity that might at first have felt whimsical starts to feel unsettling. One wonders how many buyers of prints eventually started to sense, once they had lived with them for a while, that the exaggeration of color is less uplifting than strangely alien, as if to suggest that the look of the manifest world around us is not good enough and has to be enhanced. This is the ultimately sinister impulse towards transcendence skewered by Anglican priest and scholar of Christian theology Don Cupitt when he says, "When I am not content with the manifest I start trying to go beyond it."

The experiment with color that we can see in *What Dreams May Come* closely replicates a reversal at the heart of the impulse towards transcendence described by Cupitt: "It is lost as one gains it, for it breaks the mind." Except that here we might say, it is lost as one gains it, for it breaks the classical Hollywood narrative film. Push the "Kinkade Glow" and the Bierstadt "divine illumination" a couple of steps still further in intensity, as *What Dreams May Come* succeeds in doing, and an image like the one on page 149 starts to collapse back on itself. Its intensity of color becomes an imploding scene of illusory transcendence and color returns to its pure materiality, in this case as paint.

Thanks to some remarkable visual effects work, especially for the 1990s when computer-based effects were less advanced than today, the film's "painted world" segment does the double movement described by Cupitt — out and back again — pushes color and light to their limits and in the process purges the "glow" of its claim to transcendence. Joan Didion sees Bierstadt's kind of "glow" in *Donner Lake from the Summit* as erasing the trauma after which the place was named — the experience of the 1846/7 Donner Party of pioneers heading West but driven to cannibalism when trapped by snow in the mountains. In the same vein, we might hope that the post-classical reversal in *What Dreams'* experiment with color would reconnect with the trauma (road deaths and suicide in an American family) that motivated the impulse towards transcendence in the first place. But the screenplay-driven dimension to the film just keeps pressing on with its "classical" journey towards the light.

Didion (2004), 73-75. Cupitt (1987), 147

What Dreams May Come is curiously linked to *Bunny*. In 1998 the former's effects team, led by Nicholas Brooks, won the Academy Award for visual effects. *Bunny* took the Oscar that year for best Short in the animation sub-category. The next year they shared the top prize for outstanding innovation in computer animation/visual effects in the prestigious "Prixars" competition run by the Ars Electronica media center and museum in Austria (the year that Linux operating system developer Linus Thorvalds was honored, which is good company to be keeping in the international "cyberarts" community). *Bunny*'s story is about an anthropomorphized widowed rabbit who kills an irritating moth while cooking in her kitchen, then dies in her sleep and flies with the moth into "a world of ... light" to rejoin her (rabbit) husband.

What the animators and developers at Blue Sky Studios did with *Bunny* was to pioneer a digital lighting system capable of simulating the radiosity – the interaction of hues – in real light. As such, *Bunny* has a very important place in the development of the CGI-based animation that is now delivering completely computer-generated and increasingly believable worlds. The fact that the short's content turned this new facility for light and color into a whimsical story about life after death also places it alongside *What Dreams May Come*. Both "happened to go insane with the technology" (in the words of *Bunny* director Chris Wedge), but with a common interest in how light can be used to dial up the sensation of intensity, hooking this narratively to an impression of transcendence.

In the case of *What Dreams May Come*, the underpinning technology for the "painted world" sequence we are interested in is called "optical flow" and was adapted by Pierre Jasmin (p. 150) and Pete Litwinowicz who, in addition to the team's original Oscar recognition, won a Technical Achievement Academy Award of their own in 2007 for the subsequent development of software tools for optical flow, tools described by the Academy of Motion Picture Arts and Sciences as now "ubiquitous in the visual effects industry." The effects frames from *What Dreams May Come* (p. 150) illustrate the basic principles behind optical flow.

In that example a location is "dressed" with some additional props (like artificial flowers with exaggerated colors) and material is shot with the real actors (in this case Robin Williams sliding through the flowers and sitting down). Key segments of the filmed material are then digitally analyzed into their constituent visual components which are re-mapped as "particle clouds" to which motion information is attached. This and related material is then layered together, including extra computer-generated flowers and foliage and 3D digital "paint strokes" attached to them. When the actor moves through the reconstituted image he is now moving in effect through a cloud of visual data, a flow field that can be programmed to move automatically with him, to stick to his clothes, to bend and warp, to smudge and smear.

The precursor software was originally developed by Pierre for a film called *Habitat* but not used in the end (e.g. to drive the particle cloud type effects in that film, shown on p. 150) as the computer hardware available took two hours per frame to do the work. With its huge production budget ($76 million), *What Dreams May Come* brought this down to a hundredth of a second per frame. Pete Litwinowicz, then at Apple's Advanced Technology Group, wrote a ground-breaking paper on these techniques in 1997 (called "Processing Images and Video for an Impressionist Effect") and, when Apple closed down that group, was brought onto *What Dreams May Come* to work with Pierre.

Blue Sky Studios press release, Oct. 1999

The sequence illustrated shows how "painted world" material was then combined with the other elements – live action shots filmed in Montana's Glacier National Park, 3D computer-generated terrain and background matte paintings – to produce the integrated images that, in this example, set a Friedrich-style tree and figure against Bierstadt-style "divine illumination," the whole colored with "Kinkade Glow" (some of the frames show the reference grids and orange marker balls used to synchronize the various layers when moving a camera over the composite scene).

Photograph of Pierre Jasmin by author

Pierre Jasmin (above right) is pointing out the hanger on the old Alameda naval air station in California where the effects team was based and where some of the film's larger sets were constructed and filmed (including a giant staircase for a scene we are about to look at).

Now the point of dwelling on this visual effects (VFX) work, for the book's purpose, is not merely to satisfy curiosity or for general interest's sake. Computer-generated VFX are an increasingly important part of the filmmakers toolkit, even on smaller budgets given the decreasing costs and the accessibility of powerful software tools such as those subsequently developed by Pierre and Pete. So they become part of the toolkit available for constructing the kinds of moment we are interested in here.

The pioneering work done on *What Dreams May Come* and *Bunny* in fact went in somewhat different directions. On the one hand, there is the digital 3D creation of imagined worlds from scratch as it were: from *Bunny* to *Avatar* and beyond. Here the digital VFX tools systematically enable the possible: whatever seems possible can be modeled and rendered in the computer and put up on the screen to be believed in. On the other hand, *What Dreams May Come* connected its digital VFX work back to the analog world in a particular way. The "painted world" sequence remains the most striking example of this, where filmed actuality

got transposed into the digital domain but the results (as illustrated) got re-attached to the analog world. Today's technologies blur this distinction in practice of course (so motion capture suits worn by actors capture data that is transferred into computer animations, and so forth) and films are full of computer-generated imagery that is superficially indistinguishable from filmed actuality. But the painted world of *What Dreams May Come* does not just make its VFX material simulate the superficial appearances of the analog world – it makes that material act as though it has all the thick materiality of the analog. By decomposing the digital into "paint" that acts like paint, not just looks like paint never mind light, the film pushes the intensity of its effects-driven spectacle beyond a point of extremity in a way that is unavailable to the perfect digital simulations of possible worlds.

To put this more simply, the final frame in the sequence opposite (as one example) experiments with what happens when light and color are used to ratchet up the intensity of the visual field, what happens when this intensity is attached to Friedrich and Bierstadt style representations intended to produce a sensation of affective (not just visual) intensity, and what happens (zooming in again as it were on the figure amidst the painted flowers) when the whole decomposes back into "paint" before our eyes. The answer is in that very movement into the intensity of light and color and back again. Instead of finding "transcendence" in the created sensation, the "painted world" finds sensation, curing us visually of the impulse towards transcendence. We end up in a sticky Thomas Kinkade painting – better than that, in its paint – instead of journeying on into the represented light in the expectation of transformation that way.

The result of Vincent exposing classical Hollywood narrative to an ambitious post-classical experiment with color and light is to return us to the material grounds of the affective world as the place where the transformational moment in film happens.

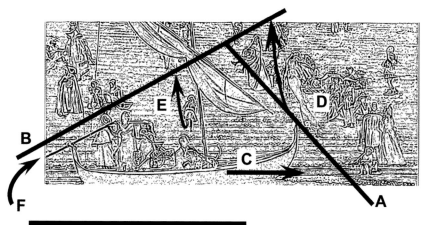

Once the intense affective visual world takes on its own life, there is no preventing it from overwhelming the classical Hollywood narrative form.

She rises in a curling, self-absorbed instant that seems slowed down compared with what is going on around her; a rippling balletic corkscrew of movement that curves around itself and rises at the same time. She leans backwards, arches her back slightly, brings up her knees. She spreads her arms languidly, closes her eyes, her vividly red hair cascading thickly over her shoulders. The movement of her body is propelling her upwards. In a scene where the ability to fly is evidently ten a penny, hers is nonetheless a distinctively eye-catching aerial competence. Yet she is merely an extra. She has no narrative point in the scene. Chris has been led now from his "painted world" by Leona (Rosalind Chow) who wears a name tag like a flight attendant's and guides him down magisterially conceived leaf-strewn steps, with a choreographed population of people from different times and places (the dead – or characters from *Peter Pan* and *Mary Poppins*?). In front of them is "the city" against another Bierstadt-style matte-painted sky.

They have now climbed aboard a boat, part gondola, part sailboat. They paid no attention to this woman, except that Chris glances up at her at the last minute, as if merely noticing the movement. But Michael Kamen's score does notice her, picks up her rising cadence and emphasizes it, adding a brief sense of closure as she rises out of the frame, her mermaid tail (for we recognize it now) undulating softly. And the camera also notices her, finding an extraordinary angle (F) from which to catch the visual cadence, with a long lens that flattens the space and affords a depth of field so shallow that almost everything else is in softened focus. Most strikingly, unlike Chris, she does not seem to be going anywhere in particular.

This scene's movement down the vast steps, which is relatively unhurried and is distracted along the way by marginal but arresting detail, ends in an elegant triangular composition as shown. The two strong diagonals A and B intersect to form a triangular space. The movement of the boat at C forms the base of the triangle and also gives the image a strong initial sense of left-to-right motion. So we pay relatively little attention to the figures grouped on the left side of the image, letting our gaze drift instead across to where the water glistens in a space defined by the prow of the boat and the strong diagonal at A. The child running up the steps at E adds a first trace of upward dynamism to the scene, so our eye senses that the triangle is not compressing the space inside so much as activating it. All of this establishes the line and the feeling of slightly languid energy for

the mermaid. She drifts upward along the line of D. The intersecting line of B then defines her exit point at the top of the frame.

A key thing about this strange moment is that it is done in two shots, not just in this one finely composed tableau. The camera finds at F an unexpectedly effective and suddenly more intimate entry point into the moment. The re-positioning of this camera and the use of a longer lens and consequently shallow depth-of-field throw Chris and Leona into soft focus. So we really focus "pointlessly" on the gently corkscrewing upward flight of the mermaid woman in shot F.

The woman is a mermaid because she derives partly from Hieronymus Bosch's medieval biblical triptych painting *The Garden of Earthly Delights*, which Vincent, production designer Eugenio Zanetti and costume designer Yvonne Blake are playfully re-making throughout this scene A few minutes earlier we have watched Chris glimpse (or imagine) his now lost wife plunging naked into the clearly icy waters of the lake in his "painted world" as it loses some of its initially vibrant colors with his mood change. Then the warm mermaid rises out of the water here. On the level of story, however, Annie is still elsewhere. In fact, we have just seen her alone and in some despair in her gloomy kitchen (see the frame sequence on the following pages). And the film, a couple of scenes later, re-attaches the mermaid image to a little card cut-out character in a flashback to Chris's dead daughter's toy theatre cum mobile (above left), complete with cardboard staircase and cast of extras, itself retrospectively then a source of much of the visual imagineering that goes on in the scene we are looking at here.

The dizzyingly post-classical interweaving of material achieved visually here may be ultimately undermined by the narrative exposition, by the story and dialogue, but it constantly threatens to reclaim the film's form as its own.

```
          LEONA
We flew to Singapore once. And my
daddy smiled at the flight
attendant who... Looked like
this. And wore the same tag.
'Leona.' He said Asian women are
so lovely. And graceful. And
intelligent.

          CHRIS
He didn't mean only...

          LEONA
I know. It was just something he
said.
```

As they boat across the lagoon, Leona reveals to Chris that she is his dead eight-year old daughter Marie, killed in a road accident some years before his own death, her present form the result of a casual remark he had made to her about an Asian flight attendant. What they have just passed through on the staircase was, in this expositional explanation, Marie's personal afterlife, just as the "painted world" was Chris's. But the mermaid and the web of images she seems to belong to in the film's visual anti-narrative affective world don't feel contained by this narrative "explanation" and the moment (see following pages) really does seem to belong more in an intensely sublime "vision" like Griffin's from *The Navigator: A Medieval Odyssey*.

As Chris (Robin Williams) visits what turns out to be his dead daughter's afterlife in *What Dreams May Come*, Annie, the only person in the family still alive, is on the verge of suicide. This scene reveals the film and its director at their most anti-narrative and "visionary" level of intensity, especially if we ignore the dialogue between Chris and Leona which is struggling here to sustain a classically straight narrative line and to "explain" things. Filmically, the scene taps into a time of arrested childhood instead and lingers there. The asterisked frame "quotes" Friedrich's painting *Man and Woman Contemplating the Moon*.

The effects team digitally extended the 40x80-foot set to six times its size and added four-fifths of the background people. Matte paintings supervised by Deak Ferrand extended this space to the horizon. Cinematographer Eduardo Serra, shooting on Kodak Super 35 film with its larger negative area, used twenty Maxi and Dino lighting units to flood the scene with softly diffused light and strong backlighting. Despite this huge effort on the visualization, Eduardo Serra still notes wryly and perhaps diplomatically that the mandated "author" on the production was ultimately the producer-backed writer ("We could not change a comma of the ... dialogue").

Eduardo Serra interviewed by Diane Baratier, AFC newsletter (Paris), September 2005

had to be there for when they called 'action' for the first time. That set was like three football fields in an airplane hangar. Way in the back is Video Village and way over there is craft services, which looks like a small restaurant. And then there's this huge set with a blue screen and a lagoon and flying people everywhere. So I get my elaborate bagel from craft services, I work my way to Video Village where I sit down in front of the monitors, next to the DP and the costume designer. I'm getting comfortable for the day. And way out on the football field is Vincent on a megaphone. And he goes 'Stephen – Stephen Book – you're here, good, come here.' So I put down my bagel and start this long lonely walk with everybody looking at me. And before I get there he announces, 'Everybody, this is Stephen – he'll be directing all the extras today – take it away Stephen.' As he walks by me he whispers, 'Just fix them.'"

Stephen Book (above right), acting coach, long-time faculty member of the Juilliard School and creative consultant on *What Dreams May Come*: "It had been another long day and now we go to the editing room where the editor has been putting together the rushes. There's just three of us, editor David Brenner, Vincent and me. We're looking at the first assemblage of the previous day's footage which is the beginning of the scene that we'd been working on that day and would be working on for the next few days. So I'm sitting there watching them pick cuts. And I said 'Look at all the people.' Robin passes through them as he comes down these steps. I said, 'Look at them all – they look like tourists who've been told to smile for the camera.' Vincent and the editor had been so busy looking at the principals and constructing this assemblage of the scene. Vincent says 'S**t, you're right, they're terrible.' So he decides to re-do it tomorrow. The next day I show up on the set. I didn't have an early call time. I just

What Stephen Book helped achieve with this scene is the remarkable fact that all the extras seem to be in their own moments, rather than being spectators watching somebody else's. A little boy takes obvious delight in running across water and taking off into the air. Another boy flicks soap bubbles in what is very much his own space, his own private moment, permitted for a few seconds to occupy the very center of the frame. A bluesman concentrates on picking out something we never hear on his guitar. A woman in gossamer floats above a child who plays with her dangling tresses of hair. Two girls splash excitedly in the lagoon, throwing up glistening arcs of water. By the time the mermaid has her moment she has become part of a second scene going on around the one with the principals, a scene made up of these moments of which hers becomes then the most perfect realization.

Stephen Book interviewed in Los Angeles, 03.01.19

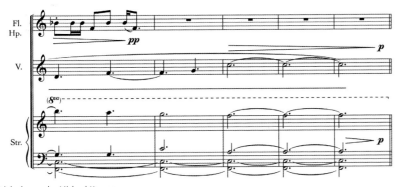

(Original score by Michael Kamen.
Extract transcribed by David Archer,
transcription copyright Soundstone Music 2010.)

Shot F as we have labeled it, the unexpected angle that isolates the "mermaid" moment, is a B-camera shot. On this scale of production the practice is to have an A-camera team covering the essentials while a B-camera typically has a little more freedom to look for shots within the parameters set by director and director of photography. In this instance, the B-camera operated by Kim Marks "finds" the particular angle at F. Editor David Brenner, with Vincent at his elbow,

then chooses to place the shot prominently within the larger context provided by the A-camera. But what makes the brief moment so striking is perhaps ultimately that composer Michael Kamen gives it its own brief but tightly synchronized underscoring (opposite), which follows the movement of her body.

Michael Kamen has said about his work on this film, "I was at an extremely profound juncture in my own life at that time, and the film produced a powerful and personal response in me." Brought in for only the final month of postproduction to replace a score written by Ennio Morricone, Kamen, with little time, tended to lightly punctuate the film, rather than producing the kind of full-blooded, omnipresent score that Morricone had delivered – and that the producers were now fearful was too intense and over-powering. In fact Morricone's score, which has since been "bootlegged," is a musical version of a Bierstadt painting and was intended to test the limits of emotional intensity in much the same way, with weighty liturgical passages based on a full choir and string-heavy orchestration and with Morricone's favored voice, Edda Dell'Orso, soaring majestically above it all. Kamen uses the female voice for a similarly "soaring" effect here but in an understated way, with flute and harp over lighter strings, and to personalize the moment rather than reaching for affective intensity.

Elsewhere, Kamen relies heavily on an existing folksy romantic ballad for the score's main theme (the song "Beside You," co-written by Kamen and Mark Snow years earlier) and this neatly, accessibly and rather predictably attaches itself to the narrative journey, which is what the producers hoped for when they dropped Morricone. In fact Kamen has said, "the 'straight lines' that the music draws [make the film] easier to comprehend." He did produce some ten minutes of orchestral drama for other parts of the film. But in moments like this one, Kamen's ability to capture the seemingly minor, fleeting detail works extremely well, in some measure perhaps because he was responding very personally himself to such specific moments. So we want to move on to thinking about how music functions in these moments in other films.

Michael Kamen interviewed by Dan Goldwasser, 09/04/99, www.soundtrack.net

This detail of the mermaid from Bosch's *Garden of Earthly Delights* is not so much a clever reference in *What Dreams May Come* (a print of the triptych appears on the wall in Chris and Annie's bedroom) as a helpful reminder that the "mermaid" we have just looked at is not about transcendence as popularly understood. "New Age" appropriations of mermaid symbolism take it determinedly in that direction, but Bosch's mermaid, with the strange armored figure beside her, has two key characteristics: she is bound up in the actual moment and, as Bosch scholar Hans Belting points out, the moment exists in a virtual world that has its own materiality (not an immaterial "spirit" world).

Michael Kamen's underscoring gives the mermaid we have been looking at her own moment – there is a very definitely self-contained and completed quality about the snippet of music – which becomes an ironic indifference to Chris's onward journey toward the light. Like all the other "extras" in the scene, she is doing her own thing. In her virtual world she has as much to do with other bodies (e.g. the ones Chris will shortly fall through from the sea of faces) as with Chris's quest (and Bosch's companion for her has affectively as much to do with the *USS Queenfish* in Vincent's *Navigator: A Medieval Odyssey* as with anything in this film).

But this moment (right) from *Map of the Human Heart* is even more instructive in this regard. We have already looked at the overall scene in some detail – Albertine and Avik in the shadowy nighttime dome of the Royal Albert Hall in London where a section of an English orchestra, far below them, has been rehearsing something that sounds like Handel. Albertine has just professed her determination to pass for white, rather than being seen as a "half-breed" in the way she thinks Avik is (with his Inuit mother and white father). Her hair whitened by dust from the German bomb that has exploded nearby, she rises slowly to her feet and composer Gabriel Yared underscores the moment with the piece

Anne Parillaud as Albertine in the dome of the Royal Albert Hall in *Map of the Human Heart*.

of music shown here, which has an untamed French-Canadian feel and a very expressive variation of the tempo (rubato) in the playing. David Archer explains: "A plaintive violin melody, through its modal tonality and use of rubato, brings a cultural contrast to the classical orchestra heard rehearsing before. Since the orchestral music is diegetic, Albertine's origins are implied even more powerfully when the solo violin is used as underscore."

So something important about the genuinely transformational moment in film (like this one from *Map of the Human Heart*) is starting to clarify itself for us here. These moments are like Hieronymus Bosch's, distributed across the surface of that great triptych known as *Garden of Earthly Delights*, and not in the end like an Albert Bierstadt painting, in the sense that *they do not assemble themselves into a single narrative image*.

Michael Kamen was brought in at the last minute on *What Dreams May Come* in order to map a simple musical straight line, as he called it, that would emphasize the narrative rather than the moments, although as we have seen

Molto rubato ♩ = 80

(Original score by Gabriel Yared.
Extract transcribed by David Archer,
transcription copyright Soundstone Music 2010.)

he was drawn personally to some of those moments. Gabriel Yared (below), on the other hand, is a composer who understands these moments and focuses on them with a clarity of musical perception that makes his meticulous and thoughtful score for *Map of the Human Heart* a deeply integral part of the film.

A narrative (the business of a screenplay) is a cartographic exercise over the body of a film. Imagine taking a pen and drawing a heavy line across Bosch's central panel, zigzagging here and there to connect a selection of its moments along the way but basically producing a step-by-step series of linkages in order to tell a story (this man crawls out of this giant egg, gets attacked by this pig, puts on this strange suit of armor, encounters this mermaid, journeys to this city in flames...). Entirely possible of course, and this indeed is what narrative cinema is expected to be able to do and quite rightly so (it sounds like a Fellini film). But the question then becomes whether the moments are allowed their own integrity.

The brief piece of music on the left utterly respects the integrity of the moment opposite. This is perhaps what composer James Horner meant when, as Yared's last-minute replacement on the film *Troy*, he said uncharitably of his predecessor, "He just doesn't have any knowledge of writing film scores – real film scores." Brought in to write a new score for *Troy* in nine days, in much the same way that Kamen had replaced Morricone on *What Dreams May Come*, Horner's job was to draw a familiar straight line for the audience to replace what he described as Yared's "lots of sort of Middle-Eastern stuff." That "stuff" represented a year of work by Yared, researching and developing material that would root the film musically in the way that even the brief piece here re-roots Albertine in who she really is, despite her protested allegiance to the idea of a more universal human being.

In short, the music is being placed *in* the moment – not used, like our imagined line drawn across the Bosch panel, to "transcend" the moment in the interests of a larger and perhaps simpler narrative image. In this case, moreover, the music ironically undercuts Albertine's denial of her own identity.

James Horner interviewed by Daniel Schweiger, *Film Music Radio*, 2006, www.filmmusicworld.com

The idea of a "narrative image" is most easily explainable in terms of film posters which tend to represent the most determined effort to encapsulate a film's narrative in one image. The two posters for Vincent's *River Queen* (opposite) show this process at work. The one on the left is a very early pre-visualization when the concept was first being developed and pitched. The one on the right is the final poster for the European release (in this case the Spanish language version).

It is interesting that some elements of setting, costume, appearance and color survived all the way from early version to release. But it is also apparent that the "narrative image" was fine-tuned along the way. The confident adventuress of the first version becomes the more imperiled woman in the later version, also picking up the film's promotional tagline "With darkness all around, only the heart can see."

This was the basis of the film's logline (or pitchable short summary): "Where the forest meets the river… In 1860s New Zealand, a young Irish woman finds herself caught on both sides of the lines during the wars between Māori tribes and the British colonial army. With darkness all around, and desperate to find her son, she discovers that only the heart can see…" It is not too difficult to recognize the effectiveness of logline, promotional tagline and poster here or how a narrative image is being conjured up to encapsulate what the film is offering.

But there is also an inevitable tension then (and this will occur in every film) between the clarity of the narrative image and the complexity and density that will satisfyingly fill out some two hours of screen time. We are especially interested here, not just in the consequences down at the level of the actual filmic moments we are looking at but also the question of music's different forms of allegiance to the narrative image and to the moment. The "straight line" that Michael Kamen talked about in the last-minute work he did on *What Dreams May Come* was very much to do with aligning the film more strongly with a narrative image (its poster if you like). The same with James Horner's last-minute work on the music for *Troy*. This is why some producers evidently expect a composer to do this kind of "fix" in a few weeks or even days — the music is being asked to function at very much the general level of the narrative image, rather than the detailed level where it is carefully "spotted" and worked into moments with their own life and qualities. So Michael Kamen's "Beside You" melody, which already existed, was used as a sort of musical version of the poster and narrative image of *What Dreams May Come*, although Kamen in the end did a few admirable moments in the film as well.

The composer on *River Queen* was Karl Jenkins. We want to look at a scene from *River Queen* (over the next four pages) with a view to understanding the role that music plays both inside the moment and over the top of the moment, as it were, in order to hook the moment to the larger narrative image. A key question is whether there will be in this any transition from one level to the other.

We know the narrative setup from our previous visits to *River Queen*. Sarah has found her lost boy, the child she had with a now long-dead young Māori man. The boy's uncle, Wiremu, had taken him in and he has been raised as Māori. We are caught up in the land wars in New Zealand (Aotearoa to the Māori), as a British colonial army clears villages and hunts down Māori rebels in the deep forest. The two forces now confront each other from entrenched positions on either side of a deep river gully. Māori working with the British ("it's a new world now" says one of them) have captured the boy and are taunting their "cousins" across the gorge by dangling him on a hook over the precipitous drop. Wiremu comes across to plead for the boy's life while Sarah has her penultimate confrontation with Baine, the British officer.

Realizing what is happening, Sarah runs through the British camp towards Wiremu and his cousin, who are bargaining for her son's freedom. "What are you going to give me for him?" "What do you want cousin?" "Your trigger finger maybe." Wiremu cuts his finger off with an axe. Sarah gets there an instant later. With this description in mind the following sequence of frames should be clear.

Samantha Morton   **Kiefer Sutherland**   **Cliff Curtis**   **Temuera Morrison**   **Stephen Rea**

Una nacción en la guerra.
Un hijo secuestrado.
Un viaje epico.

eurocine films PRESENTA

Dirigida por Vicent Ward

River Queen

Con la oscuridad a su alrededor, solamente su corazon podra ver.

SILVERSCREEN FILMS Y THE FILM CONSORTION EN ASOCIACIÓN CON ENDGAME ENTERTAINMENT NEW ZEALAND FILM PRODUCTION FUND NEW ZEALAND FILM COMMISSION
THE UK FILM COUNCIL CAPITAL PICTURES Y WAYWARD FILMS PRESENTA UNA PRODUCCION DE VICENT WARD SAMANTHA MORTON KIEFER SUTHERLAND CLIF CURTIS TEMUERA MORRISON
ANTON LESSER RAWIRI PENE STEPHEN REA "RIVERQUEEN" CASTING DIANA ROWAN Y CELESTIA FOX MUSICA KARL JENKINS EDITOR EWA J LIND
DISEÑO DE PRODUCCION RICK KOFOED Y PAUL GRINDER COPRODUCCIÓN TAINUI STHEPENS Y RICHARD FLET PRODUCCION GEOFF DIXON NEIL PEPLON JAMES D. STERN ERIC WANTSON MARK HOTCHIN
ESCRITO POR VICENT WARD Y TOA FRASER PRODUCIDO POR DON REYNOLDS Y CHRIS AUTY DIRECTOR DE PRODUCCION ALUN BOLLINGER DIRIGIDA VICENT WARD

Seeing too much leads to trauma in *River Queen* (2005), color frames courtesy of Silverscreen Films and Twentieth Century Fox Film Corporation..

River Queen (2005), color frames courtesy of Silverscreen Films and Twentieth Century Fox Film Corporation. (The diagonal on this page marks the moment we will be examining in more detail.).

When Sarah reaches the edge of the gorge and sees what Wiremu has done (we have marked this moment with a gray diagonal behind the preceding frames for clarity), time seems to stand still for an instant. We see her from Wiremu's point of view and then we see Sarah's view of Wiremu's bloody hand and axe. Having watched the soldiers watching her run through their camp in the preceding part of the scene, this moment briefly freezes another traumatic reversal of the gaze: Sarah is the one looking now and what she sees marks the point when her decision is made to go over to the other side. The boy takes advantage of his captors' distraction to unhook himself, striking the heavy tackle against the head of one of his tormentors. Wiremu fires a shot into nearby powder barrels that explode, giving Sarah, Wiremu and the boy time to leap through the embankment and down the steep slope towards the river.

The film's music editor, Peter Clarke (right), was responsible for the complex layering of the soundtrack here, with Vincent at his elbow. The first thing to point out is Peter's production of a short guitar cue – merely a snippet – to underscore the moment when Sarah sees what Wiremu has done. The music at this point needed to get inside the moment but Karl Jenkins' score (on screen opposite) was getting ready to pile on the layers of narrative drama and the forward momentum instead. Peter's introduction of the tiny segment of guitar is enough to hold the moment. David Archer explains: "This briefly tranquil but pained guitar cue allows the audience to take an emotional pause just before the action sequence. At that moment, Sarah and Wiremu are connected as she realizes the sacrifice he has just made for her son. This realization is then picked up and developed more fully by the choral cue that follows their escape. The harmonies sung there by the choir use a similar descending, then rising shape as the guitar did, which helps link the two scenes in the subtlest of ways."

In fact in postproduction Sarah's gaze at Wiremu's self-mutilation was cut into the sequence of shots in slow motion and Peter's placement of the guitar cue inside this slowed-down eight-second moment is what gives it its feeling of self-contained integrity.

Peter Clarke

(Transcribed by David Archer, transcription copyright Soundstone Music 2010.)

Throughout the second and third pages of our preceding frame sequences there is a steadily rising high-pitched drone of strings on the soundtrack, and the creaking of the ropes holding the boy as he sways, with several percussive "hits" marking the action. The guitar arrests this tension – we hear Sarah and Wiremu's breathing – and then the tension breaks when the boy swings the tackle at his captor's head on the last guitar note. So we are emotionally released over the edge much like the characters as they tumble down the cliff face and Karl Jenkins' cue with full strings, choir, drums and fanfare kicks in with explosive dramatic force. English composer Karl Jenkins has said of his score for *River Queen*: "I spent a large part of my career writing music for advertising so the process was familiar." In fact among Jenkins' best known work for the screen is his TV commercial for Delta Airlines (overleaf) that showed aircraft flying in

Karl Jenkins interviewed by John Mansell, *Soundtrack*, 2008, www.runmovies.eu

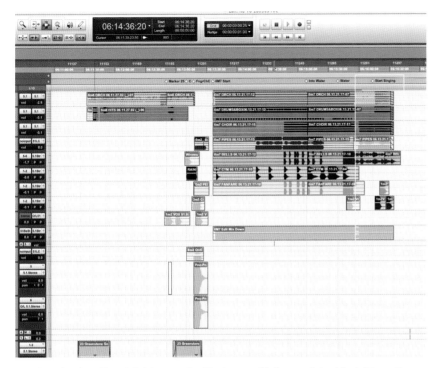

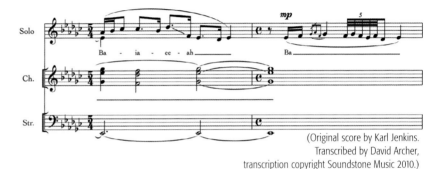

(Original score by Karl Jenkins.
Transcribed by David Archer,
transcription copyright Soundstone Music 2010.)

synchronization like dolphins, to Jenkins' song "Adiemus." Jenkins' *River Queen* vocalist Mae McKenna and "Adiemus" vocalist Miriam Stockley have recorded an album together called *Shabala* (Virgin, 1998) that demonstrates the genre of vaguely "tribal" world music which all of these have in common.

So when Sarah and Wiremu make their leap this is the world that Karl Jenkins has them leap into: a musically-evoked world that Jenkins has described as "extended choral-type work based on the European classical tradition, but where the vocal sound is more akin to 'Ethnic' or 'World' music" where the choruses sound "tribal." As Sarah, Wiremu and the boy escape towards the river, this is the sound that wells around them (see Peter's screen grab of tracks), with orchestra and choir rising above the frantic shouts and gunfire from the pursuing British soldiers.

They plunge into the water and get swept away, as much by the rising tide of music as by the river. The massive aural effect overall is in striking contrast with the fragile guitar moment we have just discussed.

Then, as they scramble ashore on the other bank to join the Māori entrenched on the hillside there, Jenkins' female vocalist rises above the choir for the last thirty seconds of the piece, accompanied by the strange tinkling of bells (the bells are the fifth track from the top on the screen grab and these thirty seconds are framed with a fine white line). This section, transcribed above, is where the cue most clearly resembles musicologist Timothy D. Taylor's description of the Delta commercial, with its promise of an elsewhere to fly off to: "This music's signification of a vague kind of spirituality or mysticism is in keeping with the clear mission of ... taking viewers away from the here and now and toward an

Taylor (2007), 196

exoticized elsewhere." This kind of music, says Taylor, echoes "centuries of western notions of other places as spiritual, in contrast to the modern West." In other words, Karl Jenkins' music, here as elsewhere in the film, may underscore the drama in effective ways but also captures and contributes to a generalized narrative image for *River Queen*. In that respect, the guitar snippet dropped in to the preceding moment by the music editor can be seen as compensatory for the score's general tendency to work over the top of the moments instead, in the interests of sustaining that more general narrative image.

So there is an important lesson here about music in films. The transformational moments we are looking for are, by and large, less concerned with that general narrative image. Where there is music in these moments it tends to be of the moment instead. And as the earlier example from Gabriel Yared suggests, it is more concerned with exploring "what it is like" for a particular character than signposting the audience's more general response.

This quality of what-it-is-likeness is going to be the next object of inquiry here as, in fact, the last major constituent of the transformational moment. So before moving on to that, it is important to note the similarity between Karl Jenkins' practiced evocation in music of a generalized exoticism or an "elsewhere" and Albert Bierstadt's painterly evocation of "transcendent" elsewheres bathed in light. Light, color and music can all be subsumed in the pursuit of that fantasy as we have seen — but they can also be deployed differently within the moment. What-it-is-likeness is a further key to these moments.

Delta Airlines
TV commercial (1994)

THE DREAM WORK OF CHARACTER-MAKING

Christopher Bollas has noted a deeper notion underpinning our term "transformation" — the idea that "the writers, filmmakers, and artists of our time are engaged in a most profound and intense transformation of the unconscious identity of a generation into consciousness." It is at exactly this point that the what-it-is-likeness of a character in film can intersect with the what-it-is-likeness, indeed with the "character," of any one of those creative artists, and Christopher Bollas further proposes that we "dream work" characters into becoming; not just fictional characters but our own characters. So this "dream work" of character-making (like Griffin's visions in *The Navigator*) crisscrosses the line between art and life. Thus in the next section we are going to attempt an imaging of just a few of those circumstances in which Vincent dreamed himself into existence. We are doing this not as an exercise somehow separate from our consideration of the films, and not at all to reduce those films to biographical explanations, but as a way of grasping how the transformation rules peculiar to an individual creative process are bound up in this kind of dream work.

Bollas (1993), 252

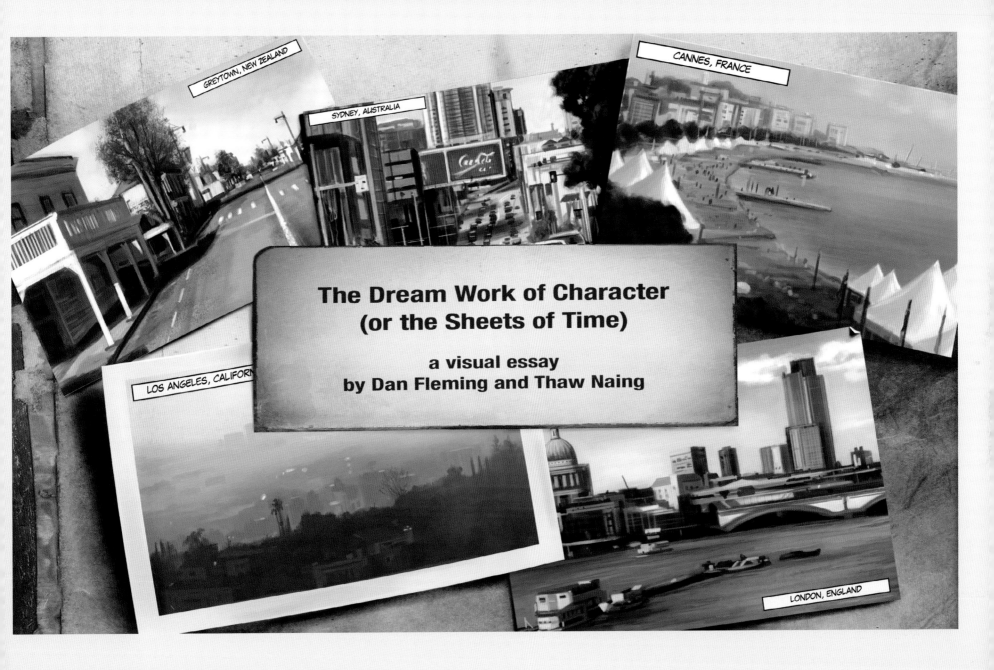

GREYTOWN, NEW ZEALAND

I DON'T KNOW HOW MUCH I CAN TELL YOU ABOUT VINCENT. HE WAS MY FOURTH CHILD AND BY THAT POINT I WASN'T PAYING MUCH ATTENTION.

IT'S ODD, THOUGH, BECAUSE I REMEMBER EVERY DETAIL IN THE ROOMS OF THE BIG HOUSE IN HAMBURG WHERE I GREW UP.

HIS FATHER WAS FIFTY WHEN VINCENT WAS BORN AND THE OTHER CHILDREN WERE OLDER THAN VINCENT.

SO HE'D GO OFF HAPPILY ON HIS OWN FOR HIS ADVENTURES. I REALLY DIDN'T KNOW WHAT HE WAS DOING MOST OF THE TIME.

Judy Ward interviewed in Greytown, September 12, 2009 (photo of Vincent courtesy of Judy Ward)

Maurice Askew (first head of the film program, School of Fine Arts, University of Canterbury) interviewed in Christchurch, January 26, 2010 (photo of Vincent Ward and Maurice Askew courtesy of John Perrone)

Louis Nowra (author, playwright and screenwriter) interviewed in Sydney, October 19, 2009

Perkins Cobb, interviewed in Cannes, May 13, 2009

LOS ANGELES, CALIFORNIA

WE GOT A NICE SOFA FOR THE OFFICE - YOU KNOW FOR THE MEETINGS - BUT VINCENT WOULD LET ANYBODY SLEEP ON IT...

...LIKE SOME CRAZY BLIND HOMELESS GUY HE FOUND IN THE MIDDLE OF THE STREET AND BROUGHT BACK HERE SO HE COULD HAVE A SHOWER AND A MEAL.

WITH MY CLOTHES STILL WET I GUESS I'LL HAVE TO STAY HERE - ON YOUR SOFA!

LATER, OVER AT THE CREATIVE ARTISTS AGENCY IN BEVERLY HILLS

MAYBE HE'S NOT GOING TO BE A GROOMABLE ASSET? DID YOU SMELL THAT SOFA?

HOW ABOUT IF WE PACKAGE HIM WITH RON BASS ON THAT HEAVEN AND HELL PICTURE?

Sarah Whistler (Vincent Ward Film Productions) interviewed in Los Angeles, January 30, 2010

Stuart Fyvie (LipSync Post) interviewed in London, June 30, 2010. Final frame shows the "rebel" Māori chief as played by Temuera Morrison in *River Queen* (2005).

The earliest record of Vincent's family in Ireland is in 1796 when Thady Ward is recorded as a tenant growing flax for the linen industry on this hillside farm at Kilnagarn in County Leitrim, then Cormac Ward as a tenant farmer here until his death aged 84 in 1870. Cormac's son Thomas stepped out of this thatched stone cottage in 1862 and looked across the waters of Lough Allen for the last time as he departed for Australia, leaving like a generation of young Irishmen whose childhoods had coincided with the Irish Famine that left the country impoverished. Thomas's younger brother Thady was present at their father's death here but by then Thomas had given up on the goldfields of Australia and settled across the Tasman Sea, in Morrison's Bush near Greytown, New Zealand, with a Limerick-born widow whom he married after her first husband died fighting a fire that swept across the whole area. Thomas was Vincent's great-grandfather. Thomas's contemporary, Englishman Humphry Butler, a commander in the Royal Navy and great-grandson of Brinsley Butler, 1st Viscount Lanesborough, owned 2,800 acres in County Leitrim as an absentee landlord, including the farm where the Wards were tenants. In Morrison's Bush, opposite, the Wards carved out their own place on what had once been Māori land, between a loop in the river overlooked by a steep cliff and a straight track that would become the road named Ward's Line.

Dan Fleming

Wairarapa Standard, 1888

"Mr Ward, a sturdy son of Erin's Green Isle, is the pioneer settler of this Line. The Line is, in fact, called after him. He has been on this property 24 years, and like other plucky settlers, conquered swamp and bush to carry out his project of forming a home for himself and his family. There are well-cleared paddocks, and orchard with trees well pruned, an infant plantation rising to protect the property from wind; oats and wheat, potatoes and vegetables. The barn and sheds are very capacious and strongly built."

Dan Fleming

The American West and the British "West" (Australia, South Africa, Canada, New Zealand) exercise a profound and continuing influence on imaginations in the Anglophone world, not least the cinematic imagination. The settler myth at the heart of these "Wests" is in many ways the deep structure behind an ongoing attachment to the myth of the "hero's journey." Associating this with more universal claims — that it is a human myth instead of a particular people's myth — keeps alive a triangulation most clearly seen in *Shane*, above (1953, dir. George Stevens). The gaze of the boy is deflected off his father (the prototype settler) onto the figure of myth. And in versions like *Shane* the original occupants of the father's land are nowhere to be seen though everywhere a potentially traumatic presence, as are the real conditions of the settler experience. Understanding the endless repetition of this pattern — this deflection toward myth but potential for trauma — is crucial to grasping why so many cinematic moments are still profoundly influenced by it. This is especially so when the landscape (including its light and color) is drawn toward myth.

(reproduced courtesy of Interscope Communications/Radar Pictures)

right: detail of a painting (oil on canvas) by Stephen Hannock for *What Dreams May Come*.
left: Vincent Ward on his great-grandfather Thomas' farm, Ward's Line, Morrison's Bush, New Zealand.

Vincent Ward, Morrison's Bush, New Zealand, 2010

184 ■ COMPOSING THE MOMENT

Vincent Ward in his studio, New Zealand, 2010, painting is work in progress
(treatment of surface resembles Stephen Hannock's luminist technique)

Vincent Ward, shearing shed, Morrison's Bush, New Zealand, 2010

'There are all sorts of markings from different strata of time – like a neighbor who shot himself in a rubbish dump with a note that his value was less than the refuse around him.' (Vincent Ward)

top: Ralph Hopkins collection, #99-291-152, Wairarapa Archive NZ. Charles Van Schaick #23745, Wisconsin Historical Society USA.
bottom: Vincent Ward, Morrison's Bush, New Zealand, 2010, photograph by the author.

Were we to design a poster for what it is like in Vincent Ward's "dream work," this painting by American artist Albert Pinkham Ryder (*Siegfried and the Rhine Maidens*, 1888) could serve as the narrative image, albeit with tongue somewhat in cheek. The artist's perhaps largely unconscious journey back to the river becomes the hero's journey, like Siegfried's here on horseback. One of the figures in the river re-appears in a painting in progress in Vincent's studio, arm bent back over her head in the same gesture. Light, color and landscape carry traces of other images and rhyming action – Friedrich's *Man and Woman Contemplating the Moon*, thus the tree in *What Dreams May Come*, the woman in the river in *River Queen*, the cliff above the river, the boy alone on the great-grandfather's farm imagining journeying heroes. The narrative image, like a film poster's, is a huge reduction of course, but this one looks promising.

There is more to this narrative image, however, than a particular biographically informed confluence of imagery and fantasy, and this is what makes it worth commenting on in the context of the book's larger interests. In fact, the key point is that this painting does not necessarily provide a way in to personal preoccupations, an individual artistic "vision," a "worldview," auteurist "themes," or any of the other ways of writing about an artist as a special individual. It only looks promising in that regard because it draws on larger forces that may have helped make the style of imagining that we encounter in a person such as Vincent.

Ryder's painting evokes what the critic Edward Said memorably described as "an atmosphere created by both empire and novels, by racial theory and geographical speculation, by the concept of national identity and urban (or rural) routine," which is to say the atmosphere of nineteenth-century imperial and colonial myths that shaped our world by continuing to shape its routines, including routines of the imagination as lived on a farm in rural New Zealand (itself there as a result of "geographical speculation").

But Ryder also taps into the trauma that shadows those routines, where the women in the river could become those escaping the fires of Hamburg or Dresden when empires clashed, or "refugees from the east" in *The Navigator*, or

Said (1993), 5

even the indigenous people of some village being "cleared" (as well as any lurking fantasy or memory of secretive pubescent sexuality), and the whole image seems imbued with the alternative "underworld" that nineteenth-century writer Hippolyte Taine saw as the new place of the imagination – not a mythical or biblical underworld but an underworld of what move us. The creative convergence of elements from these two structures – myth and trauma – defines a core space of "what it is like" to be moved.

The preceding experimental visual essay is not intended as merely a pictorial interlude in the main business of the book. It is intended to suggest something of the possible contexts for the one transformation rule we have been able to identify as a driving force in Vincent's creativity: when seeing reaches a point of sublime intensity it risks "seeing too much" and becomes traumatic. This also hints at possible sources for his intuitive post-classical sensibility as a filmmaker – the thing that set him at odds with classical Hollywood narrative even as he attempted to accommodate to it. In that respect, Vincent Ward was very much ahead of his time, anticipating the post-classical turn in filmmaking by two decades. Being out of synch in that sense, though, would not have been a professionally comfortable condition, indeed would not have been without its own trauma.

For us, on the other hand, Vincent's work brings into view the basis of those transformational moments that now take on an even greater significance, because they mark a potential transformation of classical Hollywood narrative form into post-classical form. This form is not yet clear enough for us to describe it independently of the actual work that struggles to realize it. But what we have learnt here is that new ways of handling time are very much part of the transformation.

The question of communicating what-it-is-likeness in film is a crucial one. This is often thought of as a matter of identification with or sympathy for a character. But ask yourself, glancing back at the fragment of a life story suggested a couple of pages ago, whether you felt something for the person who committed suicide amidst the rubbish pushed for years off the cliff-edge at the back of a farm? If you did, this required neither identification with nor sympathy for a character. Just a sudden capacity to feel what it was like. Those other responses could come later, given enough to attach themselves to.

Moreover, there are discernible traces of other things in that fragment. The young woman by the river on page 187 is actually from the work of Black River Falls' town photographer Charles Van Schaick who documented life in a settler community in Wisconsin in the U.S. at the time an unnamed photographer captured a neighbor of the Wards outside the Morrison's Bush Post Office in New Zealand. Author and historian Michael Lesy included the Van Schaick photograph in *Wisconsin Death Trip*, an extraordinary assemblage of images and newspaper accounts that suggests what it was like for those people. "History with a wrench" a *Newsweek* reviewer called it, and the "wrench" is the opening up of what-it-is-likeness inside the documentary detail, especially a sensation of grasping the trauma that jauntier pioneer community self-descriptions of collective and individual pluckiness tend to erase. That such descriptions also tend to erase other presences – such as indigenous people – is very much part of that trauma or that wound in the telling (and the factor we will be returning to). As Joan Didion points out in discussing Bierstadt's painting of the Donner Pass, two presences are missing from that vision – the indigenous and the traumatized voice that says, "Remember, never take no cutoffs and hurry along as fast as you can."

What we will do in the rest of this book is consider in some depth how film handles moments of what-it-is-likeness.

Didion (2004), 75

EXERCISE

This is the book's third exercise and is concerned with character.

If you can obtain the DVD, *Mister Lonely* (2007, dir. Harmony Korine) makes intriguing viewing as a way of thinking about the links between acting style and character. Werner Herzog plays a priest who accidentally drops a nun out of a light aircraft on a mercy mission to drop supplies to a jungle village. Samantha Morton plays a Marilyn Monroe impersonator in a troubled relationship with a Charlie Chaplin impersonator in a Scottish commune of impersonators. A determinedly experimental film, as you may have guessed and as is director Harmony Korine's style, *Mister Lonely*'s most revealing aspect for our purpose is Samantha Morton's performance.

The character played by Samantha Morton is fundamentally unknowable, her background and motivations obscure, her behavior fascinating to watch but hard to explain. And yet the actor delivers a mesmerizing performance of real emotional depth. The closest anyone has come to theorizing this kind of performance was probably Polish theater director Jerzy Grotowski in the 1960s who advocated acting which "necessitates the stripping away of 'how to do,' a mask of technique behind which the actor conceals himself, in search of the sincerity, truth and life of an exposed core of psycho-physical impulses" (Bradby and Williams, p.124).

The only way to grasp what it looks and feels like when an actor makes this "core of psycho-physical impulses" available, while at the same time denying us the classical knowability of character, is to watch someone like Samantha Morton at work in a film such as *Mister Lonely*. If you can, watch the film and think about how the "mask" of character-making technique is abandoned.

Mister Lonely is ultimately a playful conceit, but it was an available vehicle for Samantha Morton's acting which otherwise sits uneasily within the classical Hollywood narrative form where knowable character has to be hooked tightly into this kind of intensity in order to explain it. When "Marilyn" commits suicide in the woods near the end of *Mister Lonely* we are left instead with a puzzle.

For a discussion of Grotowskian acting, see David Bradby and David Williams (1988) *Directors' Theatre* (London: Macmillan)

PART 3

WHAT IT IS LIKE

We have looked in considerable detail at staging the moment, at composition, at narrative, at color, light and music. What it is like is the last piece of this particular jigsaw. Hippolyte Taine in 1872 (right), who is also the originator of a concept of moment not unrelated to this book's, offers an almost geological picture here of the terrain of what-it-is-likeness, as we now want to call it. But he evokes an "underworld" of proportions well beyond the scope of anything we can consider here. So what we shall do, following the lead that previous material has given us, is to consider first what it is like to die, initially from the point of view of cinematic treatments of suicide. This will raise the question of emotion in acting, which we will move on to consider as an important aspect of what it is like more generally.

So how do we start so quickly to care about somebody in a film? This happens easily in some films and not at all in others, so remains a slightly mysterious phenomenon in some ways. Opposite is the opening of *Wristcutters, a Love Story*, a film about an afterlife (2006, directed by Goran Dukic).

We watch Zia (Patrick Fugit) wake up and look around his disastrously untidy room. We feel him slump a little at the sight but then he sets to, tidying up, putting things away, arranging his desktop, watering his pot plant, cleaning (all underneath the film's opening titles), so we share quite effortlessly his satisfaction in seeing everything eventually spic-and-span. Who hasn't been there? We have a moment to admire the results as Zia goes to the bathroom in the background but then, as the camera dollies slowly in towards the bathroom door, the suspicion dawns on us that he has been putting things in order prior to cutting his wrists. The awful inevitability of what we are about to see creeps up along with that inexorable camera movement. One last look at himself in the mirror, now ashen-faced, and Zia slumps onto the tiles, his final breaths moving some clumps of dust and hair that he missed in his cleaning, to and fro in the corner of the floor.

The point about how this is done — its sheer matter-of-factness — is that it leaves us in absolute desperation to find out more about Zia one way or another,

> We have reached a new world, which is infinite, because every action which we see involves an infinite association of reasonings, emotions, sensations new and old, which have served to bring it to light, and which, like great rocks deep-seated in the ground, find in it their end and their level. This underworld is a new subject-matter

not because he has engaged us with emotionality but because we have watched him painstakingly tidy his room. As it turns out, we will get to know and like him in an unexpected afterlife that is much like this life, only a little stranger.

There was a kind of shortcut at work in that opening to *Wristcutters* — getting inside what it is like by simply watching somebody do something recognizably ordinary before the extraordinary intervenes. The unnecessity of emotion in this is worth remarking on, as a simplistic assumption might be that emotionality — for example Robin Williams's mimicking of "deep" emotions in *What Dreams May Come* — is necessary to our feeling of engagement in these kinds of moment. It is clearly not.

Indeed, there is a trick here that we can see used most effectively by director Phillip Noyce in *Patriot Games*, a film based on the Tom Clancy novel that requires us to get quickly up to speed in terms of caring about the central characters before the narrative starts piling on the action in typical Clancy fashion.

What Noyce employs, along with actors Harrison Ford, Anne Archer and a young Thora Birch, are familiar techniques to draw the audience in to what it is like to be these people right at the beginning of the film. But this version is so deftly done that it is worth looking at (p. 195). We begin with a tracking shot through a house empty of people but warmly furnished with signs of family life. A telephone answering machine kicks in and it is Ford (character Jack Ryan) asking their housekeeper to take care of some mundane things for them while they are away (like faking replacement goldfish if their daughter's have not survived). Piled-up bills beside the phone, and *Atlantic Monthly* magazine, say ordinary but smart people. Cut to Harrison Ford on the other end of the telephone, in a hotel room. A back-of-the head shot, just to play the recognition game with the knowing audience, Big Ben through a nighttime window to fill in the details, shoeless feet up despite the fairly crisp business shirt saying brief family downtime for a man with important things to do.

Wristcutters, a Love Story (2006)

Then Harrison Ford does one of the little physical actor's tricks that he is so adept at, putting the phone down and rolling over the back of the sofa onto cushions on the floor where his wife and daughter are playing Monopoly. It is that bodily "gesture," that unexpected but humanizing movement, relaxed, playful, real, which makes the moment. We like this man right away. We do not need any signs of his feelings for his family in order to understand those feelings. They are there in that one movement, telling us about how comfortable he is in the moment with his wife and daughter.

The chatter about the board game can be completely unexplicit about their relationship and at the same time say how happy these three people are together.

So everything is being communicated without being acted out, is in the physical ease of the characters with each other and in the recognizable ordinariness of what they are seen doing.

A little later the waiter delivers champagne and candles. Cathy Ryan's idea (typical of him not to have thought of it but he is glad she did) and we are set up for a conventional romantic interlude, seen on screen so many times. But again a little bit of actorly business from Ford lifts the moment. He does not quite get the scene organized before his wife comes out of the bathroom, so she catches him perched slightly comically on the bed in his business shirt and colorful boxer shorts. Ford freezes the position just long enough for us to smile, as much at the playful re-working of an otherwise utterly familiar scene as at the comical sight. Then Archer and Ford perfectly mirror each other's actions and gestures – sipping champagne, reaching for the bedside lights – in a way that says practiced but not tired familiarity with each other.

The next morning, young Sally Ryan is trying to distract a motionless guardsman outside Buckingham Palace as her mother snaps her picture. The moment is played out at more length than one might initially expect as Thora Birch does a little dance and salutes, all to no avail as the guardsman remains unmoved.

But these things have been enough. What it is like to be these three people has been telegraphed to us using basic but effective cinematic tricks and it works. The film can then throw any amount of jeopardy at them – as it does starting with a terrorist car-bomb seconds later – and we do care. At least up to a point, as a Tom Clancy story is never going to let us get any deeper than where we are already with them. That is largely enough, however, for this genre of film. And without that time spent doing this telegraphing, the action film becomes all action and very little else. While this kind of telegraphing is very conventional, Ford's roll over the sofa is a touch that lifts it beyond the over-familiar.

What becomes clear from even just the previous two examples is that what it is like may be communicated without much internality being offered to the film viewer. In *Wristcutters*, after the opening sequence, we are left wanting the film to offer us some of that internality because we have already started to care about the young man who cleaned up his room. And in *Patriot Games*, a typical but well-made piece of action cinema, we have connected with the family before we find out much about what is going on inside their heads or what kinds of feelings they may have, which are things that the genre is typically clumsy at handling in any case.

We can take this insight about the separation of what it is like from internality (the expression of feelings, emotions, states of mind) considerably further by looking at the 1998 Japanese film *After Life* (called *Wonderful Life* in Japan) directed by Hirokazu Koreeda, one of the undisputed high points in the "life after death" genre.

Set in a way station for the processing of the recently deceased, *After Life* builds slowly. We see a number of people sign-in. Each gets directed to a separate interview room where it is explained to them: within the week they have to choose one memory from their life, which will be staged, filmed and screened by the staff. Videotapes of their lives are available for them to consult if they need to. Only then can they move on and that one chosen memory is then the only memory that they will take with them when they go. We watch one after another of the dead sit on the other side of the tables recounting memories or struggling

Patriot Games (1992)

to do so (many of these are non-actors talking in an impromptu way about their own memories).

Like *Wristcutters*, the matter-of-factness is immediately seductive. The fanciful nature of the film's central premise is counterbalanced by the ordinariness of the way station, a rather time-worn place with cracked paint and rickety furniture. It is staffed by people whom we discover have been unable to choose their own memories and hence have got stuck here, processing others instead. Among these is Takashi (played by Arata), assigned with a young female staffer to interview new arrival Ichiro (Naito Taketoshi), frame 3 opposite. Ichiro, a widower, is having a great deal of difficulty finding a memory from a life that appears to have been utterly uneventful, routine and passionless. The film has an almost documentary quality in these interviews, observing silences, waiting for the words to come, the camera staging things in very simple shot-reverse-shot setups across a table.

Naito Taketoshi's performance as the older man is quietly naturalistic, revealing little by way of clues to what he is thinking or feeling. In fact for a while he could be one of the non-actors, given that so little "acting" is evident.

And yet, gradually, the film builds up a sequence of interconnections that are emotionally wrenching for the viewer. As Ichiro reviews videotape of his life, he settles eventually on one brief moment when he and his wife, whose long marriage had been politely comfortable but without much depth of feeling, sit together on a park bench (6). A good memory can come from being in somebody else's happiness, he explains. This memory is recreated in the way station's studio. Takashi watches from behind as Ichiro sits beside his wife (played by an actress) one last time (7). We are kept distant from the moment, the emotion all in the idea rather than in the performances per se.

But Takashi has realized that he himself some fifty years before had sat in that park beside a younger version of Ichiro's wife, her young first husband about to go off to war and, as it turned out, to his death. He hunts through the way station's film archive to find the memory selected by Ichiro's wife when

she herself had passed through. When he finds it, it is of her as the older woman she was when she died, but sitting beside a young officer in uniform (8). Going back to the tapes of his own life he finds that moment – two young people sitting together, one of them himself (9). Takashi has found his own memory.

Without ever trying to get "inside" its characters in any conventional way – for instance in scenes of high emotion or talk of love and loss – *After Life* builds a heart-breaking series of interconnections across their lives and stages these for us so undramatically that this very quality of restraint becomes almost unendurably moving.

After Life also illustrates a still more subtle technique for exploring what it is like. We think for quite a long time that it is Ichiro, the seemingly older man, that we are struggling to get to know behind his unresponsiveness. And indeed we do gradually get a sense of what it is like to be Ichiro. But the layering of Ichiro and Takashi's memories means that we suddenly realize how much we understand, at the same time, of what it is like to be Takashi, the "young" man who got stuck at the way station when he died in World War Two and could not choose a memory of his own.

This transference of what-it-is-likeness from one character to another is something that director Alain Resnais achieves to stunning effect in *Love Unto Death* (1984), written by Jean Gruault, who had been a star screenwriter of the French New Wave.

The film begins with Simon (Pierre Arditi) dying on his bedroom floor from what appears to be a sudden brain hemorrhage, watched by his very distraught wife Elisabeth (Sabine Azéma). So in this series of examples, this is the first instance where a conspicuous display of emotionality is foregrounded; indeed we are plunged straight into a scene of some considerable emotional intensity. But minutes after a doctor has declared Simon dead, he "miraculously" shocks Elisabeth by appearing on the stairs, complaining of a headache. The explanation – of a near-death experience and misstatement by the doctor – is

After Life (1998)

initially accepted by everyone. Almost every subsequent scene has Simon and Elisabeth touching affectionately, as if to underscore the feelings that have not just survived the experience but been intensified. However Simon's behavior gradually changes as does his mood. His affectionate moments with Elizabeth start to look almost imperceptibly like he is acting out what he should feel rather than what he does feel. These brief scenes are interspersed with shots of snow falling in darkness, accompanied by powerfully suggestive music by Hans Werner Henze, whose dislocating work is confined to these unsettling shots as if to comment on the scenes they punctuate, chipping away at any sense of emotional normality.

Simon starts to convince himself that he should be dead and is somehow living on borrowed time, dissolving away. Images of bees swarming on a tree, a farm building on fire or a tumorous growth on a plant in the laboratory where Elisabeth works, suggest something of the film's shifting tone and the notion of disturbances to a natural order. Then Elisabeth follows Simon to the riverbank and what we are suspecting becomes certain — we have been watching the stages in a person being brought to the edge of suicide. Except that Simon is shortly thereafter struck down again by the ticking bomb in his head that he had evaded for a while. This time he does die.

This, however, is where Resnais' film pulls off its structural coup. We have been so preoccupied with seeing Simon through Elisabeth's eyes that we have not quite noticed it is Elisabeth's what-it-is-likeness that we have been drawn into. And it is Elisabeth who is now recognizably depressed and contemplating suicide. Up to this point *Love Unto Death* has not used any of the familiar tricks to draw us into a conventional sympathy for the characters. There has even been something unsettlingly ritualistic about the repeated vignettes of affection between Simon and Elisabeth, the very repetition serving to distance the viewer rather than absorb them. Simon's thinking about his near-death experience has been fascinating to observe but it feels like precisely that — an act of rather detached observation.

At this point, though, it is as if a switch is thrown and we are inside what it is like to be Elisabeth, having spent the first half of the film alongside her as it were. Quietly intense drama ensues as her friends Jérôme and Judith (André Dussollier and Fanny Ardant), a husband-and-wife team of church ministers, try to talk Elisabeth out of her suicide. The question of whether she will go through with it becomes profoundly compelling, as do the to-and-fro arguments marshaled by her two friends, and the film is entirely given over to these for the remainder of its length.

So we did not get to "know" Elisabeth via any of the conventional tricks like those we saw at the beginning of *Patriot Games*. Nor, interestingly, did her early outpourings of emotion over Simon draw us in. If anything these seemed more of a spectacle to be observed (like the bright red sweater she was wearing), while we tried to figure out what was happening in Simon's head, psychologically as well as medically. Then paradoxically, Sabine Azéma's performance as Elisabeth turns still, resolute, austere and undemonstrative at precisely the stage where we suddenly find ourselves caring so much about her. So once again, the mystery of how we come to care about a character in a film has less to do with them opening up to us in some intimate and revealing way and more with the careful staging of our attention — in this instance with how we are moved, in the several senses of that word, from Simon to Elisabeth.

The capacity of Alain Resnais' *Love Unto Death* and Hirokazu Koreeda's *After Life* to be moving without being sentimental brings us to the question of sentimentality itself.

Resnais' actor Pierre Arditi (who plays Simon) has described the director's working methods in detail. He notes that Resnais did "dry takes" and "wet takes" so as to be able to modulate the affective level: in other words, scenes were shot with and without explicit emotionality from the actors, allowing Resnais very precise control over the on-screen expression of emotion. As we have seen, affective intensity for the viewer is not necessarily matched to "wet takes." In fact, in the right circumstances, as suggested by the examples we have been looking

Love Unto Death (1984)

at, the "dry take" carries the greatest affective charge, like those shots on the park bench in *After Life*.

We will be coming back to the use of "wet" and "dry" takes when we look again at the work of Samantha Morton on *River Queen*, as well as on her own directing debut, but before we do so it is necessary to develop our understanding rather more fully of the relationship between emotion and what-it-is-likeness.

The Hollywood "weepie" *Penny Serenade* (1941), directed by George Stevens and with cinematography by the great director of photography at Columbia Joseph Walker, who worked with Frank Capra and Howard Hawks on some of their best films, is a textbook lesson in handling emotion to classically full effect. Irene Dunne and Cary Gant play Julie and Roger Adams, who lose their unborn child when Julie miscarries. Unable to conceive another child, they adopt a little girl. When Roger loses his job they struggle to keep the child.

In the scene opposite, Roger has gone to the judge's chambers to support his petition to retain parental rights despite his straitened circumstances. Julie waits at home fearing the worst. Roger is accompanied by Miss Oliver, the head of the adoption agency, played by Beulah Bondi, a stalwart Hollywood character actor of great though often unremarked upon skill.

The second part of the sequence, after Roger's appearance in front of the judge, is staged with the full panoply of emotion-extracting techniques that gave the "weepie" its name as a de facto genre. With Julie, we do not know the judge's decision. Stevens and Walker frame her alone in the house, literalizing the empty family space that she fears (frame 3). Then when Roger arrives we cannot see through the pane in the door whether or not he has brought back the child (4). The camera pans with agonizing slowness from Julie towards … a grinning Roger holding the baby (6/7/8). A "wet take" of Irene Dunne reacting caps the moment (9).

The preceding scene in the sequence, however, is where the emotionality starts to grow. As well as being the cool sophisticate, Cary Grant could be an unemotional foil to James Stewart's emotional firecracker in *The Philadelphia Story* or a manically over-excited center of attention in *Arsenic and Old Lace*, but here he demonstrates his ability to stand still and slowly spill a quantity of what feels like emotional truth into the scene. Stevens captures much of this in the master shot (1), as if it wasn't sufficiently repeatable to capture from other angles in coverage. Grant fluffs his lines a couple of times, which only adds to the feeling of spontaneously expressed emotion, as he pleads at length to keep the child, in front of a judge who seems more interested in the paperwork. But Grant's "wet take" contains something else as well – a very "dry" performance from Beulah Bondi right in the center of the screen.

We know that Miss Oliver cares deeply about the couple and the child. However, Beulah Bondi acts this by doing essentially nothing. We know that Beulah Bondi could turn on the emotional tap if she wanted to, but she becomes a compelling presence in the scene by not doing so. Counterpointing Grant's plaintiveness, Bondi is the solid anchor that stops the scene short of sheer sentimentality. Moreover, her presence lingers over the sequence long enough for the button-pushing sentimentality of the homecoming to feel less manipulatively mawkish than it might otherwise have done. So the relationship between the plaintive figure of Cary Grant and the undemonstrative stillness of Beulah Bondi is what charges that scene with an unforgettable tension, whereas the tension-generating tricks of framing and a slow pan in the next scene are shamelessly exploitative of the medium's capacity to manipulate an audience's response in a more superficial way, as the "weepie" tended to do (with its persistent risk of falling into Capra's Error as we called it earlier, p. 39).

This brings us to the absolutely key question about acting, emotion and what it is like. Does the actor need to feel the actual emotion? It is very much part of the received wisdom in a dominant strand of actor training in the U.S. that the answer to this is yes, though the precise details of the answer take various forms in different "schools." The idea of an emotional truth first felt and only then expressed by the actor is a shared emphasis across a whole range of training and coaching methods for actors. A major problem with this fact, however, is that

Acting in *Penny Serenade* and *Fail-Safe* is discussed in Mamet (2008), 169-73

Penny Serenade (1941)

much of the best research into acting, such as Elly Konijn's work in the Netherlands, suggests that "emotional truth" in the sense of self-exposed interiority is largely a misreading of what happens in practice.

Pierre Arditi, one of the two leads in *Love Unto Death*, jokes that director Alain Resnais told him he would be able to shed tears on demand because it was in his contract. A joke maybe, but also a reminder that it is behavior a spectator sees. David Chambers of Yale School of Drama has praised Elly Konijn's research for counterbalancing the "fog banks of sanctimonious mystification, psycho-jargon, and charlatanism [that] obscure the craft of acting," by which he means in large measure the persistent characterization of acting as a quest for emotional truth found through an inward rather than a task-orientated focus.

Konijn's work (from which the simplified diagram below is extracted) finds

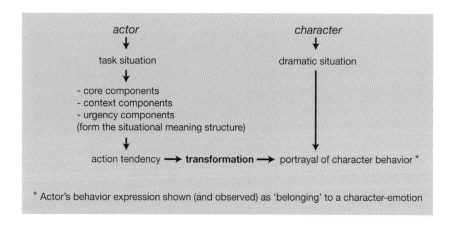

instead that acting in practice is largely task-focused, where the actor faces a series of well-defined task situations that produce what she terms an "action tendency." This leaning towards a specific action or set of linked actions is what gets transformed in performance into a portrayal of a character's behavior. This transformation is what produces the observable impression that an actor's behavior-based expression "belongs" to a character's emotion.

So this kind of transformation will be an indispensable last component to our moments, if we can separate it from the "psycho-jargon and charlatanism."

We can see how this works in Sidney Lumet's *Fail-Safe* (1964), one of Henry Fonda's best performances (though the film's release was overshadowed by Kubrick's satirical *Dr. Strangelove* coming out at the same time on the same topic). Fonda plays the American President, dealing with a failure in the nation's Cold War strategic bomber control systems that sends a group of aircraft past their "fail safe" point and towards the Soviet Union with erroneous instructions to drop their nuclear bombs. Negotiations are started with the Kremlin in order to avert catastrophe, the contact taking place over the "hotline" telephone, with Larry Hagman playing the interpreter on the American side (we never see the other side). Re-staging the scene opposite makes a great exercise for acting class.

Using Konijn's model (simplified here), we can see how Fonda and Hagman are dealing first with a specific task situation: they have to make these protracted telephone conversations believable. The core components of this situation include sounding like who they are meant to be (President and professional interpreter) and then looking and sounding like they are actually having these conversations. The context components include looking and sounding like they are in the larger situation (the historical moment, with certain requirements in terms of likely behavior) and expressing both familiarity with the general situation and the unexpectedness of the particular turn of events. The "urgency" components, as the narrative develops, are those factors that determine the required level of tenseness. According to the model, getting these layered components of the task situation right then triggers a transformation into behavior in which the audience "sees" the characters' emotions within the represented dramatic situation.

In other words, the observed emotion does not have to be felt by the actors. It is read into the observable behavior. Fonda and Hagman generate edge-of-seat tension through their performances, not by conspicuously "emoting" (e.g. on the basis of what they are really feeling as actors) but by crafting their behavior

Chambers in Konijn (2000), 8; figure simplified from Konijn (2000), 91

Fail-Safe (1964)

within Konijn's "situational meaning structure" in ways that are utterly believable and riveting, including small details such as briefly fumbling with a strip of security tape stuck across the "hotline" telephone (it genuinely looks as if the President has never used this phone before).

This is not to say that actors do not bring a palpable intensity to performing roles such as these ones in *Fail-Safe*. Fonda and Hagman both look completely absorbed by the situation they are in and physically tense when things get especially tricky in the life-or-death negotiations, and they seem particularly aware of each other's subtlest shifts of mood and attitude, something that the self-absorption of an actor's quest for their own inner emotion does not always facilitate. Elly Konijn's research allows that personal emotion will be drawn on by an actor from time to time in a kind of re-tuning process as the performance dial shifts between components of the task situation and appropriate things that an actor may find themselves feeling. But she uncovers little evidence that strong performances may mostly be driven emotionally from deliberately plumbed personal depths. Instead task-emotions, or emotions stimulated in the actor by doing the tasks required by the situation, become a principal emotional resource for generating around the transformation (as diagrammed) what Konijn, quoting Josef Kelera, calls a "radiance," the feeling of convincing on-stage or on-screen presence that spectators sense. Kelera, however, was referring to actors trained by Jerzy Grotowski whose approach melded technical precision with material drawn from deep inside the actor's private life, and Kelera spoke of the result in terms of "light" and "illumination." Konijn's research with actors recognizes a less mysterious "radiance" effect but produces no convincing evidence that it comes from anything other than the actor's task-emotions in the given situation.

So here we have in fact yet another evocation, on the one hand, of intensity as light, as illumination, of the transformational moment as impelled towards transcendence. In this case, not the light in a Bierstadt painting but the "illumination" generated by the actor looking deep inside his or her own emotional life and triggering a kind of fission there. David Chambers' "fog banks of sanctimonious mystification" have sprung up around this impulse towards transcendence. The analysis of acting reported on here, on the other hand, identifies a much more situation-specific kind of intensity of concentration in performance.

With this insight in mind, we have reached a point where we can return to the question of Samantha Morton's problematic role as Sarah in *River Queen*, which we touched on throughout the book. We are looking at this, not as some local instance of trouble on a film set, but because it raises some important questions about how emotion is handled in film, especially now that we have prepared the way by considering some key aspects more generally of the relationship between emotion and what-it-is-likeness. Samantha Morton is the volatile and talented two-time nominee for an Academy Award as actor whose own (made-for-TV) directing debut in 2009 won that year's British Academy of Film and Television Arts award for "Best Single Drama." *The Unloved* (opposite) is a semi-autobiographical account of a young girl in the north of England who, beaten by her father, is taken into a children's home in the British social services' care system.

We see Lucy (Molly Windsor) being threatened by her father (Robert Carlyle) and hear her being beaten from outside the open door to their living room. After this and other moments in the film we see Lucy's reaction in "dry takes," often looking at something past or behind the camera, usually with unsettling stillness and always without emotionality. A glowing sunset over the drabness of the town is less spiritually uplifting than a mutely ironic commentary on Lucy's colorless reality. When the social worker takes her into a medical examination room for assessment, the door is closed in our face. We see Lucy being driven to the children's home — she gazes impassively out the car window. The film's one memorably "wet take" is at the end, when Lucy tries to connect with her troubled mother (the parents are separated) who keeps her at arm's length, tells her that their living together is out of the question, and puts her on a bus back to the children's home. At the last moment the mother (Susan Lynch) breaks down, but only long enough for one protracted embrace before the bus takes Lucy away. We watch Lucy sitting at the back of the bus for a very long time before the end credits roll.

The Unloved (2009)

While writing and training for film actors in the West is still full of the language of emotional self-expression on the part of the actor and still often concerned with finding techniques for matching that interiority to a character, it remains relatively rare on screen these days to find somebody who looks and feels like they are really testing that paradigm. Samantha Morton is one of these, which is why her work (e.g. in Oren Moverman's *The Messenger*, 2009, or Cecilia Miniucchi's *Expired*, 2008) occasions considerable interest. Reviewer David Edelstein in *New York* magazine said of Morton's performance in *Expired* that her "skin barely covers her soul."

Evocations of "Method" acting are often ritual inclusions in this sort of discussion but there is not one school of self-expressive, emotion-excavating acting any longer that can be so neatly labeled. And Samantha Morton's personal method is clearly rather different, tapping something that, as noted, might have come from theater director and innovator Jerzy Grotowski's ideas – the notion that emotion gets wired through to the muscles. Whatever its sources (and some of this may just be intuitive) Samantha Morton brings a very particular way of working to her film parts. The scene opposite from *River Queen* is an especially clear example.

Sarah, who has spent years searching for her lost son, is being taken up-river by boat to the Māori stronghold. She has realized that Wiremu, her son's uncle, has taken the boy in and raised him as his own. We have already looked at a later scene where Wiremu cuts off his own finger to save the boy, a moment that seals Sarah's decision to leave the white world for ever. But at this point she is still wanting to reclaim her son and take him back. Still blindfolded (so as not to betray the location of the Māori stronghold), she reaches out to touch an old scar on the boy's knee, the proof of who he is.

Samantha Morton, though blindfolded, succeeds in giving Sarah here a blistering but tightly wrapped intensity of feeling. There is something about her body, her hands and her mouth that – even with her face half covered – expresses the stored up emotion in that Growtowskian sense of a wiring through to the muscles. What is especially interesting in practice though is that Samantha

Morton refused to touch the boy's knee when shooting the scene. The hand in the close-up is a body double's.

Four things are going on here and we need to unpick them in order to discover something crucial about overall success and failure in this kind of filmic moment. The first is the huge risk that the self-absorbed, inward-orientated, emotion-plumbing method of acting presents to a film as a whole, which is the risk of failing to connect with much else that is going on in the film unless all of that is being centripetally organized around the one performance (and in *River Queen* it was not). A risk of closing out the other actors goes hand in hand with that. The boy (Rawiri Pene) is being given nothing to work with here and you can see this even from the frame stills.

Second, the most intensely inward-looking forms of acting if brought to this kind of moment, especially if there is a Growtowskian wiring of emotion to the muscles, run the internal risk of that bodily involvement being easily discharged or dissipated – for example through the simple action of touching somebody else, like a stored current going to ground. Samantha Morton is protecting her own "charge" here.

Third, there is an ideal narrative means for handling this sort of pent-up tension and psycho-physical interiority, which is storing it up for a symbolic release at a key chosen point in the narrative. This is what Samantha Morton hoped to do in *River Queen* but this method got progressively out of step with the kind of film it was – an expansive, multi-layered narrative with a complex time structure and very little by way of a centripetal organization of narrative material around only one role. However, we will look at that idea being played out as far as it could be in two further moments over the following pages.

Fourth, Samantha Morton was resistant to handing over to the film any "classical" emotion-laden resources – like a touch between mother and son – that could be too casually re-directed into what critic Tara Brabazon calls "a womb with a view," which is to say visible emotionally expressed motherhood, etc. which ultimately becomes all that the woman is (like Irene Dunne in *Penny Serenade*).

New York Magazine online (nymag.com/listings/movie/expired/); Brabazon (2002), 80

River Queen (2005)

Sarah watches as WIREMU gives TIMOTI a tender hug, then
sends him off.

                    WIREMU
          Sarah . . .

She stares at him, not really seeing.

                    WIREMU
          It's a war, Sarah. You didn't start
          it. He touches her face but she
          pulls away -

                    SARAH
          I have to go. I have to leave here -

                    WIREMU
          It's too late. They're almost on
          us. You can't go back downriver
          alone. If the kupapa find you
          first...

He doesn't finish. She stares straight ahead.

                    WIREMU
          You'll go to the sanctuary where my
          wee lad and his mum have gone.

He plucks a branch off a nearby tree, strips the leaves off
and fans them into a bouquet. He hands them to her.

                    WIREMU
          Kawakawa. For luck. But it doesn't
          heal everything.

He reaches to caress her but she stiffens; he pulls back. He
goes. She's alone again.

In the run of frames on the two preceding pages (scene 105 in the screenplay, left) we initially see the sort of thing that Samantha Morton was wary of in *River Queen*, as Wiremu has a Dickensian "Tiny Tim" moment with one of her boy's cousins by the river bank, an image of overt sentimentality placed in deliberate contrast to the images of rapacious soldiery (including kupapa or pro-British Māori) approaching through the forest.

As filmed and edited, this scene adds several distinct features to what was scripted and deletes others. Cinematographer Alun Bollinger's camera stays well back off the characters, filming them closely and edgily through a long lens, which isolates them and also gives the camera a feeling of trying to stay in touch with the two as they move around each other tensely. This visually dramatizes the evasive nature of their exchange, and the refusal of connection as Wiremu reaches for Sarah and she backs off. This distinctive operating of the camera also creates a space for Samantha Morton to turn inwards again (frame 17), visually disconnecting her from the background with the shallow depth of field.

Sarah in fact snarls "Get off me!" (frame 11) and Samantha Morton, much more insistently than in the screenplay, refuses Wiremu's advances. The piece of business with the "bouquet" is dropped. Some extra dialogue is dubbed onto the backs of heads in postproduction to "explain" that in fact she is resisting Wiremu's attempt to have her leave (the scripted line "I have to go…" is dropped along with several others). In short, the scene as it ends up is much more clearly an example of Sarah/Morton creating another moment of refused connection, "directing" the film from inside her performance on the way towards the climax (right) where she finally does let a touch pass between herself and her son.

After the battle, Sarah has her penultimate encounter with Baine, the English officer, who points out a white woman being stoned out of camp for a liaison with a Māori man. Then Doyle, her one white friend, dies and she and Wiremu make love. Her boy is captured by the kupapa but rescued by Wiremu. The three of them escape together via the river and take refuge in a cave where the boy, who has learnt tatooing and skin chiselling from his Māori grandfather, cuts a

moko (facial marking) into Sarah's chin. As she washes her now marked face in the river she is shot from the riverbank above. We watch her blood swirl away in the water.

The big question we have been heading for here is in one sense very simple. Do we care that Sarah has just apparently died? Enough extracts from *River Queen* have been included in the book for you to feel something of the reach of this question. If you can watch the film you will be in the best position to answer this question but I am going to predict the answer anyway. That answer is "not enough." Understanding why this is so – in the context of our discussion of what it is like – is a very important question in terms of understanding the transformational moment that the preceding scene might have been.

Why do we not have a sufficiently strong sense of what it is like to be Sarah for us to care sufficiently about her death? After all, we cared about Zia after only the opening moments of the film *Wristcutters, A Love Story*.

Scene 105 from the *River Queen* screenplay was included in full here because this was the last point in the film where it was going to be possible to draw the viewer into what it is like to be Sarah, the last moment to establish something that would make us care, the last available moment to ensure that the later scene of her shooting in the water wrenched our guts out. We have not been breaking down the narrative structure of *River Queen* as we did in detail with an earlier film, but this was what we can term the second turning point narratively. It established Wiremu's – and hence the Māori world's – invitation to Sarah. So it mattered.

What is extraordinarily instructive though is the reason the scene falls short. The scene in the screenplay sets up a task situation (with reference to Elly Konijn's model). This task situation involves Wiremu giving Sarah an improvised bouquet of kawakawa tree leaves. This task situation has a role to play within the situational meaning structure of that part of the film and of the film as a whole.

However, what we witness is one character's dramatic situation being directly addressed, bypassing the particular task situation, and through an inward-focused,

emotion-plumbing moment of self-absorbed intensity. Samantha Morton looks totally convincing in frame 17, the emotion absolutely believable on one level. Who knows what personal experience or memories she tapped into here, and in the knee-touching scene, in order to express this moment of self-contained emotional truth. But it closes actor Cliff Curtis out along with his character Wiremu. The given task situation is bypassed in the interests of a free-standing moment of individualized "illumination" in the Grotowskian sense.

What we see in frame 17 is extraordinary acting but the snarled "Get off me!" at frame 11 might as well have been directed at the spectator. By frame 17 we are like Alun Bollinger's camera – standing off in awe and detachment. So no, when Sarah is shot in the river after the actual and symbolic crossing over from the white world, we do not care enough, which is a small tragedy in terms of the film's commitment to classical narrative form. We have suggested, in referring to the scene where Sarah touches the boy's scarred knee, some of the reasons informing this withdrawal.

Fired but re-hired for postproduction, Vincent felt compelled to look for ways of compensating: a diary-type voice over to tell us more about what it is like to be Sarah, with discarded diary pages filmed by Vincent himself in the River Thames, a lot of back-of-the-head dubbing of new lines during ADR (automated dialogue replacement) to add explanations, inserts shot with a double.

The task situation in scene 105 with the bundle of leaves might have been like the dusty hair on a bathroom floor, a casual forward roll over a sofa in a hotel room, two people sitting on a park bench. And what-it-is-likeness might have become a shared and transferred quality. Cliff Curtis might even have been Samantha Morton's Beulah Bondi. Given a fully developed task situation here, with all its components attended to, we might have "got" how the situation functioned as a turning point, drawing us more engagingly into the immense drama of Sarah's marginalization from the white world and the invitation open to her. Instead, we observe an extraordinary actor digging deep into her own emotions. We have discovered here that what it is like cannot be left to depend on that alone.

But rather than seeing this as a failure, we have to understand finally what it tells us about the tensions that are arising between classical Hollywood-style narrative film form and what we have been calling post-classical sensibilities in film. Both Vincent Ward and Samantha Morton have these sensibilities — an urge to find new ways of using film to express things that the classical form is now struggling to express. That is why Vincent gravitated towards Samantha Morton for the role of Sarah in the first place. An Irish-born British actor such as (for instance) Susan Lynch, with impeccable theater and film credentials, would have reclaimed the character of Sarah for a classical treatment and everything else in *River Queen* would probably have fallen neatly into place (including an Oscar nomination or two). But Vincent wanted something else: the "radiance" referred to by Elly Konijn but ratcheted up to a unique level of intensity, which is where Samantha Morton tends to abandon the masks of conventional character-making technique, as we have noted in discussing *Mister Lonely*.

Vincent, however, is still looking for ways of hooking these kinds of post-classical intensity to the core classical form (right). So *River Queen* presented Samantha Morton with a series of task situations (we have just been describing some of these) that were thoroughly embedded within the classical narrative form. The most important connections did not in the end get made between her acting and those situations, in part because it was such a risky experiment to attempt (and she would have preferred to abandon many of the conventional task situations in favor of something else).

Similarly, as we can now see more clearly, Vincent's pursuit of a visual intensity through images in *What Dreams May Come* ran into a disconnect with story and dialogue still thoroughly embedded in the classical form.

Why does a brilliant filmmaker whose first three films were all Cannes official selections not repeat that achievement? Because those films consolidated his early intuitive post-classical sensibility as an artist and he then set out to discover whether he could connect the forms of cinematic intensity he was intrigued by with the classical form. To date there have only been partial successes with this.

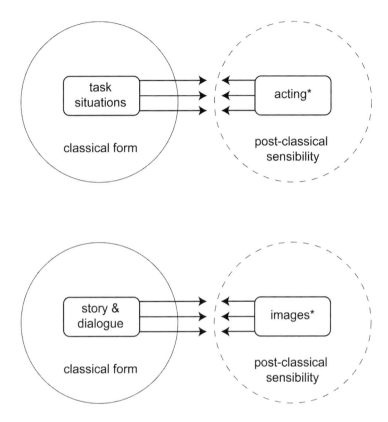

*Acting and images as the repositories of Vincent Ward's post-classical pursuit of intensity ("seeing too much").

But the attempt continues to be one of the most instructive we can find anywhere, not least as other filmmakers catch up and begin to explore post-classical alternatives. The development of "puzzle" forms has, to date, been the most successful partial solution to bridging the kinds of gap identified above. Vincent Ward has not been much interested in that particular solution, but this book has definitely been drawn to it in order to tell its own story.

EXERCISE

This is the final exercise in the book. Appropriately then, it concerns endings.

Multiple endings due to disagreements between directors, producers and "studio" executives have become a fact of life in the film industry. Vincent's films *Map of the Human Heart*, *What Dreams May Come* and *River Queen* all have endings different from originally intended.

This exercise is to script and plan another ending for *Map of the Human Heart*.

In the film as we see it, Avik (the Inuk who follows cartographer and military planner Walter to wartime Europe) drops bombs on the city of Dresden on the night of February 13, 1945 (which historically may have been the largest ever single-event killing of civilians). As the aircraft in which he is a bomb-aimer is hit by German anti-aircraft fire, Avik calls for his grandmother. The last time he did so was on seeing her commit suicide by tumbling into the Arctic waters from the Inuit boat that was leaving Avik behind as an outsider, tainted by the white man's world and no longer accepted by his people.

Having seen too much at Dresden when he parachutes into the city where even the river is on fire — Avik returns to his Arctic homeland. He will die there alone on an ice floe after an accident on his snowmobile.

As he dies, Avik imagines turning up at the wedding of the daughter he conceived with Albertine in wartime England but had never seen as a child, and taking Albertine away with him in a hot-air balloon. At the end he thinks he is in the sky with Albertine looking down at his own body on the ice as it sinks into the water.

In the original screenplay, Avik and Walter meet one last time in Germany in the closing days of the war, before Avik's return to the Arctic. In the released film, the scene with Walter, Avik and the automaton that we looked at in detail is the last time they see each other. This leaves things unsaid between Avik and Walter and, in a sense, perhaps lets Walter off the hook dramatically.

So this exercise is to write a final scene between Walter and Avik, modeled loosely on the scene opposite from Robert Altman's *Buffalo Bill and the Indians*.

Written by Robert Altman and Alan Rudolph, *Buffalo Bill and the Indians, or Sitting Bull's History Lesson* (1976), based on Arthur Kopit's award-winning 1969 stage play *Indians*, deals with William "Buffalo Bill" Cody's Wild West show and its attempts to turn Sitting Bull into a star attraction for paying customers. Sitting Bull (Frank Kaquitts), who has his own reasons for getting involved, is reported to have been shot and killed by agency (reservation) policemen in South Dakota near the end of the film.

In this extraordinary scene (right) Cody (Paul Newman) wakes in the night and thinks he is seeing the dead Sitting Bull (who appears motionless at various places in the room), to whom he tries to explain himself.

So this exercise is to imagine a somewhat similar scene to end *Map of the Human Heart* – a coda after Avik's death on the ice – in which Avik "appears" to Walter. Let us imagine that Walter has become a senior military planner for NATO during the Cold War. Perhaps he is helping coordinate the nuclear submarine *USS Queenfish*'s operations under the Arctic icepack? Perhaps it is a time of particular global tension (think *Fail-Safe*). In the middle of a sleep-deprived night (perhaps he has been drinking?) he "sees" Avik one last time. What would Walter and Avik have to say to each other?

The exercise is to script the scene and then to block out its staging and camera positions and to make some notes on the use of color and light. But you could also give some thought to how you would want to see the scene acted. Is this an opportunity for emotionality in one or both performances? Is it about getting "inside" the head of one of the characters? Is it about situating them in some broader framework? What task situations will you set for the actors? Where will you set the scene? In other words, this exercise is about how you would construct a moment. There is an opportunity here to think about the gaze as a structuring factor in the visual organization of a filmic moment. And there is an opportunity to think about cinema's power to deploy intermeshed layers of time.

Viewing *Buffalo Bill and the Indians, or Sitting Bull's History Lesson* for comparative purposes after doing this exercise should prove instructive, especially if attention is given to the way the camera is used, the very limited use of tight shot-reverse-shot cutting, the "panoramic" approach to staging, even in interior scenes like this one, and acting that deliberately skirts opportunities for feverish intensity (even though we know that Newman, with his Actors Studio training, could deliver that).

Jonker, Peter (1988) *The Song and the Silence: Sitting Wind* (Edmonton: Lone Pine). The biography of Canadian First Nations chief Frank Kaquitts, the Stoney Indian also known as Sitting Wind who played Sitting Bull opposite Paul Newman in Altman's film.

"Grandma" The real Puhi (page 216, photo courtesy New Zealand Film Commission) and Puhi played by Rena Owen in *Rain of the Children* (opposite page, bottom frames).

the manifest and the latent

Rain of the Children (2008) is a drama-documentary feature by Vincent Ward that returns to an area and a subject he first made a film about when still a student over a quarter of a century earlier. Back then, he had taken himself off into New Zealand's forested Urewera mountains, homeland of the Tūhoe (pronounced roughly "two-hoy"), the Māori tribal grouping that resisted European penetration longer than any others, refused to sign the principal treaty and remains determinedly hostile to white dominance.

The early student film. made there over eighteen months with the help of young cameramen Alun Bollinger and Leon Narbey, documented the life of an old Tūhoe woman in her eighties called Puhi and (according to the outside world's labeling) her "schizophrenic" adult son Niki. Over the intervening years, Vincent had learnt more about Puhi's involvement in some key historical events and *Rain of the Children*, made immediately after his big-budget feature *River Queen*, embeds extracts from the earlier documentary in an exploration of that history, which is viewed as far as possible from Puhi's point of view. *Rain of the Children* goes back to the period of the land wars, New Zealand's civil war and the setting of *River Queen*, even including some out-takes from *River Queen* (far right opposite) as historical re-enactments. Then in several layers, with actors of various ages playing Puhi, the film builds an account of her life.

One of these layers is Vincent's first visit to Puhi's long-abandoned house since he had filmed there years before (middle row right). Since a main objective of the film is to have us care about its subject, we can relate some of our findings from the previous section to how this is achieved in *Rain of the Children*.

The old documentary material establishes the ordinariness of Puhi and Niki's daily lives (top row right). We watch Puhi cook for them both, we watch her hands, we watch the simple actions of putting food on a plate, we listen to the everyday sounds. We have seen in our previous examples how this very ordinariness affords a quality of what-it-is-likeness so essential to our starting to care. There is an element of "telegraphing" about this (shortcuts to sympathy) but it is deftly handled and persuasively genuine in its observational honesty.

Then the film starts to construct its several layers. We saw how director Hirokazu Koreeda drew us into a series of initially unanticipated connections in *After Life*. Much the same happens here as the visit to the present-day location, the old film, historical re-enactments, and documentary material (including interviews in the community) reveal points of connection that gradually form a web within which Puhi comes alive for us as a multi-faceted person in history, not just an old stooped mumbling figure in the clips from the original film.

The affective "charge" that this film starts to generate comes very much, initially, from observational acuity without emotionality. Although we watch Vincent trying unsuccessfully to find Puhi's grave in the long grass, and he is clearly moved by his return to the old house, it is the slow accumulation of details and the growing web of connections that draw us in, rather than any overt appeal to sentiment. As the film's construction skillfully works its way through the techniques for creating what-it-is-likeness that we looked at in the previous section, this becomes a "constructed" Puhi, of course — how could it be otherwise? — but it is difficult to resist the conviction that we will never come any closer than this to feeling what it was like to be this woman in this place at this time.

The historical "layer" culminates in an attack by white police on Puhi's community in the hills in 1916. Puhi, at the age of sixteen, has married the son of Māori "prophet" and land rights activist Rua Kenana, and is living in a community he founded at the foot of Tūhoe's sacred mountain Maungapohatu. A police raid on the village, ostensibly to root out illegal alcohol sales there, replicates any number of colonial raids on indigenous communities in different times and places to root out difference on whatever local pretence was convenient. Puhi is caught in the middle of the raid (following pages).

While the staging of the raid on the village is at the center of the web of connections through which we come to care about Puhi, the film also effects a powerful move that we have seen before in other examples. By observing Puhi caring for Niki, even in the simplest of ways (like painstakingly unwrapping his ice cream, right), the film slowly teaches us to care about Niki ourselves.

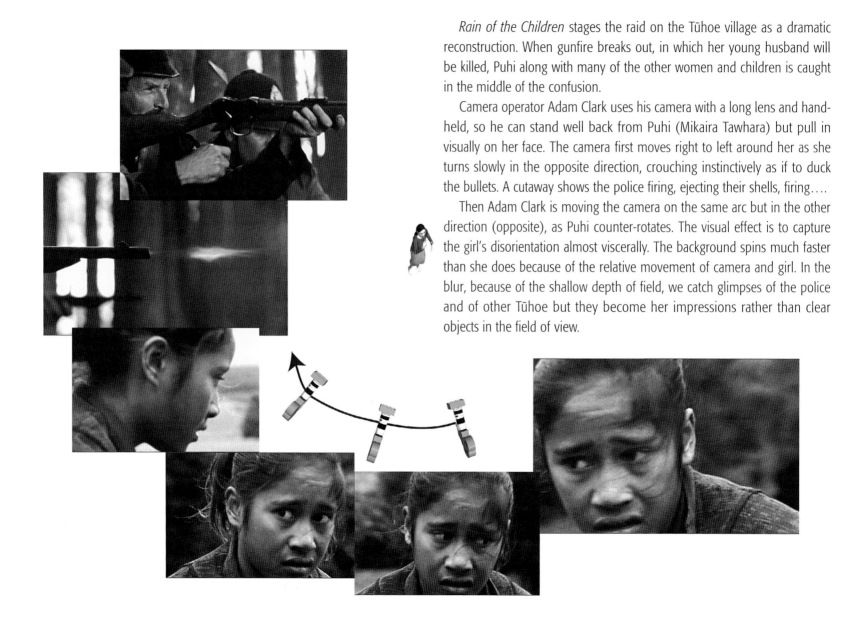

Rain of the Children stages the raid on the Tūhoe village as a dramatic reconstruction. When gunfire breaks out, in which her young husband will be killed, Puhi along with many of the other women and children is caught in the middle of the confusion.

Camera operator Adam Clark uses his camera with a long lens and hand-held, so he can stand well back from Puhi (Mikaira Tawhara) but pull in visually on her face. The camera first moves right to left around her as she turns slowly in the opposite direction, crouching instinctively as if to duck the bullets. A cutaway shows the police firing, ejecting their shells, firing….

Then Adam Clark is moving the camera on the same arc but in the other direction (opposite), as Puhi counter-rotates. The visual effect is to capture the girl's disorientation almost viscerally. The background spins much faster than she does because of the relative movement of camera and girl. In the blur, because of the shallow depth of field, we catch glimpses of the police and of other Tūhoe but they become her impressions rather than clear objects in the field of view.

In fact the scene's power starts to derive from an unexpected quality of abstraction at this point. Puhi as a girl and the specific event in which she is caught up, while physically captured with a quality of dynamic naturalism, are also simultaneously lifted by these techniques out of the specifics. What we referred to before as an "elsewhen" is powerfully evoked — or rather a series of "elsewhens" in which this kind of event has happened to other people.

And most powerfully of all, there is the "elsewhen" of a police raid in 2007 (right) on Tūhoe communities in the same area, carried out under the authority of a Terrorism Suppression Act brought into law with the encouragement of U.S. authorities in the post 9/11 global climate. The staging of the scene seems to spin out dizzyingly to connect with the village clearance depicted in *River Queen* and with the 2007 anti-terror raids in one web of historical interconnection. At the same time, canisters of compressed air were used to puff Mikaira Tawhara's strands of hair here, in synchronization with the sounds of passing bullets.

Whakatane Beacon

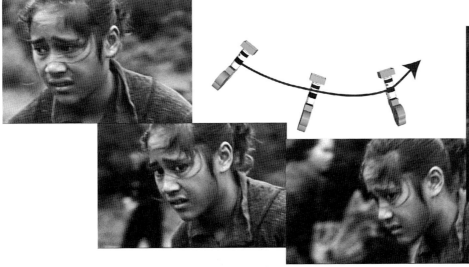

Having drawn us deep into the life of Puhi, the Māori woman, *Rain of the Children* then takes our accumulated interest and our sense of what-it-is-likeness and transfers it to her troubled son Niki, especially after Puhi's death when he is left on his own.

Niki at the outset is not an obvious sympathy-eliciting figure. A sullen, sometimes violent, overweight, non-white "schizophrenic," whose rheumy eyes peer suspiciously at everything and whose talk, when he does talk, seems by turns paranoid and ominous. Try pitching that in a logline to a Hollywood producer. But by the closing stages of *Rain of the Children*, and not through any sentimentalized discovery that Niki is other than he is, we are heartrendingly interested in this person.

When Niki (Waihoroi Shortland) is found drunk and naked in the middle of the street, the transformational moment is not a transcendent one. The white light is not heavenly but from the streetlights in a little town on the edge of Empire. It is not the Archangel Michael who comes to the fallen one but a neighbor's white horse to which he has been attached and which seems to understand him. And Niki himself is both just that – himself – and at the same time carries the awful weight of a history that has made him who he is. Our anguished interest in him is in part a felt recognition of the sheer magnitude of those crippling forces.

So the illumination of the transformational moment when it comes is not derived from the intensity of a divine light in a Bierstadt painting or from the intensity of a revelatory performance that uncovers a depth of psycho-physical interiority. Rather, it is found in the surfaces of things marked by trauma, which is to say the wound that opens up between how things are and how they might be.

Vincent Ward's instructive thirty-year project in pursuit of transcendence through film ends up for the time being on this street in this moment and with the realization that the transformational moment in film is here.

Gustav Doré *The Last Judgment* (1897)

The true stories of our time
have to be able to reconcile
a pile of clothes in a drawer
with world historical
upheavals. (John Berger)

The search by actors for
the truth within themselves
has now gone too far.
(Tyrone Guthrie, *In Various Directions*)

The debunkers are probably
right, but they're no fun
to visit a graveyard with.
What the hell. I believe
in ghosts. (Mary Roach, *Spook*)

CONCLUSION

We are finally in a position to "model" the transformational moment in film (opposite). As we saw at the outset, staging broadly conceived is where the creative process that begins with loglines and screenplays proceeds to engage with the raw material from which the transformational moment will be constituted.

The camera is always confronted by the persistent givenness of things. Whether it is that dog looking lost in Griffith's *The Massacre* or any of the details we have picked out throughout the book, the lens captures scenes that are fraught with background. Much of what is latent in the manifest detail is nowhere to be found in a screenplay and only appears in the staging, which is one of cinema's major differences from literature of course. At the start of the book we hypothesized, with Eric Auerbach, two styles of imagining defined in large measure by their attentiveness or otherwise to the resonances of such latency. As we have seen, the transformational moment as defined by this book re-balances things in favor of more attentiveness.

The other major component of the manifest in these moments is the actors' engagement with the particular task situation. "Manifest" implies little by way of *required* interiority in acting. We have seen how the actor's plumbing of interior emotion risks intensifying the performance to a point of disconnect with the kinds of task situation that typify classical Hollywood narrative. While that way of re-orientating acting from the manifest to the latent has its place, the moments we have looked at tend to be much less reliant on it than they are on the actualization of solutions to a task situation embedded in the film's larger situations at that point, where an actor arrives at appropriate externally connected solutions rather than turning inwards in search of something else.

The solutions arrived at then connect across to the latent dimension of the moment, where what-it-is-likeness insists on drawing us in to the potential experientiality being offered. This is where, as spectators, we *affectively connect* with film (mediated, as we have seen, by aspects of staging such as the gaze).

The other aspect of the latent dimension that we have discovered is what we have termed "elsewhens," a virtual world of other times layered into the moment. Borrowing a phraseology from Gilles Deleuze, we have referred to these as "sheets" of time, some describable biographically, some historically, some cinematically (with reference to other films), and sometimes all three at once.

For anybody hoping that there are generative rules for producing these moments, the news is discouraging. The transformation rules themselves are

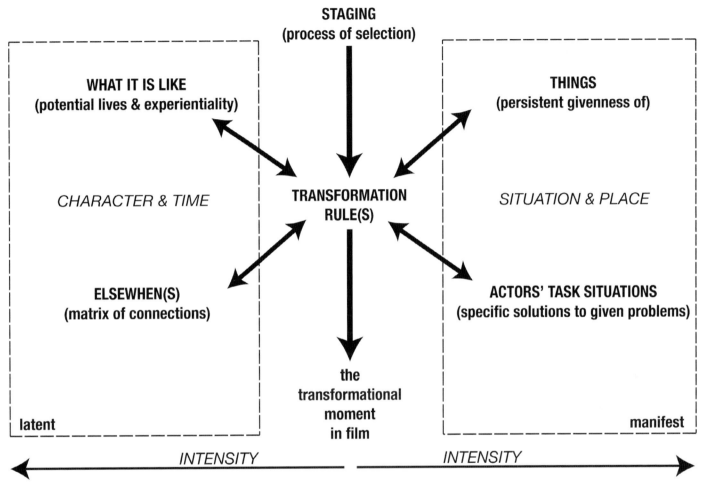

STAGING
(process of selection)

WHAT IT IS LIKE
(potential lives & experientiality)

THINGS
(persistent givenness of)

CHARACTER & TIME

TRANSFORMATION
RULE(S)

SITUATION & PLACE

ELSEWHEN(S)
(matrix of connections)

ACTORS' TASK SITUATIONS
(specific solutions to given problems)

the
transformational
moment
in film

latent

manifest

INTENSITY

INTENSITY

usually unique to the creative process in each case, which may mean unique to the situation of the creators. Vincent's work has demonstrated this for us, driven as it has been by the unique transformation rule that seeing, when it reaches a sublime intensity, risks seeing too much and becomes traumatic (in ways that can even spill over into the circumstances of production). Such "rules" are not invented by the filmmaker so much as derived from who he or she is and which, in turn, come into view as another aspect of the latent dimension above. So this book is making the point that there are no short cuts to film artistry, no "rule book" that can be slavishly copied. But it is also demonstrating the potential painfulness of the making, especially if the power of the image is being used as a means to work through a transformation rule by repeating it, which may be one of the characteristics of art.

SHEARING SHED

**The old farm, Wairarapa,
New Zealand, the present**

--duration: 1:47

PHOTO OF VINCENT AS BOY,
  (3D EFFECT AS CAMERA
   PANS/TRACKS WITH PRESENT-DAY
   SHED IN BACKGROUND)

CRANE UP SLOWLY INTO
LOADING BAY...

PULL IN ON WALL,
BIRDS FLUTTERING IN BACKGROUND,
STIRRING UP DUST IN THE SHAFTS
OF LIGHT...

THE POSSUM - (AUDIO FX) HISS
& SUDDEN BLUR OF MOTION AS IT
LEAPS PAST CAMERA, SHRIEKING.

SHEARING FLOOR.

DOLLY OUT ACROSS FLOOR
OF SHEARING SHED...
CHALKED MARKINGS ON STALL...
LIGHT CUTTING ACROSS THE SPACE.

TEETH OF HAND PIECE WHIRRING...

VINCENT PUSHES DOOR OPEN,
LETTING IN BLAZE OF LIGHT...

18-YR OLD SELF IN THE LIGHT.

VO: I am a child of eight exploring alone. Up in the loading bay the birds beat against the walls but, though they can, they refuse to leave. There will be warm eggs hidden here in the nest they are protecting. I know where it is. Visible only in a leak of light, a giant hook hangs above the double shuttered doors used for hoisting bales down onto the cargo trucks. Beside the shutters, in a cleft in the wall, will be my treasure. It's shielded in a barely boarded space that separates inner wall from outer. With excitement I gently reach into the hollow dark shaft. Ahead of time I sense the tingle of the fragile warm egg running across expectant finger tips. But I feel exquisitely soft fur and then the teeth bite. [AUDIO FX LEFT] Teeth, fur and hard sandpaper snout leap past and graze my face. A guttural choking hiss that exploded into a tortured-kettle-shriek. I think that sound was the opossum but if opossums could speak she might have said it was me.

VO (cont.): Now I am 18, promoted to fleeco, making neat folds of the fleece and pulling it away quickly to throw out flat like a gilded bird onto the fleeco's table. All the shearers have crew cuts while my hair is down over my shoulders. So I get the usual comment about looking like a girl. He is holding his whirring hand piece with its violent blade twitching towards me. His lips move but it takes me a moment to hear the words. He's offering to shear me. He will drag me down to the floor. He'll use his elbow as a fulcrum burying it between my ribs and curl me round at a sharp angle

- 24 -

(SHEARING SHED CONT.)

AUDIO FX: MEN LAUGHING AND
CALLING 'BE FAST BOY, CATCH
HIM..'

VINCENT CLIMBS OUT,
DOWN THE OLD DIPPING SLIDE...

AUDIO FX: MEN'S LAUGHING VOICES
FADE...

DOLLY BACK SLOWLY INTO THE
SPACE...

LEAVING THE SHEARING SHED
DESERTED...

HOLD THE SHOT...

THE BOARDS CREAK SLIGHTLY,
SOUND OF BIRDS FLUTTERING,
ONE OF THE STALL DOORS CREAKS
OPEN SLOWLY ON ITS OWN.

FADE TO BLACK.

winding me like any other sheep being shorn. Then he'll run the blade through my scalp, leaving a furrow of ripped tissue. No, none of this yet - just the threat, the rest in my imagination. But the calls from the gang are very real.

VO (cont.): Several of the shearers race after me, keen to 'shear' the joke and break monotony but I am slight and fast and flee - back through the pen, the gate springing up on its pulley, along the narrow chutes and out down the dipping slide, just missing the large deep trough with a floating putrid lamb carcass in vile black liquid. Thinking, hoping that perhaps they have no intention of catching me but taking no chances, I keep a watchful distance until the beers are brought in and quiet the place.

- 25 -

SUMMARY #2

(q) Our affective involvement with the moment and the always immanent reversal of the gaze can connect with the screen as a field of potential intensity
(primed by meta-compositional forces).

(r) Intensity is not only about turning up the dial (visually or emotionally),

(s) It is about what it is like and the intense affects this affords.

(t) So the transformational moment in film is not in the end about transcendence

(u) but about the manifest's articulation with the latent

(v) and about artists such as Vincent

(w) who "strike out over the hills of possible time" (Heinlein)

(x) to imagine elsewhens

(y) for us, and for those who share the post-classical sensibility,

(z) even at the risk of seeing too much.

The 26 points in the book's two summaries are in the end about the cinematic staging of affect in new ways, which is the basis of a filmmaking sensibility
capable of renewing the form of narrative film today.

AFTERWORD: A CONVERSATION

This conversation between Perkins Cobb and Dan Fleming takes place at a sidewalk café in Cannes during the 2009 film festival. The café's white canvas-backed chairs have the names of film stars printed on them.

DF: So, we're having this conversation at a point when you're finishing your documentary called *Holy Boy: Looking for Vincent Ward* and I'm finishing my book, which sees Vincent Ward's career in films both as an artist's journey to Hollywood and back and as what the science fiction writer Robert Heinlein called a journey over the hills of possible time. But we are both interested in broader topics about film. In your case it's the fate of the auteur. In my case it's what I call the transformational moment in film. I guess the first question is, why have we chosen to see these larger topics partly through the lens of Vincent's life and work?

PC: Well, I'd say because of that journey you've just suggested. A lot of things about the nature of filmmaking today come into view when you follow somebody who goes all the way from film school to art-house success, the Cannes festival three times, big-budget Hollywood movie-making, back to the margins, and then a kind of border crossing in his latest work when he goes back into a non-First World, indigenous community where he seems

to have discovered some of his film artistry in the first place.

DF: And seemed to have been affected by the Māori way of thinking about time – that the past is in front of you. I think that's where some of the creative tension comes from – the interesting trouble his work often has with the determined forward movement of classical film narrative, perhaps even where his early intuitive post-classical sensibility has its roots.

PC: So you can see film in a different way, whereas a filmmaker who is all small-budget art-house or all Hollywood blockbuster or all inter-cultural cinema only gives you one angle.

DF: I'd add that Vincent's work over thirty years has been a major experiment. The writer Louis

Nowra has said that Vincent wanted to make films that would "stun." I think he wanted to see what kinds of intensity film is capable of. But I know you have a slightly different take on that. Do you want to talk about it?

PC: Well, you know what my view is of the so-called auteur filmmaker in the mainstream system, especially since Coppola's attempt to run an auteur-friendly studio failed.

DF: That at best they only have it in them these days to make the one great film and everything else is just repetition?

PC: Not just repetition, but a betrayal of their singular achievement.

DF: Because of what I call Coppola's Prediction – that trying to make a film "one of a kind" leads to excess, over-ambition, self-identifying as an auteur in a way that becomes personal myth-making…?

PC: Definitely all of the above.

DF: But this is the point. You don't quite see Vincent in that way.

PC: I do and I don't. I think he set out, whether entirely consciously or not, to try a series of experiments as you put it, after his extraordinary first film *Vigil*. Have you written about *Vigil* in your book?

DF: Actually no, not until this point at least. That's partly because it's a perfect little crystal of a film (that's how its producer John Maynard described it to me) whereas everything that came after was reaching more riskily for something – the limits of narrative, a visual intensity through digital effects, an emotional intensity by pushing actors to the limit. So those increasingly big high-risk experiments are more instructive. We really can learn things about film from them.

PC: Ah, that's the teacher in you coming through. But I agree up to a point. Anybody who can make a film like *Vigil* could have kept on just re-doing that, if they could get the money, though of course I don't see the point in doing that! What's interesting is exactly the fact that he didn't repeat himself in that superficial way. What attracted me to this, though, was the seemingly self-destructive element at work. The bigger, the more different the experiment, the more there was to go wrong. So the "Holy Boy" I've been looking for was that self-destructive artist who didn't play safe, as if he knew that superficial self-repetition was a different, slower, less dramatic form of self-destruction.

DF: Did you find him?

PC: Yes, I think so.

DF: Where?

PC: As a boy, in a sheep shearing shed on the old farm imagining he was about to be shorn for being different.

DF: For being an artist?

PC: Ultimately yes, though I guess he didn't really know that at the time. And a lot attaches to that – to do with the twinning of a visionary impulse with the self-fulfilling expectation of being punished for that impulse. If you really believe that, you can manage to find a lot of ways of being punished, of being shorn….

DF: This relates closely to what I call in the book a traumatic reversal of the gaze – seeing too much. But that background is often seen as tying him specifically to a strand in New Zealand culture – in its national cinema – the isolated figure in the

elemental landscape as source of a distinctively New Zealand sublime. Also maybe the punishment of pretensions.

PC: But you've included most of his films in a book about film generally that's much broader and intended for a much wider readership?

DF: Absolutely. I don't discuss New Zealand cinema at all in the book. That's because I see Vincent's work in film as concerned primarily with asking a sort of semi-religious question, which is whether film as a medium can be transformational of its raw material in the way Robert Bresson proposed and whether this is about transcendence. There have only been a handful of New Zealand painters and poets interested in that sort of question, so in that central respect he's profoundly atypical of the country that produced him. And in that central respect, he's been asking something of film as a medium that has much broader interest. His way of testing that question was to take narrative, light, color and emotion – very much the building blocks of cinema – and look for the limits, the breaking points in them all.

PC: That reminds me of the scene in *Vigil* – do you recall it – where Ethan does that trick for the girl – remember, with the bottles and light in the old shed?

Vigil (1984)

To fill in some brief context here, Vigil, *1984, is often referred to as an "iconic" New Zealand film. It observes a period in the life of Toss, a young girl on a hill-country farm, whose father dies trying to rescue a ewe from a cliff face at the back of the farm. Life with her mother and grandfather is complicated by the hiring of Ethan, a poacher who found her father's body and brought it home. Ethan becomes involved with her mother. As plans are made to dispose of the farm and move away, Toss must cope with the threat of change, puberty, new insights into adult life, her own imagination unsettled by images in the old family Bible, and Ethan's presence, all against the unsentimentalized backdrop of a harsh natural environment.*

DF: Ethan draws the curtains of sacking over the windows in the old shed on the farm where they let him stay and he turns it into an improvised camera obscura. He sets up some bottles to catch the beams of light and creates a light show for the entranced Toss, all deep blues shot through with fragile rainbow hues, like light through a cathedral window instead of a half-derelict shed on a remote settler farm somewhere in the British "West."

PC: Of course, the name Ethan reminds us of Ford's *The Searchers* and how that mission ended with an attack on an Indian village. And Toss is that somewhat androgynous child who appears in Vincent's films – like the daughter in *What Dreams May Come*. They're "Holy Boy" as well, even if they're female.

DF: But I don't see any of that as quirks of an auteur filmmaker's personal obsessions. I see that scene in *Vigil* as setting up everything else. It's about the question of cinema – of light through glass. The question then becomes how far you can take that light show and how to reach what it is like to be Toss at that moment. Those two questions drove Vincent's subsequent work, but they're also fundamentally intriguing questions about the inner workings of cinema for anybody interested in the medium's capabilities.

PC: And the prototype of your transformational moment.

DF: I guess so. The scene goes in two directions simultaneously – outwards towards the light and inwards towards what's latent in the manifest detail – the dusty bottles, the texture of the old sacking, the atmosphere in that particular shed in that particular place. That's the paradox of cinema. The association of those two styles of imagining.

PC: Ecstatic truth, Werner Herzog calls it. The strange secret beauty of the latent in articulation with the manifest. You're making me think of Herzog's penguin.

DF: Ah, in *Encounters at the End of the World*?

PC: The documentary about Antarctica. There's this one crazy penguin that insists on walking off on its own away from the sea and towards the mountains. For some barely comprehensible reason it's a really moving moment, even though there's almost nothing in the image except the one penguin in the empty landscape. *(Laughs)* So a director like Vincent is that lonely penguin?

DF: Well, the post-classical sensibility that a director like Vincent always had is certainly a big part of what's isolated him while working in the mainstream. But we're now at a moment more generally when a much more widespread post-classical sensibility among filmmakers is desperately in need of workable ways to connect with and then transform classical narrative film form. This has a good deal to do with the intensities of experiencing film, which is what "cinema" still means even when removed from old-style cinema-going. So Vincent's remarkable pursuit of those intensities and those solutions is very instructive at the present moment.

What did he discover? First, that cinematic intensity pursued through color and light too readily comes unhooked from classical screen narrative requirements rather than transcending them. Then that cinematic intensity pursued through an actor's interiority also easily becomes unhooked in much the same way. However, the third approach seems to work. Intensity pursued through building into a film an affective map of connections in time can really begin to transform the classical screen narrative.

When Avik bombs Dresden and calls in anguish for his dead grandmother, personalized causality (the reduction of events to individual actions) is briefly but powerfully replaced by a post-classical intensity focused on time. As this book has illustrated, an affective mapping of connections in time may be the most promising way forward in bridging this gap (right), in order to extend the reach of classical narrative filmmaking and then to transform it.

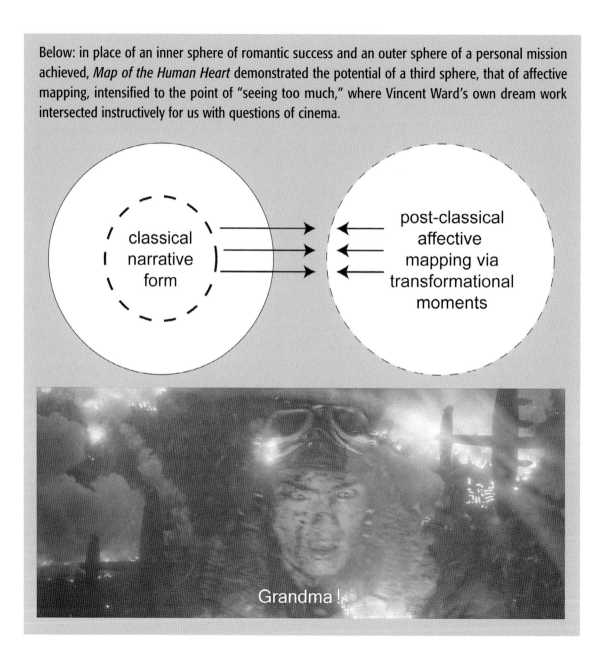

Below: in place of an inner sphere of romantic success and an outer sphere of a personal mission achieved, *Map of the Human Heart* demonstrated the potential of a third sphere, that of affective mapping, intensified to the point of "seeing too much," where Vincent Ward's own dream work intersected instructively for us with questions of cinema.

classical narrative form

post-classical affective mapping via transformational moments

Grandma !

FILMOGRAPHY

After Life (1998) dir. Hirokazu Koreeda. Engine Film.
Alien³ (1992) dir. David Fincher. Twentieth Century Fox Film Corporation.
A Matter of Life and Death (1946) dir. Michael Powell and Emeric Pressburger. The Archers; J. Arthur Rank Film.
Apache Rifles (1964) dir. William Witney. Twentieth Century Fox Film Corporation.
Apocalypse Now (1979) dir. Francis Ford Coppola. Zoetrope Studios.
Arsenic and Old Lace (1944) dir. Frank Capra. Warner Bros. Pictures.
Avatar (2009) dir. James Cameron. Twentieth Century Fox Film Corporation.
Bunny (1998) dir. Chris Wedge. Blue Sky Studios.
Burden of Dreams (1982) dir. Les Blank. Flower Films.
Citizen Kane (1941) dir. Orson Welles. Mercury Productions; RKO Radio Pictures.
Clear and Present Danger (1994) dir. Phillip Noyce. Paramount Pictures.
De weg naar Bresson (1984) dir. Leo De Boer, Jurriën Rood. Prodimag.
Dr. Strangelove (1964) dir. Stanley Kubrick. Columbia Pictures Corporation.
DreamChild (1985) dir. Gavin Millar. Thorn EMI.
Encounters at the End of the World (2007) dir. Werner Herzog. Discovery Films.
Expired (2007) dir. Cecilia Miniucchi. Aga Films; FR Productions.
Fail-Safe (1964) dir. Sidney Lumet. Columbia Pictures Corporation.
Family Guy (1999-) dir. various (animated TV series). 20th Century Fox Television.
Fatal Attraction (1987) dir. Adrian Lyne. Paramount Pictures.
Fitzcarraldo (1982) dir. Werner Herzog. Werner Herzog Filmproduktion.
Fort Apache (1948) dir. John Ford. RKO Radio Pictures.
Good Morning, Vietnam (1987) dir. Barry Levinson. Touchstone Pictures.
Hearts of Darkness: A Filmmaker's Apocalypse (1991) dir. Fax Bahr, George Hickenlooper. American Zoetrope.
Heaven's Gate (1980) dir. Michael Cimino. United Artists.
Holy Boy: Looking for Vincent Ward (unreleased) dir. Perkins Cobb. Clue Productions.
Hondo (1953) dir. John Farrow. Warner Bros. Pictures.
Inception (2010) dir. Christopher Nolan. Paramount Pictures.
In Spring One Plants Alone (1981) dir. Vincent Ward. Vincent Ward Films.
Jaws (1975) dir. Steven Spielberg. Universal Pictures.
Lady in the Water (2006) dir. M. Night Shyamalan. Warner Bros. Pictures.
Lost in La Mancha (2002) dir. Keith Fulton, Louis Pepe. Quixote Films.
Love Unto Death (1984) dir. Alain Resnais. Philippe Dussart; Les Films Ariane; Films A2.
M (1931) dir. Fitz Lang. Nero-Film AG.
Map of the Human Heart (1993) dir. Vincent Ward. AFFC; Les Films Ariane; PolyGram Filmed Entertainment; Working Title Films.
Mary Poppins (1964) dir. Robert Stevenson. Walt Disney Productions.
Minority Report (2002) dir. Steven Spielberg. Twentieth Century Fox Film Corporation.
Mirror (1975) dir. Andrei Tarkovsky. Mosfilm.
Mister Lonely (2007) dir. Harmony Korine. Love Streams; RPC; O'Salvation; Agnès b; Film4.
Mouchette (1967) dir. Robert Bresson. Argos Films.
Nosferatu (1922) dir. F.W. Murnau. Jofa-Atelier Berlin-Johannisthal.
Now Voyager (1942) dir. Irving Rapper. Warner Bros. Pictures.
Pandora's Box (1929) dir. G.W. Pabst. Nero-Film AG.
Patriot Games (1992) dir. Phillip Noyce. Paramount Pictures.
Patton (1970) dir. Franklin J. Schaffner. Twentieth Century Fox Film Corporation.
Penny Serenade (1941) dir. George Stevens. Columbia Pictures Corporation.
Rain of the Children (2008) dir. Vincent Ward. Wayward Films; Forward Films.
Rescue Dawn (2006) dir. Werner Herzog. Metro-Goldwyn-Mayer.
River Queen (2005) dir. Vincent Ward. Silverscreen Films; Film Consortium; UK Film Council; New Zealand Film Commission.
Road House (1989) dir. Rowdy Herrington. Silver Pictures.
Roma (1972) dir. Federico Fellini. Ultra Film.
Salt (2010) dir. Phillip Noyce. Columbia Pictures.
Savoy-Hotel 217 (1936) dir. Gustav Ucicky. UFA.
Siegfried (1924) dir. Fritz Lang. UFA.
Soldier Blue (1970) dir. Ralph Nelson. AVCO Embassy Pictures.
Stakeout (1987) dir. John Badham. Touchstone Pictures.
Star Wars (1977) dir. George Lucas. Twentieth Century Fox Film Corporation; Lucasfilm.
The Bone Collector (1999) dir. Phillip Noyce. Columbia Pictures.

The English Patient (1996) dir. Anthony Minghella. Miramax Films.
The Last Samurai (2003) dir. Edward Zwick. Warner Bros. Pictures.
The Lion King (1994) dir. Roger Allers, Rob Minkoff. Walt Disney Pictures.
The Lovely Bones (2009) dir. Peter Jackson. DreamWorks SKG; WingNut Films.
The Massacre (1914) dir. D.W. Griffith. Biograph Company.
The Messenger (2009) dir. Oren Moverman. Oscilloscope; Omnilab Media.
The Navigator, a Medieval Odyssey (1988) dir. Vincent Ward. Arenafilm.
The New World (2005) dir. Terrence Malick. New Line Cinema.
The Pacific (2010) dir. various (TV mini-series). DreamWorks SKG; HBO.
The Philadelphia Story (1940) dir. George Cukor. Metro-Goldwyn-Mayer.
The Quiet American (2002) dir. Phillip Noyce. Miramax Films.
The Searchers (1956) dir. John Ford. Warner Bros. Pictures.
The Stalking Moon (1968) dir. Robert Mulligan. National General Production Inc.
The Unloved (2009) dir. Samantha Morton. Film4, Revolution Films; EM Media.
Top Gun (1986) dir. Tony Scott. Paramount Pictures.
Touch of Evil (1958) dir. Orson Welles. Universal International Pictures.
Troy (2004) dir. Wolfgang Peterson. Warner Bros. Pictures.
Vertigo (1958) dir. Alfred Hitchcock. Paramount Pictures.
Vigil (1984) dir. Vincent Ward. John Maynard Productions.
What Dreams May Come (1998) dir. Vincent Ward. PolyGram Filmed Entertainment; Interscope Communications; Metafilmics.
Wrath of Gods (2006) dir. Jon Einarsson Gustafsson. Artio Productions.
Wristcutters, a Love Story (2006) dir. Goran Dukic. No Matter Pictures; Crispy Films; Adam Sherman; Halcyon Pictures.

BIBLIOGRAPHY

Auerbach, Erich (1968) *Mimesis* (Princeton NJ: Princeton University Press)
Badham, John and Craig Modderno (2006) *I'll Be in My Trailer: The Creative Wars Between Directors & Actors* (Studio City CA: Michael Wiese Productions)
Ballinger, Alexander (2004) *New Cinematographers* (New York: Collins Design)
Barrie, J. M. (1987) *Peter Pan* (New York: Henry Holt and Company)
Belting, Hans (2007) *Hieronymus Bosch: Garden of Earthly Delights* (New York: Prestel)
Berger, John (1985) "Afterword" in Hugh Brody and Michael Ignatieff, *Nineteen Nineteen* (London: Faber and Faber)
Bergerey, Benjamin (2002) *Reflections: Twenty-One Cinematographers at Work* (Hollywood: ASC Press)
Biddick, Kathleen (1998) *The Shock of Medievalism* (Durham NC: Duke University Press)
Biskind, Peter (2005) *Down and Dirty Pictures* (London: Bloomsbury)
Bollas, Christopher (1993) *Being a Character: Psychoanalysis and Self Experience* (London: Routledge)
Booker, Christopher (2004) *The Seven Basic Plots: Why We Tell Stories* (London: Continuum)
Boorman, John et al. (1995) *Projections 4: Film-makers on Film-making* (London: Faber and Faber)
Bordwell, David (2006) *The Way Hollywood Tells It: Story and Style in Modern Movies* (Berkeley CA: University of California Press)
Brabazon, Tara (2002) *Ladies Who Lunge: Celebrating Difficult Women* (Sydney: UNSW Press)
Bruno, Giuliana (2007) *Atlas of Emotion: Journeys in Art, Architecture, and Film* (New York: Verso)
Burch, Noël (1973) *Theory of Film Practice* (London: Secker & Warburg)
Carroll, Lewis (1865 & 1871; 2009) *Alice's Adventures in Wonderland* and *Through the Looking Glass* (London: Penguin Books)

Caruth, Cathy (1996) *Unclaimed Experience: Trauma, Narrative, History* (Baltimore: The Johns Hopkins University Press)
Cavell, Stanley (1979) *The World Viewed* (Cambridge MA: Harvard University Press)
Cupitt, Don (1987) *The Long-Legged Fly: A Theology of Language and Desire* (London: SCM Press)
Deleuze, Gilles (2005) *Cinema 2: the Time-Image* (London: Continuum)
Didion, Joan (2004) *Where I Was From* (London: Harper Perennial)
Frost, Jacqueline B. (2009) *Cinematography for Directors* (Studio City, CA: Michael Wiese Productions)
Gilbert, Helen, ed. (2001) *Postcolonial Plays: An Anthology* (New York: Routledge)
Gulino, Paul Joseph (2004) *Screenwriting: The Sequence Approach* (New York: Continuum)
Heinlein, Robert (1988) "Elsewhen" in *Assignment in Eternity* Vol.1 (London: Hodder and Stoughton), pp. 89-127
Herman, David (2009) *Basic Elements of Narrative* (London: Wiley-Blackwell)
Holloway, John (1979) *Narrative and Structure: Exploratory Essays* (Cambridge: Cambridge University Press)
Hollyn, Norman (2009) *The Lean Forward Moment* (Berkeley CA: New Riders)
Koestler, Arthur (1975) *The Act of Creation* (London: Pan Books)
Konijn, Elly A. (2000) *Acting Emotions* (Amsterdam: Amsterdam University Press)
Lesy, Michael (1973) *Wisconsin Death Trip* (Albuquerque: University of New Mexico Press)
Lewis, Jon (1995) *Whom God Wishes to Destroy… Francis Coppola and the New Hollywood* (Durham: Duke University Press)
Lévy, Pierre (1998) *Becoming Virtual* (New York: Plenum)
Macnab, Geoffrey (2009) *Screen Epiphanies* (London: BFI/Palgrave Macmillan)
Mamet, David (1992) *On Directing Film* (New York: Penguin)
Marks, Dara (2007) *Inside Story: The Power of the Transformational Arc* (Studio City, CA: Three Mountain Press)
McGowan, Todd (2007) *The Real Gaze: Film Theory After Lacan* (Albany: State University of New York Press)
McKee, Robert (1999) *Story* (London: Methuen)
Naficy, Hamid (2001) *An Accented Cinema: Exile and Diasporic Filmmaking* (Princeton NJ: Princeton University Press)
Proust, Marcel (1913-27; 2003) *In Search of Lost Time* (New York: The Modern Library)
Rancière, Jacques (2006) "The Child Director" in *Film Fables* (New York: Berg), pp. 63-70
Said, Edward (1993) *Culture and Imperialism* (London: Chatto & Windus)
Sarris, Andrew (1962/3) "Notes on the auteur theory in 1962" in *Film Culture* no. 27, pp.1-8
Sebald, W.G. (2004) *On the Natural History of Destruction* (New York: The Modern Library)
Spivak, Gayatri Chakravorty (1990) *The Post-Colonial Critic: Interviews, Strategies, Dialogues*, edited by Sarah Harasym (New York: Routledge)
Stewart, Kathleen (2007) *Ordinary Affects* (Durham: Duke University Press)
Taine, Hippolyte (1872) *History of English Literature* (New York: Holt & Williams)
Taylor, Timothy D. (2007) *Beyond Exoticism: Western Music and the World* (Durham: Duke University Press)
Thanouli, Eleftheria (2009) *Post-Classical Cinema: An International Poetics of Film Narration* (London: Wallflower Press)
Thomson, David (1991) "The True Story of Perkins Cobb, King of the One-Shots" in *Movieline*, April, pp. 50-54
Thomson, David (1992) "Perkins Cobb Revisited" in *Movieline*, April, pp. 44-47, 88-89
Thomson, David (1997) *Beneath Mulholland: Thoughts on Hollywood and Its Ghosts* (New York: Vintage Books)
Truffaut, François (1954) "Une certaine tendance du cinema Français" in *Cahiers du Cinéma* no. 31, pp. 15-29
Vogler, Christopher (1992) *The Writer's Journey: Mythic Structures for Screenwriters and Storytellers* (Studio City, CA: Michael Wiese Productions)
Ward, Vincent, Kely Lyons and Geoff Chapple (1989) *The Navigator: A Medieval Odyssey*, screenplay, with foreword by Nick Roddick (London: Faber and Faber)
Ward, Vincent, with Alison Carter, Geoff Chapple and Louis Nowra (1990) *Edge of the Earth: Stories and Images from the Antipodes* (Auckland: Heinemann Reed)
Ward, Vincent, with Lani-rain Feltham and Louis Nowra (2010) *The Past Awaits: People, Images, Film* (Nelson NZ: Craig Potton Publishing)

ABOUT THE AUTHOR AND ILLUSTRATOR

Born in 1956, Dan Fleming is the same age as Vincent Ward. Growing up in Northern Ireland during the "Troubles," Dan found respite in his local cinema, chaired a cinephile film society that screened three films every week, and learnt to make 16mm films of his own. He then gained the first doctoral degree to be awarded by a Scottish university in the new subject of film studies. Ironically, however, he abandoned film and joined the early "Sony Portapak" revolution, becoming a community video activist and practitioner. While working with community groups and educators to help develop hands-on media literacy using the new video technologies, Dan edited the grassroots journal of the Association for Media Education in Scotland (AMES) and taught video art and documentary at a community college. Over the next twenty-five years, Dan became Professor and chair of two university film and media studies departments, first in Ireland and then in New Zealand where he currently lives. Along the way, he was awarded a Winston Churchill Memorial Fellowship and a Distinguished Teaching Award, wrote three books, lectured in Brazil, dabbled in screenwriting, held a Research Fellowship at British Telecom in the team trialing Video on Demand systems, presented at 17 international conferences, edited a textbook, and raised alpacas. Dan is a member of the University Film and Video Association. The London *Times Educational Supplement* called his first book "a work that perfectly meets the moment." Dan says that "meeting the moment" is one theme of his work in general. Another is his belief that the cinematic image still has the power to return to people a capacity for experience that other modern technologies have tended to take away. For more information, please visit *http://www.transform-film.info*

Thaw Naing, co-creator of the "graphic novel" section of this book, was born in Rangoon, Burma in 1986 and grew up in Fiji and New Zealand. He attended Massey University in New Zealand, specializing in illustration, and has illustrated for a wide range of projects including children's books and graphic novels. Thaw has also worked in film as a concept designer. He lives and works in Wellington, New Zealand. For more information, please visit *http://www.thawnaing.com*

(Portraits on this page painted by Thaw Naing.)

How will you create, plan and communicate your vision?

FrameForge Previz Studio is the must-have previsualization software for today's top filmmakers. Its optically correct storyboards will save time and money throughout the production process. **Start calling the shots with FrameForge Previz Studio.**

"Accurate camera placement within a given space is not something that old-style storyboarding was much concerned with. But this is where FrameForge really excels. That's why I used the software throughout my book to visualize the staging of scenes and the precise camera placements that are essential to a scene's effectiveness. Much more than a storyboarding tool, FrameForge is the real deal for accurate scene visualizations."

– Dan Fleming, author, *Making the Transformational Moment in Film: Unleashing the Power of the Image*

FrameForge® Prē•viz Studio 3

Save 10% off FrameForge Previz Studio by entering coupon code UNLEASH at the checkout cart at www.FrameForge3D.com

Storyboarding and Previsualization Redefined.